Ray & Joan

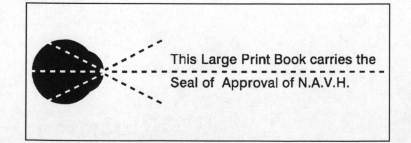

This Large Print Book carries the
Seal of Approval of N.A.V.H.

Ray & Joan

THE MAN WHO MADE THE MCDONALD'S FORTUNE AND THE WOMAN WHO GAVE IT ALL AWAY

Lisa Napoli

THORNDIKE PRESS

A part of Gale, Cengage Learning

GALE
CENGAGE Learning·

Farmington Hills, Mich • San Francisco • New York • Waterville, Maine
Meriden, Conn • Mason, Ohio • Chicago

GALE
CENGAGE Learning·

LIBRARY OF CONGRESS CIP DATA ON FILE.
CATALOGUING IN PUBLICATION FOR THIS BOOK
IS AVAILABLE FROM THE LIBRARY OF CONGRESS

ISBN-13: 978-1-4104-9670-6 (hardcover)
ISBN-10: 1-4104-9670-8 (hardcover)

Published in 2017 by arrangement with Dutton, an imprint of Penguin Publishing Group, a division of Penguin Random House LLC

Printed in Mexico
1 2 3 4 5 6 7 21 20 19 18 17

For my mother, Jane,
who has shown me that
generosity has little to do with money

From everyone who has been given much, much will be demanded;

and from the one who has been entrusted with much, much more will be asked.

LUKE 12:48

CONTENTS

1
JEWELS

Even before she married Ray Kroc, Joan learned it was possible to outsource bad news. When she agreed to Ray's proposal the second time — six years after first accepting and reneging — Ray had his lawyer break it to his then-wife that he wanted a divorce. Ray was notorious for having his trusted secretary fire employees for the slightest infraction, like wearing what he deemed an inappropriate hat or drinking the wrong cocktail. (Manhattans, he thought, were for sissies.) Inevitably, the next day, in the hazy aftermath of the heated moment, he'd wonder why the person hadn't shown up for work.

After he died in 1984, leaving her heir to a fortune greater than one person could reasonably spend in a hundred lifetimes, Joan followed Ray's example. Having decided she no longer wanted her former son-in-law to serve as her proxy on the board of that "chauvinistic corporation" McDonald's, she sent her Gulfstream jet to Chicago to pick up her chief advisor and bring him to her home in San Diego for a chat, then dispatched him back to company headquarters in suburban Chicago to relay her wishes — despite the fact that the ex-son-in-law lived just up the street from her. Feeling betrayed by a once-beloved cook who deigned to ask for a modest raise after years of service, she turned to another member of her personal staff to dismiss him.

Now, in June 2003, faced with the harsh reality that she was dying, Joan requested her personal physician break the difficult news to her immediate family.

It was early summer in southern California, a gloomy gray blotting the morning skies. Leaves on the eight hundred trees in and around Joan's meticulously manicured thirteen-acre estate, Montagna de la Paloma — built on land owned long ago by the earliest movie stars — feathered softly in a light breeze. The fragrant scent of blooming roses sweetened the dry desert air. She'd humored her head gardener, who'd pleaded for the go-ahead to plant hundreds of the thorny bushes. He liked having a ready source of cut flowers. With the door to the family room closed and Joan nowhere in sight, the doctor held up a scan of the matriarch's brain, riddled with cancer.

"This is the saddest day of my life," he said solemnly, explaining the nuances of this particular menace, a glioblastoma that had been slowly impeding Joan's vision, her speech, her balance. The diagnosis clicked into focus what the family had been observing for a while. Linda, Joan's only child, and Linda's four children, all women now, felt something had been off in the typically buoyant seventy-four-year-old's step. In March, she had radiated joy at the gala opening of one of her pet projects, surprising the crowd as she took to the stage with the hired entertainment for the night, Tony Bennett. And yet, to those who knew her, there was something not quite right.

At this point, the doctor revealed, the cancer would begin to grow at warp speed, wending its way through her brain, impacting every bit of her function, with the terrible, inevitable outcome: Joan had three to nine months to live.

A moment of silence pierced the room as the sad information soaked in, after which a few of the girls began to sob. The others froze in shock.

Only after she was sure the message had been relayed did Joan hobble in, masking her fractured gait as best she could. She had always been a blur of motion and cigarette smoke, action and forward momentum. Joan vibrated with life so intensely, it was impossible for anyone in her orbit to imagine a day when she wouldn't be present. So game, so intrepid, so opinionated and tough, Joan was a wildly unpredictable study in extremes. She'd hop into her jet — her prized possession — as casually as if it were a convertible, off to Vegas to gamble for sixteen hours straight, winning or losing a million bucks; or rouse her great-grandson for a trip to the convenience store for a hot dog in the middle of the night. Yet she was just as likely to feast on a simple salad for dinner and retire at seven p.m. after phoning to find help for some itinerant soul she'd discovered in the parking lot of her neighborhood McDonald's. Publicly, she'd appear meticulously put together in stylish Givenchy or elegant St. John, perfumed with a spicy hint of Yves Saint Laurent's Opium, her hair so neatly coiffed it wouldn't move in a strong breeze. Many mornings after waking, she might whisk down the hill, hair wrapped in a turban to mask the impact of a night of sleep, so she could grab a Diet Coke (for her) and a Big Mac (for the lucky pooch who got to ride along). Occasionally, she'd forget her purse and the kind cashier, who had no idea who she was, would wave her through; other times, she'd proffer a hundred-dollar tip.

Even her collection of a half dozen dogs exemplified her lopsided nature. She had a thing for strays, among them a three-legged creature. She'd drive her staff bonkers by crossing the border to Tijuana, dognapping some mangy critter from a sad, destitute existence on the streets, whisking it back in the trunk of her Mercedes to a luxurious life of filet mignon. Others in her collection were prissy purebred Cavalier King Charles spaniels with pedigrees worthy of the royalty they were bred to serve. She'd fallen in love with a particularly cute one named Ralph she'd seen on a website, and sent her plane to transport both the doting breeder and the dog from Ohio. When the critters passed away, they were laid to rest with reverence in a pet cemetery on her grounds.

Halloween would never be the same without Joan dressed up in costume, gaily dispensing Snickers bars to the trick-or-treaters traipsing around her tony neighborhood, Fairbanks Ranch, one of the wealthiest in the nation, where armed guards at the entrance gate added a layer of protection to Joan's already impenetrable life.

On the day her family learned the news, she was as resolute as ever. "I don't want any tears," she said, waving her hands, facing her heartbroken family. "I've had a great life. Let's make the most of the last days I have." She intended to fully live those few weeks and months, not die them.

The next morning, she kept her appointment to grab breakfast at McDonald's with one of her granddaughters and her great-grandson, pausing for just a moment when they arrived home, with the boy safely out of the car, to allow the young woman to cry. There was much work to be done. With the help of the coexecutors of her estate, Dick Starmann, a former McDonald's executive, and Nancy Trestick, a woman who'd risen through the ranks in her secretarial pool, Joan set about attacking the business of dying with the same chaotic zeal with which she'd lived, working through the details of her last wishes as if she were making the guest list for a party. Before she breathed her last, she'd throw a party for herself, too.

All tallied — this property; her Gulfstream IV jet, decorated in her chosen mauvy pinks and as lush as a Ritz-Carlton; jewels fit for the royalty of several kingdoms; $100 million in a wide-ranging art collection of serene impressionist florals, majestic Renoirs, comely nudes, and Rockwell Americana; and the seemingly endless pools of cash and investments — Joan had about $3 billion at her disposal. Three billion dollars — a fortune amassed because of a roadside hamburger stand started six decades ago by two hard-up brothers she'd never met, a hundred long, dusty miles north of where she now sat. Joan, who arrived on this earth the year before the Great Depression gripped and paralyzed the nation; whose father struggled without work for seven years, and ran the numbers for the neighborhood; whose mother sold coffee beans door-to-door to help the family survive. There were challenges besides money. Joan had long been at odds with her mother, though time and age had mellowed the fierce battles of her youth. Scars from her early days had never healed; she carried a pain that never abated. She'd hint at it at odd moments, usually with people she didn't know well, and then tuck the secret back away.

Adulthood hadn't tamped the trials. When Joan's own daughter, Linda, so sweet and blond and all of five years old, claimed the fifty-dollar first prize for her rendition of the cheerful song "Oh, You Beautiful Doll!" on the live local TV contest *Toby Prin's Tal-*

17

ent Hunt, the winnings allowed the family to pay that month's rent.

Another person might have been happy — even eager — to shelve the struggles of the past and fully inhabit the splendor of her current life. But Joan never felt entitled to simply revel in the fast-food fortune. The unfathomable sum she had at her disposal, at her complete discretion and control, enveloped her with awe. She was forever amused and amazed by it, as if it were a living, breathing organism she'd been entrusted to nurture and tend. If Ray hadn't met and made the deal with those brothers . . . If she hadn't been playing the organ that night he walked into the dining room . . . If her boss at the supper club hadn't hired Joan's first husband, Rollie, to manage the McDonald's franchise he bought . . . If, then, if, then — where might life have taken her? Had she stayed with Rollie all these years, life wouldn't necessarily have been *bad.* But it would hardly have been as *big.* She would never have befriended and supported some of the great thinkers of her time: a former president; a mystic priest; a children's TV star; a crusading journalist who'd discovered, he believed, the secret to healing pain. She never would have experienced the joys and challenges of

18

presiding over a major league baseball team! Of all the experiences a poor midwestern girl could only have imagined, her giving had been her greatest gift — to herself. The pleasure and thrill of helping faceless strangers. She wasn't deluded enough to think she could fix the world's problems, but she had loved making a tiny dent where she could. And, oh — when people learned what she was about to do. *That* would knock their socks off!

Joan knew all too well that life was hard, that for so many people on earth, its unpredictability took difficult, sometimes devastating, twists. No one was exempt from trouble; wealth most certainly didn't insulate one from life's tribulations. She and Ray were proof of that. Her marriage to an incredibly wealthy man had come with an enormous price. It had complicated her life immensely, in fact, and in many ways intensified the pain. Her husband's affection for the rotgut whiskey Early Times, which he'd come to love before he could afford much better, ratcheted up his already irascible personality to a tempestuous boil. Fierce battles inevitably followed. She had begged him for years to stop. There was no reasoning, no pleas or threats ("If you loved me . . .") that would sway him into realization, acknowledgment, or acceptance that his drinking was a problem. He was Ray Kroc, the hamburger king! Help was something *other* people needed — not the founding chairman of McDonald's, impresario of an international corporation that had changed the way the world ate and rendered rafts of people in his orbit impossibly rich. Members of his inner circle trained themselves to be complicit, to delicately referee Ray's volatile skirmishes with Joan, while keeping enough distance and playing Switzerland, lest they appear to be meddling. The couple was a less Hollywood version of glittering stars Liz Taylor and Dick Burton, whose passionate scuffles and equally passionate reunions were the stuff of legend. Joan's daughter had even made that comparison to a reporter: "Ray loved my mother so hard." Each of them, Linda said, had such a strong personality.

And yet, *despite* the volatility, they all lived well. If they had to endure his wrath, so they would. Joan herself had come to the same conclusion. She'd taught herself to see light in the darkness, to turn her feelings of helplessness about her unhappiness into action. She'd rallied the finest addiction counselors and morphed from aggrieved wife to activist, film producer, publisher, benefactress of an entire medical curriculum, agitator in major league baseball — all in the name of sharing the ugly truth about drinking and its impact on the family, and with nothing more than a high school education, sheer will, and a slice of the fortune. Through it all, there was never a question of Ray's adoration. She believed he loved her more than anyone ever would. It might have been easier to leave if he hadn't.

Whether she reciprocated almost didn't matter. What was love, anyhow? In these last few years — he'd been dead for nearly two decades now — Joan had started to open up, hinting ever so slightly to a reporter or someone new in her orbit about the reality of life with her husband. It wasn't a full confession, but, as time passed, she no longer felt compelled to maintain the whitewashing mythology that had been constructed around him — the all-American, the humanitarian, the modern legend. She had helped perpetuate it in her own way. While he was alive and receiving awards from the likes of the Boy Scouts commending him for being a fine, upstanding American, she didn't remind anyone that she'd once filed for divorce because of his violent temper. After he'd died, she'd dropped into interviews the publicly known fact that he'd entered rehab, but with no elaboration.

In the entryway of the palace to physical fitness she'd underwritten in a run-down section of San Diego, she smiled slyly the first time she saw a portrait of her, Ray, and one of the long-ago pets. "I liked the dog," she said sardonically, gesturing toward the photo. Though Ray was long gone, she'd insisted on putting his name, both their names, on the center — an ironic tribute to the man whose name was synonymous with greasy food. The boys' club at McDonald's would say the tribute was the least she could do. It was *Ray's* money she was giving away, after all. He had earned the fortune, and the old guard cringed at how she was spending it — almost as much as some of them cringed at the forbidden, dreaded words "fast food" that characterized the product that had made them wealthy, too.

Becoming caretaker of the fortune was, in a way, Joan's reward for having endured life with Ray. But even when she learned her dire diagnosis, she was hardly resolute about how she would pass it along. Over the years, she'd changed her last will and testament a thousand times, as whimsically as a teenager deliberating the perfect outfit to wear to the mall. Each time she rewrote the will, the people or the causes that owned her heart at that moment got the lion's share. Then, like a tote board flipping furiously to chart the changing action at the racetrack, her focus and attention would switch, and another person or cause would suddenly land in first place.

All the while the fortune ballooned from the $500 million or so she inherited when Ray died. To diversify, Joan would unload shares of McDonald's stock; shortly afterward, it would split, leaving her with even more than before. It was pure, almost unfathomable abundance, a spigot that could not be shut off — the exact opposite problem of the first thirty-odd years of Joan's life, when there had never been enough and she'd longed for more.

Now, with a lifetime behind her and the future so brief, the meting out of this fortune was no longer abstract. The deadline was fast approaching. She pondered the possibilities while she sat in a contemplative spot near her Olympic-size swimming pool, the place she reserved for big decisions.

Joan knew one thing for certain: She was not going to leave family the bulk of what she had. She'd give them enough to be comfortable, but not more. She'd tried to instill in her granddaughters how fortunate they were — that their access to a lifestyle of privilege had been an accident of birth. Joan had harbored tremendous ambition for Linda's girls: Allison, the eldest, whom their mother described as athletic and brainy; Amy, the intuitive; Amanda, funny and compassionate; and Holly, full of life. They had been born in the age of women, and would never face the limitations Joan had experienced. To Amanda on her twenty-first birthday, she'd put forth something of a manifesto in a letter. Love, instead of hate, she admonished her; think positive thoughts, not negative ones; find joy between the covers of a good book; believe that a life of service is a happy one to lead:

Love your fellow man — keep hate out of your soul. It has soured the lives of many who could have been messengers of joy.

She would do what she could to help her succeed, Joan finished the letter. What she would have given to have such a promise made to her! Even if money had been available in her younger years, she had grown up in a time and in circumstances where a woman had to fight to transcend her traditional place, behind her husband, which had suffocated Joan during her early years of marriage to Ray. She had struggled so hard to buck that role — and won.

In orchestrating her legacy, Joan defied what was most practical and common for the enormously rich — indeed, what was almost expected for a person with her means: to isolate the lion's share of the fortune within the safe and conservative confines of a nonprofit foundation. Joan had had one of her own, once — the Joan B. Kroc Foundation — but she'd closed it long ago, beleaguered by the bureaucracy and worry involved in managing it. She became tired of the loss of privacy from the required paperwork, of grappling with the endless piles of unsolicited requests. The more Joan gave, the more people crept out of the woodwork, asking for more, hoping for a donation toward some project or cause or idea they were absolutely certain would dazzle and inspire her to open her checkbook. Even her household staff routinely got hit up around town by people eager to get their precious cause before Joan's eyes. She opted for giving from her own checkbook, and, whenever possible, insisted on anonymity.

More than once these last years, she'd

been urged to consider the long-term wisdom and benefits of reviving the foundation. With $3 billion invested carefully and doled out to worthy causes bit by bit, her advisors argued, Joan could ensure a legacy that would keep both her name and her money alive, growing and helping others for decades to come. The magic of wise investment strategies and compound interest! Nestled this way, the fortune would multiply over time and therefore achieve far more good, far into the future.

The appeals had fallen flat; Joan couldn't be persuaded. It had been hard enough to find people to trust while she was alive. She never could shake Ray's joking comment that he'd "never seen a Brink's truck following a hearse." The truck, in his case, had detoured in her direction. And so, Joan figured, faced with this death sentence, the fortune she'd inherited should die with her. Let the people who ran the organizations to which she had chosen to leave her money steward it, and her name, going forth.

Her approach was in every way the opposite of the carefully constructed McDonald's philanthropy, a master stroke of public relations in an age long before the trendy catchphrase "corporate social responsibility." From the very start, Ray and

26

the company had been advised to give, strategically, as part of an ongoing campaign to infiltrate the communities where they set up shop, to counter the negative association with fifteen-cent hamburger joints. Franchisees had been encouraged to sponsor high school sports, to be present at disasters, to become "Mr. McDonald's" in their towns — this sort of community involvement boosted their image, magnetized customers, and was cheaper than advertising. As McDonald's mushroomed into an international force and started trading on the public markets, the company was singled out as a target by detractors: What about the high fat content of the meat? What about the environmental impact of all the Styrofoam packaging? The breakdown of society caused by eating meals, even breakfast, on the run? There had been a time when the mere suggestion of a sign that declared "McDonald's" riled up the neighbors. Joan remembered it well: It was one such delay that allowed her the chance to get to know Ray. Calculated benevolence aimed to offset the dissent. When he turned seventy in 1972, Ray grandly announced the gifts he was giving, donations of $7.5 million — to the zoo, the planetarium, the hospital, a prison education program, the neighborhood church from his youth, which he no longer attended, and to his own foundation, which was focused on funding medical research. The gesture grabbed the headlines his advisors had hoped it would. How could McDonald's be bad if its founder cared so much about the community?

His politics had been as calculated as his philanthropy. A staunch conservative, he'd donated more than $250,000 to President Nixon's re-election campaign in 1972. Later, after the Democratic party railed against him for trying to curry favor with the administration for permission to raise the price of burgers and squelch the cost of labor, he claimed the gift had merely been a hedge against the opponent, George McGovern, who was perceived as anti-business. The liberal-minded Joan, whom Ray called a "patsy," had chosen to swallow her tongue, even though the gift had been made in her name, too. Before that, Ray had ordered the flags at a McDonald's hoisted to full staff, in defiance of demands they be lowered to memorialize students killed by the National Guard in the bloody Vietnam War peace protests at Kent State. After Ray died and she ceased to suppress her politics, Joan later explained to a reporter that it wouldn't have been "ladylike or proper" to have disagreed with Ray's boorish stance. On his seventy-fifth birthday, she'd toasted him for doing things his way. But it was she, really, who had forged a singular path. As soon as he was gone, her transformation from wife to woman had been swift.

He would be remembered for hamburgers, as it should be. But she, at least, wanted the name Kroc to be remembered for giving.

Two months before her death, her final wishes had been spelled out on paper and shrouded in mystery from all but her closest advisors. She'd insisted there be no public funeral and laid out the plans for a modest memorial service — personally inviting the speakers in advance. As the days tripped by and the cancer took up greater residence in her frame, there was little else she could do but thumb through the leatherbound Bible given her by the late Father Henri Nouwen, from whom she'd sought spiritual counsel. She meekly signed the documents that set forth her wishes. It was even tough, eight weeks before her demise, to wield a pen, as evidenced by her feeble scrawl of a signature on her last will and testament, in place of her once perfect cursive writing.

In the shimmering material representations of her wealth, she took solace — her collection of jewels, chief among them one not intended to be worn: her prized translucent royal-blue Pine Cone egg, trimmed in gold, created in the year 1900 under the supervision of the great designer Fabergé. The egg's velvet interior contained an exquisite surprise: a tiny elephant made of silver, its tusks fashioned out of authentic ivory, its back bedecked with a saddlecloth trimmed with a triad of shimmering diamonds. An accompanying gold key, when inserted into a hidden keyhole, animated the animal, causing it to amble side to side and rear its head and tail. The "McEgg," she called the gem for which she paid more than $3 million.

"It's a little Republican." Joan had laughed in her throaty midwestern twang as she'd showed off the treasure to the cohost of television's *Today,* Jane Pauley, on the air in 1988. Joan's art dealer had just placed her winning bid in Geneva. While she identified more as a "donkey," and though, after Ray's death, she had given the first-ever million-dollar donation to the Democratic Party, Joan was proud to say she was registered as an independent. She could see myriad points of view. That her egalitarian bent didn't line up with her opulence didn't seem to faze her. Neither did her choice of jewelry. A confidante advised her that it was a bit too much for breakfast-time TV.

On camera, Joan nonchalantly fidgeted the precious oval, palm to palm, as if it were a trinket from the county fair. She'd bought it so it could be displayed with others like it as part of the "Treasures of the Soviet Union" festival her friend Maureen O'Connor, then the mayor of San Diego, had orchestrated — the most passive of the many gifts Joan had given her adopted hometown.

She'd amassed a trove of other jewels. Bulgari, Cartier, Van Cleef & Arpels: The forty-two-carat pear-shaped yellow diamond necklace. The twenty-two-carat diamond ring, flanked with triangular-cut diamonds, set in platinum and gold. The rare dark blue-gray diamond; pink diamonds, colorless ones, yellow, too. Pear-shaped, rectangular, square-cut, trapeze-cut. An exquisitely perfect string of twenty-nine cultured pearls. The Holly Wreath necklace by the designer Harry Winston — precious stones, suspended without a trace of metal evident. Collecting these sparkling gems had brought Joan much joy. The simple pleasure of sunlight refracting through them conjured up a sense of the elegance she'd steadily lost with the weight of the disease.

She wasn't afraid. When Ray had been close to the end of his life, after years of declining health, she'd lamented to a reporter how hard it was for Americans to accept their own mortality. By denying it, she said, we missed out on the day-to-day beauty of existence. She'd lived each day so vividly since then.

"Our world hangs like a magnificent jewel in the vastness of space," her friend the children's television star Fred Rogers had once said. "And in the perspective of infinity, our differences are infinitesimal. We are all intimately related. May we never pretend that we are not."

If we were all connected, then we never truly died.

Each day of her final weeks on earth, Joan Kroc's attendants would carefully work her deteriorating physical body into a meticulously pressed outfit, as if she were headed out to a ball. They'd style and primp her hair, and paint her now distorted face so that, from a distance at least, Joan looked like the radiant blonde she used to be, the beauty who had captured Ray fifty years ago, changing the course of her life. They'd complete the look with a set of gleaming treasures. Piece by piece, she wore them all, reveling in their everlasting magnificence, until she took her final breath on October 12, 2003. It would be up to her executors to reveal her final wishes, scattering her fortune around the universe on her behalf, like ashes in the wind.

2
LAND OF CRAZED SPECULATION

Before southern California's glorious, golden landscape was etched with eight-lane superhighways and tangles of concrete fly-overs choreographing a continuous vehicular ballet; before families became enchanted with the thrill and convenience of popping TV dinners into the oven; before preservatives and GMOs allowed food in mass quantities to be processed, preserved, and transported in refrigerated trucks and served up in disposable packaging at fast-food franchises for quick consumption on the go by harried, hungry travelers, there were oranges. Millions of oranges, fragrantly punctuating thousands of acres.

In this plentiful agricultural bounty at the dawn of the automotive age, visions of dollar signs danced in entrepreneurs' heads. They erected giant facsimiles of the brightly colored orbs, cheerful and whimsical and visible from a distance to motorists as they bumped and bumbled their way down the open road. Inside these stands, they pressed fresh, thirst-quenching juice, a nickel a glass, an elixir to revive the overheated motorist. (For this was before air-conditioning in cars, too.) After experimenting with lemonade, one particularly enterprising fellow in the northern part of the state, a Mr. Frank Pohl, launched a dozen stands under the rubric "Giant Orange" and tried, unsuccessfully, to sue any rival who included the name of the fruit in their own stand's name.

Squeezing citrus was hardly the aspiration of two brothers named McDonald from frosty Manchester, New Hampshire. They'd watched as their father had been kicked to the curb after forty-two years of employment at the G. P. Crafts shoe factory, told he was too old to be of use anymore. Just like that, his working days were done. The indignity of his dismissal impressed upon his children the urgency of taking control of their own futures in order to avoid such a fate. Older brother Maurice, known as Mac, trekked west first, followed by Dick, seven years his junior, in 1926, two among the first crop of speculators to blaze the trail millions more would tread in the decades to come. Their hope was to find fame, or at least unearth fortune, in the burgeoning industry of moving pictures and to become millionaires by the time they turned fifty.

To pay the rent, the brothers wound up sweating for a paycheck at Columbia Movie Studios, hauling sets and working lights during backbreaking shifts on silent film sets. Their twenty-five-dollar-a-week salaries were hardly enough to allow them to live like kings and certainly not enough to guarantee their futures.

Unable to work their way into the more alluring behind-the-scenes ranks of the business like producing and directing, Dick and Mac scrimped and saved in order to partake in another, less glamorous part of the industry: screening films. In 1930, they purchased a theater twenty miles east of Los Angeles, in the center of a quaint, growing orange-belt burg called Glendora. Newsreels and double features turned a trip to the cinema into an all-day affair. To dissuade patrons from toting their own food to the movies, the brothers installed a snack bar in the lobby. It seemed a sure bet. The 750-seat Mission Theater was situated just down the block from City Hall, on the tree-lined thoroughfare of Foothill Boulevard. The brothers recast the venue with an optimistic new name, the Beacon, and the local newspaper, the *Covina Argus,* touted its virtues: "The Beacon is one of the nicest, most comfortable theaters in any of the small cities of the valley, and the management is ever on the lookout for the latest and best films which are shown as soon as they are released." But despite the blustering promise, the Beacon faltered during those lean years of the Depression, and the brothers were perennially behind on their bills. They even buried some silver in the backyard as a hedge against bank closures. The only person who seemed to be making any money was the proprietor of a root beer stand named Wiley's. And so, after seven years in business, Dick and Mac sold the theater in 1937 and shifted industries from entertainment to food service.

In the next town over, Monrovia, on a decade-old thoroughfare called Route 66, they crafted some borrowed lumber into an octagonal open-air food stand and cut a deal with Sunkist to buy fallen fruit, twenty dozen oranges for a quarter. What they christened the "Airdrome" derived its name from its proximity to the Foothill Flying Field, which fancied itself "America's Friendliest Airport." From this spot, a brisk twelve thousand passengers a year were ferried magically into the clouds. This air traffic drew all manner of gawkers, eager to get out of the house and marvel at the magic of flight: takeoffs and landings and the thrill-seeking parachute jumpers who filled the skies each Sunday. Since the field's sandy acreage was enlisted, on occasion, for film shoots, there was always a chance of catching a glimpse of stars like Laurel and Hardy. Fortified by spectacle, satisfied day-trippers would then sidle over to the Airdrome to sate more basic needs, their thirst and hunger, with a fresh orange drink and a hot dog. This venture was so successful that the brothers were able to import their parents from New Hampshire and open two more stands.

Eager to consolidate and try their luck in larger pastures, the brothers decided to venture yet farther east, to the growing desert city of San Bernardino, a long-established trading hub sixty miles from Los Angeles. For close to thirty years, San Berdoo, as locals called it, had served as home to the National Orange Show. Each February, millions of pieces of citrus were fashioned into ornate sculptures, attracting hoards of fun-seeking sightseers, which put the city on the map as a tourist destination. Soaring mountains — believed by the earliest settlers to emanate healing powers —

along with abundant mineral springs added a touch of California mysticism to the area.

The brothers briefly entertained the dream of a new establishment they'd call the "Dimer," where every menu item cost ten cents, but rejected the idea as too Depression-era. The future, they were certain, involved appealing to drivers. Soon, they believed, the workweek would shrink to under four days, leaving Americans with abundant leisure time in which to tool around in their cars — and stop to eat. Their optimism about the future buoyed them through rejections from bank after bank, until they finally managed to talk their way into a five-thousand-dollar loan from a lender wowed by the location they'd chosen downtown at E Street and 14th. They'd asked for — and needed — 50 percent more than that, but they knew they were lucky to get any backing at all. Financial types were dubious about investing in the uncertain trade of restaurants, and the only collateral the brothers possessed besides their dreams was their tired old octagonal juice stand. For two hundred dollars, they hired a mover to slice the structure in half to fit on a truck and haul it from the site to its new home, fifty miles away. This time, the entrepreneurs plastered their surname on their reincarnated establishment, followed by the featured menu item: "McDonald's Barbeque." To lend an air of sophistication to the title offering, wood chips were imported from the faraway, exotic state of Arkansas and tended to by a prized employee named Ralph Evans, whose expertise cost the brothers a pricey thirty-five dollars a week.

Like other roadside restaurants of its day, McDonald's Barbeque offered food delivered direct to the customer's car via a fleet of attractive young women called carhops, so named because of their practice of jumping up on the auto's running board to claim a patron as their own. Ever thrifty, Dick and Mac outfitted these ladies in usherette uniforms recycled from the Beacon, embellishing the already theatrical flourish of service to your window.

McDonald's survived the challenging deprivation of the war years, when creature comforts and pleasures were duly rationed. The declaration of armistice allowed the curtain to rise on an era of playful abandon, which suddenly swept over the most banal aspects of life. Americans had been banking both their money and their desire for fun, and now they were making up for lost time. Henry Ford's production lines began turning out cars after the wartime halt, vehicles priced for the average consumer. By 1950, forty million cars jammed the roads. Taxes collected on fuel sales allowed the construction of wide new thoroughfares offering access to large swaths of America and new possibilities for adventures. All this meant a need for expanded services: gas stations and restaurants and motels. The journey became as critical as the destination. Cars were the chief accomplices of the developing suburbs and allowed them to expand; babies boomed, and daily commutes became common routines of the day. The increased travel time was seen as a worthy trade-off for more square footage, space to fill with more children, new appliances, modern conveniences. Eating meals outside the home became not just socially acceptable but a sign of carefree affluence. Eating a meal delivered directly to the window of your beloved new vehicle punctuated the feeling of delight that car ownership allowed.

Roads that had once been thick with orange groves were now dotted with quick-serve restaurants. While once a mound of ground beef was considered to be a tasteless and suspect blob of glop, suddenly the hamburger was de rigueur. But to the consternation of the family-minded, food wasn't all that could be had at these stands. Drive-ins became minefields of unsavory behavior, filled with loitering teenagers who smoked and blasted the jukebox and engaged in sexual shenanigans in the parking lot with the hired help. Staff seemed to churn through a revolving door; employees would quit or no-show, regularly leaving their employers in the lurch. The McDonald brothers found the dishwashers to be particularly unreliable: "winos and floaters and just plain bums."

None of this served to diminish sales. A steady flow of customers kept a cast of twenty carhops hopping and the parking lot, with room for 125 vehicles, brimmed to capacity, the go-to place in town for the younger set. In the face of this success, in 1948, Dick and Mac made the bold, perhaps foolish, decision to step back and reassess, closing their doors for a hiatus. Their "hoss and buggy system" desperately required updating, Dick said, in this "age of jet propulsion." While some rivals modernized by handing walkie-talkies to their carhops and installing spiffy conveyor belts, Dick and Mac decided to tackle the issue of speed organically, and asked themselves how they could prepare hamburgers, fries, and shakes as efficiently as possible. How, they wondered, could they streamline operations for maximum profit? How could they distinguish themselves from the other drive-ins? How could they speed up service?

In their quest for answers, they drew inspiration from East Coasters named Levitt. This enterprising family applied Ford's Model T–like assembly-line logic to housing, needed in abundance to fill the rapidly expanding suburbs. Lumber, they'd discovered, could be cut off-site, then shipped with the necessary hardware for efficient construction. This life-size Erector set allowed thirty houses a day to rise in cleared-out potato fields of Long Island, creating insta-neighborhoods. The McDonald brothers' goal was to mimic this prefab mentality in the preparation and serving of food: "Levittown on a bun."

To begin with, the brothers analyzed their business receipts to identify the best sellers, and slashed their menu from twenty-five items to the nine most popular, nixing the pricey and labor-intensive barbeque. Dick deviously posed as a freelance writer and ventured into Los Angeles to sleuth out trade secrets from the candy industry. In a hand-operated confectioner's cone used to form peppermint patties, he found inspiration. Dick enlisted a mechanically minded friend to fashion an automatic condiment dispenser that doled out a precise squirt of ketchup or mustard at the push of a button. A mechanized press allowed for the quick formation of beef into patties. To keep up with demand for milk shakes, Dick and Mac purchased eight blenders called Multimixers. These workhorses possessed enough spindles and horsepower to churn out frothy drinks — five at a time per machine. Surplus could be stored in the fridge, ready for the asking. Crucially, in the brothers' new business model, the customer was not allowed to request substitutions. Offering choice, the brothers said, dashed the speed.

To execute the next phase of their makeover, they retreated, in the dark of night, to the tennis court behind their home. Using thick chunks of red chalk to plot the action, they choreographed an assembly line of food preparation and delivery, where workers could most efficiently grill the meats (forty patties in 110 seconds), fry the fries (900 servings an hour), and dispatch an entire meal to a hungry customer in just twenty seconds. After they'd called it quits, a rare desert rainstorm struck, washing away the marks they'd charted out. Unfazed, the next day the stoic brothers plotted it out all over again.

This hamburger dance allowed Dick and Mac to address the costly issue of personnel. The alluring carhops were swiftly marched out of the picture: Customers would have to get out of their cars and — gasp — walk to the window to order. And while they were there, they could gaze inside the "fishbowl" and marvel at the meticulous, efficient kitchen where their food was being prepared. The new staff was to be all male, outfitted in tidy, conservative paper hats and white uniforms that imbued them with an air of surgical cleanliness and precision. Women employees, the brothers believed, presented an unnecessary distraction.

To cap it off, paper goods and wrappers replaced glass and chinaware, erasing the need for problematic dishwashing personnel. An even more important trait: Paper goods were more reliably sanitary than glass, a key selling point in the years after the deadly 1918 flu pandemic, when Americans were first tutored in the hazards of germs.

The pièce de résistance of the reincarnated operation was the price list. Factoring in the lower labor costs, the brothers could now charge crucial pennies less than the competition. Fifteen cents for a burger, ten cents for a bag of fries, and twenty cents for a creamy, triple-thick milk shake. Dick and Mac were counting on the math of their reduced operational costs, plus a high volume of sales, to add up to a handsome profit.

As a final touch, to advertise their reconfigured business, the McDonald brothers hoisted up a flashy neon sign featuring a chubby animated character rakishly attired in chef's hat and bow tie. His name summed up the promise: "Speedee." As the lights blinked, Speedee winked and moved, brisk and charming, a grin permanently etched on his pie-shaped face. The customer's time, the smile implied, would not be wasted here.

Re-opening night on December 12, 1948, proved ominous when a freak snowstorm hit the area. Speedee's welcome did not compensate for the confusion created by this new system. Customers roundly despised it. Some drove into the lot, only to peel off when no carhop appeared. Others lamented the loss of the old, longer menu and the inability to customize. The brothers took to having employees park in front of the restaurant, so the place didn't look so dead. All to no avail. Slack receipts and the empty parking lot were dire indications to the brothers that they'd goofed. The face-lift was a disaster.

Four months in, a miraculous turnaround occurred, for no particular reason. Cabbies came, then construction workers, then kids, and, soon, lines of hungry customers began to crowd the counter, and the presence of those customers attracted others. Sales were so brisk the brothers commissioned a painting of a rising thermometer in the front window, a neat visual to boast the sales. When the number reached a million, Dick said, the painter would add an explosion to the top. The brothers had gambled correctly. Profits soon soared to a bounteous $100,000 a year, which allowed them to partake in their own personal automotive fantasy, upgrading to the newest Cadillacs on the market — three of them, including one for Mac's wife. (Dick had yet to marry.)

Hamburger seekers, it seemed, were indeed willing to trade choice for speed and price. The quality of the food wasn't the main draw. The exception, perhaps, was the brothers' fries, the paragon of crispy freshness. Mac had become a wizard of the spud, applying principles of chemistry and perfecting a recipe through painstaking trial and error. The magic step involved drying Idaho russets in the desert air to break down the sugar content, a crucial if time-consuming step. Patience was as virtuous as precision: Improperly blanching, or in any way trying to hasten the process, was sure to yield greasy, limp potatoes, the sort fried up by the competition. It was the one arena in McDonald's recast formula in which slow and deliberate were essential and allowable ingredients.

Aside from the long lines, the brothers had another indication that they had a hit on their hands. Would-be imitators arrived to study the operational ballet on display behind the store's glass windows, a half dozen at a time, hanging around the periphery of the parking lot, sketching. When these copycats pressed for details on what they couldn't see, Dick and Mac cheerily shared trade secrets. Eventually, it dawned on them that they could put a price tag on their formula and pocket some extra cash. In 1952, a few months after their shortening provider, Primex, ran a piece in the trade journal *American Restaurant* lauding the prolific French fry operation at McDonald's, the brothers took out an advertisement themselves. They promised readers "The Most Important Sixty Seconds in Your Entire Life." The ad's centerpiece was a picture of their unique hexagonal building, glowing. Their "revolutionary development in the restaurant industry" was now available for sale to interested parties. A cover story echoed the hype, trumpeting McDonald's sales of "one million hamburgers and 160 tons of French fries a year" and revealing a whopping gross annual take of $277,000. That cinched it. For aspiring hamburger barons, San Berdoo became Oz.

The more honest in the bunch plunked down a $950 franchise fee for the formula, instead of just paying a visit and stealing the idea. First in line was an oil executive from Phoenix named Neil Fox whose family considered him nuts for jumping into this déclassé hamburger racket. Dick and Mac thought Fox was nuts, too — for wanting to use *their* name on the stand he intended to build, and not his own. The word "McDonald's" meant nothing outside San Bernardino, they said. Fox explained to the brothers that he thought their name "lucky."

Besides the name, for his money Fox got an operating manual, a counterman on loan for a week to show him the ropes, and, capping off the brothers' reimagination of the drive-in, a hot-off-the-press architectural blueprint from which to build a specially designed red-and-white-tiled restaurant — suitably eye-catching and accommodating of the sacred automobile. Even Dick and Mac hadn't yet rebuilt their own store from these plans. Finding an architect to execute their vision for a new structure had been a challenge. Dick, the younger and more marketing savvy of the pair, was insistent about his vision: He imagined parabolas hoisting up the structure. A growing backlash against the scourge of billboards lining new roads was forcing designers to fashion the structures themselves as signs. Bold, even wild, designs were sweeping the roads, becoming standard markers for roadside joints and restaurants, the better to grab the eye of motorists and punctuate the landscape with soaring roofs, boomerangs, and starbursts shooting kaleidoscopes of colors.

One prospective architect balked and tried to talk the brothers out of the idea of arches; another complained about being told what to do and suggested the arches were so harebrained that Dick must have cooked them up during a nightmare. At last, in Stanley Meston the McDonald brothers found an accomplice. Meston sketched out a twelve-by-sixteen-foot red-and-white-tiled workspace, easily approachable by and visible to customers. As instructed, he attached neon-trimmed golden arches to this structure, rising from the side of the building

50

like rainbows, which made the building look as if it were ready for liftoff. The building itself now served as a sign — all the better to catch the roving eye of motorists. The happy, animated Speedee blinked brightly and urgently from atop one arch, a visual reinforcement of the McDonald's message: A hungry customer could buzz up in his car, sate his hunger quickly, and have fun, too.

After franchisee Fox's brothers-in-law witnessed the clamoring lines of customers outside this new, second McDonald's in Phoenix, they shelved their snootiness and plunked down their own franchise fee to get in on the game. In 1953, store number three debuted in Downey, California. A handful of other interested parties paid up and constructed their own stores around the state.

Hundreds of inquiries streamed in from around the rest of the country. The dairy supplier Carnation was eager to swoop McDonald's and its winning formula into its corporate fold. Hoping to encourage sales of ice cream, the company's brass tendered an offer to replicate McDonald's nationwide. The brothers considered the alliance and ultimately refused; they were happy with the status quo and disinclined to have their enterprise and their personal lives enveloped by a large bureaucracy. The extra work hardly seemed worth the potential payoff. "More places, more problems," lamented Mac. "We are going to be on the road all the time, in motels, looking for locations, finding managers." It was easier just to sell the manual and blueprints and to pocket the $950 fee. To handle the added chore of wrangling prospects, the brothers enlisted a franchise agent, William Tansey.

One day, among the steady stream of curious looky-loos on E Street was a compact, well-dressed, hard-up fifty-two-year-old salesman from Chicago, on the hunt for a lucky break. His name was Ray Kroc.

The emerging automotive landscape of the midwestern United States wasn't, as in California, dotted with oranges, real or facsimile. A motorist on the back roads of, say, Illinois was more likely to encounter simple cinder-block structures festooned with turrets. Prince Castles, they were called, a play on the name of the business's cofounder Earl Prince. From these makeshift fortresses, creamy, fresh Frozen Gold brand ice cream was scooped with signature square dippers from behind clear glass cabinets — an innovative inside peek that dazzled customers.

Prohibition had transformed booze-starved Americans into ardent consumers of sweets, particularly of the frozen variety. Electrical freezers were a pricey luxury, beyond the reach of most families. Ice cream was a treat to be purchased from a vendor. Dollars that parched Americans could no longer (legally) spend on alcohol were diverted to purchase 300 million gallons of ice cream a year — three gallons a person. What could be better fare for a family on an aimless road trip than an ice cream cone?

A bit of marketing wizardry set Prince Castle apart from the competition. Instead of one large scoop for a nickel, customers got a double dip — comprised of two smaller scoops — for the same price. The ice cream purveyors stayed vogue by riffing on current events for new dessert innovations. The year 1936 inspired two: the Quintuplet Banana Split, named in honor of the five Dionne babies, whose miraculous birth had captured headlines. And the One-in-a-Million malt, named for the film of the same name, which starred the popular, perky Olympic gold medal–winning figure skater turned movie star, Sonja Henie. This particular frosty treat contained four thick scoops of ice cream. Churning a shake like that in a regular blender burned out the motor pronto. So proprietors Earl Prince and Walter Fredenhagen engineered their own state-of-the-art contraption, which they christened the "Multimixer."

Another innovation from earlier in the century made the growth of roadside businesses possible: paper cups. Before they'd arrived on the scene, shops served customers in glasses, and a thirsty soul away from home would sip from a communal drinking dipper at a public water barrel, hardly conducive to the emerging grab-and-go lifestyle. A populace learning to love the pleasure of eating outside the home demanded assurances of both portability and sanitation. The chain of Liggett's soda fountains bragged in newspaper ads about spending a whopping $250,000 a year on disposables for the well-being of their patrons and to safeguard the public health.

With more than forty Prince Castles across Illinois, the midwestern ice cream empire plowed through five million sixteen-ounce cups in a year. The turreted castles from which their goods were served dazzled their supplier, Ray Kroc, a star paper cup salesman from Chicago who was happy to count Prince Castle among his customers.

He saw so much promise in the operation that he asked Prince and Fredenhagen to let him take their business national. Think how many cups he'd sell then! The food service industry was his stock-in-trade. Ray had witnessed the paving of the open roads, seen them filling up with not just cars but the likes of quick-serve outposts like Carvel Dari-Freeze, Howard Johnson's, and White Castle. The men refused. They were content with their success and wary of giving up control of their creation. They also found this Kroc fellow a bit too pushy.

There was no middle ground about Ray. People either lapped up his magnetic, no-nonsense candor or were repelled by it. What persuasive charm he possessed could be tempered by an eruption of fury at the slightest perceived affront. The sales pitch came naturally to him, in part because of his fearless gift for gab. He was born with a hail-fellow-well-met demeanor that made it easy for him to approach and chat up anyone who would listen. He loved to be at the center of attention, the life of the party. Even as a young man, he acknowledged in his autobiography, he'd been "cocky and probably annoying to be around." He was prone to snap judgments, too; if a man's hair was, in his conservative estimation, too long, or his shoes improperly polished, Ray would decide he was stupid or slack and freeze him out.

Ray had been born in 1902 in Chicago to hardworking immigrants from Brasy, Bohemia. His mother cultivated his first love, music, calling him in from street-side after-school baseball games to practice piano every day. But classical music and hymns were too slow, too precise for his high-octane demeanor. He scandalized the choirmaster at church by irreverently punctuating practice with the cheeky riff "shave and a haircut, two bits."

Eager to burst from the tedious confines of the classroom, Ray briefly opened a sheet music shop outside Chicago proper in leafy Oak Park, where his parents had moved to accommodate their expanding family. Flush with patriotism, and tired of school, he dropped out to participate in the world war, lying about his age so that he could train as an ambulance driver. Ray deemed a fellow underage corps-mate named Walt Disney peculiar because he preferred doodling on his sketch pad to skirt chasing. Yet before either future chief executive could serve his country, armistice was struck on November 11, 1918. At his parents' insistence, the restless Ray gave high school another try. Sit-

56

ting at attention in a classroom was still not in his constitution, and after a semester, he dropped out for the second time.

Next summer, when he was seventeen, Ray's flair for the dramatic landed him a gig at a popular summer resort spot in the nearby town of Paw-Paw Lake, Michigan. His assignment: to regale vacationers from behind a piano perched on a steamboat — a live, floating advertisement for the dime-a-dance fun available inside the Edgewater Bandstand. As a coworker shouted through a bullhorn to anyone within earshot that they should join in the fun, Ray played his heart out.

His enthusiastic performance attracted an admirer in the form of a demure strawberry blonde, Ethel Janet Fleming, the daughter of a local innkeeper. Dazzled by Ray's blue eyes, skillful musicianship, and dapper dress, Ethel canoed with her sister Mae from their parents' place on the lake to delight in Ray's serenade. Afterward, they'd all row in the moonlight in search of wiener roasts and late-night fun. The romance continued back home after the season's end, and even survived the Kroc family's brief move east to New York, after Ray's father's promotion at a subsidiary of Western Union. Father Kroc forbade the couple from marrying until his son landed proper employment, so Ray tapped into his non-musical talent: talking. This was an essential skill for a salesman. Lily Paper Cup gave him his break, which allowed a wedding to occur on June 2, 1922, just a few months before Ray turned twenty-one.

Neither a new bride nor his nine-to-five obligation tamped his passion for music. The invention of a new and exciting medium called radio captured his fancy. By day, Ray would make the rounds of restaurants and other prospects in Chicago with his sample briefcase. He'd catch the train to Oak Park, devour a quick dinner at home, then rush over to serve as music director at the radio station WGES, headquartered in the ballroom of the local hotel. He'd play his beloved piano live on the air, with gusto, until the station went dark for the night at two a.m. Part of his job involved developing other on-air talent. Ray deemed the singing of the duo Sam and Henry "lousy," but felt that they possessed some promising comedic banter. So he nudged them to reinvent their act with an offer of five dollars each, and ultimately they morphed into the popular Amos 'n' Andy.

Even on Mondays, when the station was off the air, Ray couldn't relax. He'd pick up gigs at clubs in Chicago. Ethel complained that her husband was never home, but Ray couldn't, and didn't want to, tamp his ambition.

Restlessness served him well selling disposables. In a city dotted with 3,500 drugstore soda fountains alone, there were ample prospective customers for his wares. With his pitch perfected, he rose to become the area's highest-producing salesman. Paper was a wise investment, he'd tell them. It allowed for the customer to be moved away from the counter once his order was filled so that another could be quickly served. A win-win scenario: the more customers, the more cups. Another of Ray's customers hardly needed to be convinced of his product's merits: his beloved baseball team, the Chicago Cubs. Paper was a natural tool for the concession stands at Wrigley Field, making it easier for fans to drink beer while keeping an eye on the game.

Such seasonal business froze up with the temperature during winter, so after the birth of baby Marilyn, in October 1924, Ray took advantage of the lull to try his hand at a different sort of peddling — of property, in sunny Florida. The prospect of owning a slice of land in the Sunshine State captivated the newly mobile nation. Word spread that a plot bought one day could be sold at a stratospheric profit the next. Newspapers around the country brimmed with ads promising riches to anyone wise enough to invest. Ray couldn't resist the fever; he wanted in on the action. He loaded up his family in his beloved Model T, convinced Ethel's sister Mae to come along, and off they trundled, south down the Dixie Highway. On arrival, he landed work with an entrepreneur named W. F. Morang, one of the wealthy developers bankrolling the property scheme. Morang's team was carving out the most desirable real estate, "water-front" lots, by dredging canals in Fort Lauderdale.

Anyone who agreed to a free tour of this emerging paradise received a free fresh fish dinner. Ray figured out a clever way of finding prospects: He asked the Miami Chamber of Commerce to provide him a list of arriving visitors from his hometown.

"I'd call them and fill them in — one Chicagoan to another — on an exciting development I'd found in this palmy land of crazed speculation," he explained. The unsuspecting tourists, intoxicated by the sunshine and his spiel, eagerly opened their wallets and plunked down nonrefundable $500 deposits. There was one problem: The plots they were buying were literally under-water. The crazed speculation screeched to a halt after muckraking newspaper columnists blew the lid off the scheme, cautioning would-be buyers to keep their hard-earned money away from the scam-riddled Florida real estate madness. Virtually overnight, and much to Ray's chagrin, this spectacular speculative bubble burst.

Out of work, with a young family to feed, Ray saved his bacon with music. He lucked into a gig at a fancy Prohibition-era night-club called The Silent Night as the sub for pianist and popular composer Willard Robinson. The headliner was drinking himself into a stupor after a divorce and had been ordered to stop performing after he toppled off the piano stool.

Ray felt a bit guilty that one man's misfortune created his next opportunity, but no sooner had he got over the guilt and settled into the job than his good luck disappeared. A police raid on the club landed the entire staff in jail, an uncomfortable three-hour experience that soured Ray on Florida for good.

Ethel herself was not only fed up with the unpredictable nature of her husband's life-style, but homesick, too. Her playmate was gone — her sister had moved into a place of her own in Florida. Ray packed up his wife and child and put them aboard a train back north to Chicago, then trundled up the Dixie Highway alone in his Model T to rejoin them.

His paper cup employer awaited his return. Ray redoubled his commitment to sales, vowing that piano would now occupy only his spare time, as a hobby. Though he was home more now than when he'd juggled two jobs, his presence hardly deepened his relationship with Ethel. The onset of the Great Depression, naturally, had taken its toll on the cup business. His boss informed the staff that in order to keep everyone on the payroll, he was implementing an across-the-board pay cut. Incensed by what he took as a slight, the superstar Ray quit in an insolent huff. Knowing his wife would be equal parts worried and outraged, he concealed his joblessness, dressing each day and taking the train into Chicago as if he were still going to work. He'd while away the hours in a cafeteria, reading the want ads, which, given the times, were pitifully thin. When his boss phoned his house to ask him to return to work, Ethel fielded the call, and her discovery of Ray's ruse sparked a domestic conflagration. In the end, Ray returned to the job with his pre-Depression pay rate restored.

It was during his routine sales calls that the Prince Castle founders had shown Ray their Multimixer machine. Ray was enamored of the design, as well as its sleek efficiency. A drink mixed right in the cup minimized waste, a joyous outcome for the parsimonious salesman, who was deft at stretching his expense account by cutting corners when he was on the road.

Heeding Ray's enthusiasm and his knowledge of the industry, and despite their concern over his large personality, the Prince Castle founders signed an agreement enlisting him as the exclusive sales rep for their invention. The contract they signed even gave Ray the right to use the name "Prince Castle" in the corporation he formed to distribute their workhorse machines.

The only thing standing in the way of Ray's exciting new venture was his job. His employer, it turned out, wasn't keen on letting this demanding salesman sell another product on their watch. When Ray insisted on striking out on his own and incorporating "Prince Castle Sales," the boss responded that he deserved a piece of the action for Ray's having made a deal on company time.

Ray took out a second mortgage on their new house to pay the debt, escalating the tensions at home with Ethel to a crescendo he later described in his memoir as a "veritable opera of Wagnerian strife."

But personal drama and financial roadblocks and even a contentious conflict with his employer weren't going to stand in the way of this opportunity. He'd perfected the art of stress management with a self-styled brand of hypnosis. He imagined his mind was a blackboard filled with messages and envisioned a hand with an eraser wiping it clean. Then, he'd mentally relax each part of his body, from head to toe. By the time he was done, he'd be nestled in a deep sleep. Even with just a few hours of rest, he'd be primed and ready to face the day, unfettered by petty concerns.

Over the next few years, convenience food stands continued to crop up around the country. Aimless road trips meant brisk business for roadside restaurants and, by extension, for Ray. In one year, he and his team sold eight thousand of the mixers to customers like Tastee Freez, Dairy Queen, Willard Marriott of A&W Root Beer, and a roadside hamburger stand in San Bernardino called McDonald's, whose owners inventively chopped the ends off the machines' spindles to accommodate their cups.

Strict rationing of metals during World War II took a toll on production of the Multimixer, and rationing of sugar led to a reduction in the ice cream supply. To fill in for his diminished business, Ray began hawking a milk shake mix made from a revolutionary sugar substitute called corn syrup. It wasn't the same as the real thing, but it sated the public's desire for the sweets they were denied with the rationing of sugar. This helped him stretch through the war years, but the dawning of peace in 1945 didn't mend his troubles completely. Rival manufacturer Hamilton Beach now was peddling its *own* multi-spindled mixer. Americans were streaming out of the cities toward the suburbs, and Ray's mainstay customers, neighborhood drugstores and their soda fountains, were going the way of the dodo bird. New ways of living, of eating, were emerging. The ultimate symbol of the change? The trade magazine called *Soda Fountain Service* reincarnated itself as *Fast Food.*

The future of the product that was his mainstay was just one of Ray's concerns. His relationship with the Prince Castle founders grew increasingly tense. The family-minded Prince and Fredenhagen had

had it with Ray and his irascible, volatile personality. He was, after all, the public face of their product. Knowing he was under scrutiny and with waning sales, Ray began to grasp about for additional outlets for the Multimixer, for something — anything — new. From his years in the field, Ray had determined that fries and hamburgers sell a "devil of a lot of milk shakes" more than an ice cream stand. He approached the owner of a popular hamburger place in Los Angeles, the Apple Pan, hoping to entice him to let Ray franchise the operation. His overture was refused. Desperate for a product to sell, he invested in a Murphy bed–style folding kitchen table called the Fold-a-Nook. It flopped.

That's when Ray's West Coast representative, William Jamison, phoned in another order from that drive-in in San Bernardino — for eight machines. Maybe there was something to be learned from this customer in the desert. It was worth a trip, Ray figured, to see the place in action.

Driving east from Los Angeles on Route 66 en route to San Berdoo, Ray didn't know as he whizzed by the former location of Dick and Mac's Airdrome that he'd passed a spot of history that had paved the way for his future. His mind was squarely focused on the now. Arriving on E Street in 1954 during the frenzied whirl of lunchtime activity, he found himself enthralled by the lines of customers forming to place their orders — mesmerized by the spare efficiency of the food preparation line; the fervor with which the griddlemen worked; the French fry operation; the symphony of whirring Multimixers; the customers digging hungrily into their food; the immaculate grounds . . . Forget Florida. To a man who had spent much of his life inside the chaos of food operations, *this* was Shangri-La.

His reaction was instantaneous: "Son of a bitch, these guys have got something. How about *I* open some of these places?" Not having the capital made this an idle fantasy.

The icing on the cake came when Ray learned that Dick and Mac were earning enough money to upgrade their three Cadillacs each year. This was, in the salesman's estimation, the "eh-pit-o-mee of the eh-pit-o-mee" of modern American success. By now, the McDonald brothers were immune to such dazzled reactions. Requests to franchise continued to stream in; nine stores had been built, with twenty other deals in the works. Still, they were happy to greet the man they called "Mr. Multimixer," and made plans for dinner. That night, they proudly showed their visitor blueprints for their new building, a glimmering jewel anchored by those space-age neon arches.

Ray couldn't rest that night, back in his motel, for the starry vision of an empire stretching across the American landscape — each one requiring the purchase of at least several of his mixing machines. The vision carried him all the way home to Chicago. Even the name, he thought — no, *especially* the name — was a guarantee of success. Didn't every child in the nation grow up singing about a farmer called McDonald? He liked the ring of it. It was "all-inclusive . . . Irish to the Irish, to the Scotch it was Scotch . . . A typical English, American word. It flowed. *McDonald's.*"

It was wholesome and genuine, Ray believed, not gimmicky like the Burger Chefs and Burger Queens and Hamburger Handouts proliferating across the land. And certainly not Kroc's. No one would ever eat *there.* The McDonald's Speedee system was, to Ray, in every way a winner. A bit corny, perhaps, but, he later blustered to a reporter, he knew raw talent when he saw it. The hamburger stand's potential intensified his long-unfulfilled desire to conquer the world. Though he was the same age as

Mac, and burdened with physical ailments — gout eroding his hip joint, diabetes, bad hearing — he possessed the ambition and enthusiasm of a much younger man, a passion and drive amped up now by what he'd witnessed in the desert.

As it had in Florida, once again another man's misfortune opened a door for Ray. Tansey, the brothers' franchise agent, suffered a stroke, which forced him into immediate retirement. Word of the matter reached Ray, who, seizing the opening, hopped a plane and flew back to San Berdoo. Ever the salesman, he persuaded Dick and Mac to give him a shot at the job of propagating golden arches across the land. This Kroc was as aggressive as Tansey, the brothers decided, just the personality trait necessary for the job.

The men signed a contract drafted by the brothers' attorney. The terms were clear. Going forward, Ray would keep any $950 franchise fee he collected. New franchisees would now fork over 1.9 percent of their gross sales. Of that, 1.4 percent was earmarked for Ray to sustain and expand the business; the remaining 0.5 percent went to Dick and Mac as a royalty for use of their name and idea. If Ray wanted to change the blueprints or formula in any way, he needed approval in writing from the brothers; he also had to sign over each new outpost to them. To get Ray started, they handed over a list of deals they'd struck and a large stack of inquiries that needed answering.

Back home, Ray plunged into the task. Thousands of miles away from the founders, he behaved as he had with Prince Castle — not like a hired man, but more like the boss. He formed a new corporation, McDonald's Systems, Inc., and set up shop in the offices of Prince Castle Sales that he'd long maintained at 221 North LaSalle Street in the heart of Chicago. Indeed, what income Ray continued to make from the sale of Multimixers would help sustain the new business, as well as his family, for years. A fresh twenty-four-page offering plan was drawn up, and eventually Ray convinced the brothers to raise the initial franchise fee from $950 to $1,500.

What Ray needed now, he felt, was to build his own prototype as a proof that what worked so well in San Berdoo could transfer to a completely different climate. To deal with inclement weather, he'd have to amend the architectural plans a bit, swapping out the swamp cooler on the roof of the desert store for a basement, where a heater would be needed for the long, cold Illinois winter.

Lacking capital or the credit to raise any, he tried to cajole Earl Prince and Walter Fredenhagen into joining him. They deemed the operation — not to mention continued association with Ray — too risky. Besides, they'd recently added hamburgers to the Prince Castle menu. It didn't surprise them that Ray would consider, after their seventeen-year alliance, launching a new operation that, in essence, competed with theirs. They were so peeved they even consulted a lawyer to see if they might get out of their Multimixer agreement. They were advised against it.

Besides his lack of personal capital, the other obstacle in the way of Ray's hopes for his own McDonald's was a contract for a franchise the brothers had previously sold. The Frejlack family had paid $25,000 for the right to develop McDonald's anywhere they liked in all of Cook County, Illinois — Ray's home turf. Dick and Mac had been dubious that their idea would translate to a colder climate, since their restaurants had no indoor seating. They'd taken the money anyhow. This existing agreement, though, now meant Ray couldn't open his own store in the area, nor sell any others. Furious, he insisted on buying out the Frejlacks, mortgaging his home again to come up with the necessary money. To keep the peace, the McDonald brothers paid half.

Ethel was beside herself, certain that this time her husband had gone certifiably mad. Hamburgers? There were hamburger stands all over the place. Why on earth did these men in the desert need Ray, all the way in Chicago, to help them start more restaurants? What did anyone need with a formula to make *hamburgers*? And why did Ray need *his own* McDonald's? This new scheme was as impractical as it was humiliating. What about their future? As if all this wasn't bad enough, Ray set about corralling other friends to buy into his plan — the ones who didn't think the idea of investing in a hamburger stand was a harebrained risk and tried to talk him out of it. The suave young gent with slicked-back hair and bright blue eyes had charmed Ethel way back in the carefree Paw-Paw Lake days. When they'd been kids, Ray's boisterous personality, his sense of wonder and possibility and fun, had sparked joy in the quiet Ethel and melted her heart. But thirty years in, that same spirit enraged her. Why couldn't her husband grow up, settle down, put the family first?

She had done without for years in the service of his fancy, sewing her own clothing so that he could spend their money on custom suits. In recent years, Ray had done well enough that they could join the local country club, hire help around the house, and take the occasional vacation. The prospect of going back to the days of sacrifice, especially in the name of French fries, infuriated her. Marriage had proven to be a lonely disappointment for Ethel Kroc. But her latest despair didn't deter Ray's sharply focused determination. This was a life-or-death situation. If McDonald's didn't work out, he was lost for what he'd do next.

To soak up the routine of the hamburger assembly line under the neon-lit double rainbow, Ray sat for hours on the ice cream freezer at the franchise in Downey, California, angling to perfect and improve the dance, thunderstruck by the possibility of an empire. Imagine the possibilities, he told anyone who'd listen, if he could open a thousand stores!

Finally, on April 15, 1955, he managed to open one. Ray smooth-talked a friend into footing the cost of building a winter-weather McDonald's prototype in the Cook County suburb of Des Plaines. It was right around the corner from a Prince Castle. At its debut, he preened so grandly, friends said, it was as if this were the birth of a child.

It was as he scoured the country in search of coconspirators that he was struck by a thunderbolt that rivaled the sensation he'd felt when he'd first laid eyes on the busy desert burger stand. This thunderbolt, though, hit him square in the heart.

3
BLOND BEAUTY

Smoke curled from the ashtray perched on top of the Hammond organ. Votive candles flickered shadowy light throughout the seductively darkened dining area. The starched white tablecloths were smoothed to perfection. Dinner hour was about to begin at the Criterion on University Avenue in St. Paul, Minnesota.

Each day, guests from all over the country streamed into this room for a meal. The Criterion was considered one of the finest restaurants in the nation. The menu boasted that it was "Known for Good Food by People Who Know." Beautiful women and powerful men dined here; the place was just up the street from the gleaming white Minnesota State Capitol, an architectural masterpiece inspired by the grand dome at St. Peter's Basilica in Rome. Because of the Criterion's proximity and elegance, lawmakers were frequent customers, using a break from the day's proceedings to continue hashing out important matters beneath the restaurant's wood-beamed ceilings. At lunchtime, the ambiance was that of a royal hunting lodge; at night, the Criterion felt like an exclusive speakeasy.

Filet mignon, lamb chops, and sweetbreads were standard fare on the menu, but the place was best known for serving up treats from the sea. Customers could choose their own lobsters from the fish tank stationed by the front door. Then there were the giant fluffs of dough served with generous portions of butter. Diners always raved about the Criterion's popovers.

The food wasn't all that was memorable. No one entering the dining room could help but notice that Hammond organ, perched on a pedestal, framed by a lush, red-velvet wall. Neither could a diner miss the beautiful, poised woman who sat behind it. A perfectly positioned mirror hung above her, tilted to provide a close-up of her manicured hands gliding gracefully across the keyboard as she provided the live sound track. Joan Beverly Mansfield Smith, age twenty-eight, loved performing and being on display.

The dinner customers were beginning to stream in. Her cigarette would have to wait. The owner, Jim Zien, hated it when Joan lit up while working. That overhead mirror also broadcast the ashtray to the entire room, and Zien felt it looked unprofessional. This was a supper club, not some cheap bar, and a woman smoking in the spotlight sent the wrong message. But Joan couldn't help herself. She was addicted to the habit, the sensation, the hot drag of air that filled her lungs as she inhaled. She wasn't too worried about upsetting her boss. He had a big meeting tonight, so he'd be preoccupied. Besides, she knew she could charm him out of any momentary anger he might feel. She was too much of an asset to the Criterion for Zien to hold a grudge.

Each night, Joan played masterfully to her audience in the crowded dining room. Her blond hair elegantly styled, her dress hugging her bosom, she was the picture of glamour. Here in this swank dining room, she could forget the eternal struggle to pay the bills. She'd grown into the looks she hated as a child, her pug nose and freckles. Her beauty now had as much to do with her bold personality — a sense of fearlessness and confidence made her stand out in a room full of other attractive women.

"Baby Girl" Mansfield debuted at St. John's Hospital in St. Paul at four thirty in the morning on August 26, 1928, according to her official birth certificate, although she always claimed August 27 as her birthday. As the Great Depression took hold of the nation, her family relocated to Los Angeles in search of new opportunities. Her only sister was born there before the Mansfields moved back to St. Paul, when her dad scored work on the railroad.

As a child, Joan harbored dreams of becoming a star ice-skater. Or, perhaps, a veterinarian. She loved animals and relished treating the neighborhood pets when they were sick. Her skating hadn't been good enough for goal number one, though, and studying to be a vet was out of the question for different reasons. College would have been beyond her family's means, and besides, Joan didn't have the necessary grades to launch her into medical science. Her GPA at Humboldt High School had hovered just below a two, ranking her number 114 out of 197 in her class.

Though she would never make valedictorian, Joan excelled in the music lessons she'd started at age six, proudly traveling on the streetcar after school to the prestigious MacPhail School of Music in Minneapolis, the twin city next door, to perfect the skill that came so naturally to her. Her talent on the keyboard provided an escape, even if it also got her into trouble. Once, instead of listening to a symphony during music class, she played a rollicking boogie-woogie, and got kicked out for the infraction.

It was a difficult time to be young. Levity was in short supply for the class of 1945. Life was punctuated with war, rations, and dissent, as evidenced by the ticker tape–style chronicle of events that marked senior year, provided in the Humboldt yearbook:

Seniors choose navy and white caps and gowns . . . Hitler gives pep talks . . . Senior Girls College Tea . . . Mussolini killed . . . Honor Society initiated . . . Butter twenty-four points a pound . . . Students broadcast war efforts at Humboldt . . . Hitler's death reported.

The quippy poem yearbook editors had written to accompany the photo of Joan Beverly Mansfield, drama club member, had proven prophetic:

Though other blondes may fade and tire, Joan will set men's hearts afire.

A year after graduation, Joan boldly trekked solo a thousand miles on the Milwaukee Road railroad to Whitefish, Montana, where a summer job as a pianist awaited her at the Cadillac Bar and Hotel. She was desperate to flee the pain of her childhood home — the battles with her mother, her father's unpredictable state of mind — and eager to make her way in the world.

Right after her arrival she was swept up by romance. The handsome Rawland F. Smith had just returned to his hometown from Idaho, honorably discharged from a wartime posting as a pharmacist's mate in the navy after an injury on the base. This dashed his hopes of defending the honor of his older brother, who'd given his life in the war. Arriving at the Cadillac, Rollie found himself so intoxicated by Joan's looks and music that he joined her in song at the piano, his glorious tenor voice ringing out to fill the room. He couldn't help himself; this young performer from another state had cast a spell. Six weeks after that fateful first meeting, on July 19, 1946, the couple married in the county seat, Kalispell, sixteen miles south; Joan listed her age on the marriage certificate as twenty-one, even though she was actually a month shy of eighteen.

Three months later, she was expecting. With a baby on the way, proximity to home, and a big city, held allure. Rollie could go to work on the railroad in St. Paul and Joan's mother could help out once their daughter, Linda, arrived on July 12, 1947. With her mother serving as family babysitter, Joan could more easily juggle her three jobs: entertaining at the Criterion, teaching keyboards to a dozen students, and providing musical accompaniment during the midday programming at the local television station, KSTP. Joan's good looks and musical talent had inspired the powerful local broadcasting pioneer Stanley Hubbard to hire her for the midday slot on live TV. Hubbard's roots in the industry were deep: He'd started with radio twenty years earlier, at the dawn of the medium, launching WAMD ("Where All Minneapolis Dances") in 1925, with live music broadcast out of a hotel ballroom. When he merged with KFOY ("Kind Friend of Yours") in next-door St. Paul, Hubbard was on his way to becoming a titan of entertainment. Recognizing the need to serve both the Twin Cities equally, he headquartered KSTP on the precise border of Minneapolis and St. Paul, so that citizens of each could claim the media innovation as their own. Before television became an indispensable fixture in American homes, he invested in one of the nation's first studio cameras from RCA,

81

so he was poised to expand his broadcast empire.

An attractive blonde making lovely music live on the air was sure to be a hit, Hubbard reckoned, in this new, visual medium. It certainly created a buzz at the studio. One of the news readers, as soon as he was through delivering the nightly headlines, would speed east down University Avenue straight to the Criterion to moon over Joan. By then she'd shifted from the organ in the dining room over to the restaurant's lounge, where she continued playing piano for customers enjoying after-dinner drinks or nightcaps. The love-struck journalist would sit as close as possible, sighing as he nursed a cocktail. Dizzy with lust, he climbed to the roof of the Smith home on State Street in order to peer into Joan's bedroom window and rolled off onto the ground, breaking his arm.

Good-natured Rollie was accustomed to this sort of reaction to his wife. Diners at the Criterion routinely approached her, sometimes proffering twenty-dollar bills, dreamily reciting special requests. (One snippy patron boldly snatched the bill back when her husband wasn't looking.) Rollie had witnessed his bride evolve over the past decade from a confident, strong-willed teenager into the full flush of womanhood, tenacious, self-possessed. While a wife with such pluck might have intimidated another man, Joan's doting husband, solid, handsome, and kind, was swept up in her feisty zeal for fun.

Together, they would do whatever they could to give Linda the opportunity to excel at her studies so she might obtain the higher education Joan herself never got to have. The modern world would be more accepting of a woman going to college and choosing her own career path. Since war's end, the possibilities were multiplying, and this excited Joan. Her daughter could travel a different course, go out and live and explore fully before being saddled with the responsibility of husband and family — or, perhaps, she might opt out of that life direction entirely. For now, Linda loved the glamour of the mysteriously darkened Criterion, where she'd go with her father to fetch her mother from work, and the chef treated her to a special plate of popovers made to order.

Joan was consumed by her passion for her music, and her yearning to find a bigger role for herself in the world, a place and position beyond her own small universe. How to do it with a family and no education was the challenge. How to save money to pull out of the treadmill of constant financial pressure? This work offered a joyous diversion from what was shaping up to be an otherwise ordinary life. The nods from her appreciative audience at the Criterion were an essential element of this escape. Wearing a dress that flaunted her figure was another. She was proud of her looks; she loved to flirt, to chat up strangers. Most of all, she loved being an active part of the community into which she'd been born. The candlelit dining room provided a window into a more exciting, expansive universe. Business deals and legal matters were negotiated within these walls; lovers enjoyed the elegant treat of a ten-dollar champagne dinner for two; night after night, the place brimmed with life. With her music in the background, the Criterion offered an elegant backdrop for an elite segment of the population, and for locals celebrating a special occasion. Joan considered this work an honor.

The Criterion music songbook propped up on the organ was just for show. She practiced the music in it at home and could play most of it from memory, a human jukebox. The top of one of the pages carried a snippet of a poem, "The Voiceless," by Oliver Wendell Holmes — a cautionary passage:

A few can touch the magic string
And noisy fame is proud to win them
Alas for those that never sing
But die with all their music in them.

Joan might not find "noisy fame," but it would be impossible for her to keep the music bottled up inside. She could hear Frank Sinatra's voice as if she were accompanying him live, right here, as she played her favorite song, the dreamily romantic Gershwin brothers' tune "Our Love Is Here to Stay."

Joan's boss, Jim Zien, was well known and well regarded around town, a successful businessman of fine stature, and civically involved. Postwar antipathy toward Jews like Zien loomed large, and organizational efforts by the tight-knit Jewish community in the Twin Cities had given rise to a private hospital, Mount Sinai, that refused to discriminate against doctors or patients of any race or creed. Zien was proud to be able to contribute, to support the cause.

Like his father and grandfather before him, both merchants, Zien was possessed of an entrepreneurial spirit. With his sister Ruth's husband, Sim Heller, he'd built his own reputation — and a sizeable fortune — as an owner of local movie theaters. He'd then taken a well-situated restaurant called Harry's and upscaled it to this, the glowing dining room over which Joan now presided. More than anything, Zien loved toying around with marketing and advertising. Building a business was exciting, but the creative challenge of attracting customers was the piece of the puzzle he relished. To tout the latest shows at his theaters, he'd turned cars into moving billboards by affixing banners on their sides. And he'd hired a glamorous performer for the dining room.

The Criterion had been a fruitful departure into another, differently demanding, business. Zien was prepared to diversify again, investing in something completely far afield from this elegant establishment. Tonight, a salesman he knew named Ray Kroc was about to arrive from Chicago to discuss a new opportunity.

"Mr. Multimixer" had tried in the past to entice him to buy one of his pricey $150 machines, though there wasn't really any need for one in a fancy supper club. To make his case, Ray had invented several cocktails he hoped might make his workhorse a necessary staple at the bar; he'd printed the recipes in a newsletter he sent out to customers and prospects as a marketing tool. He dubbed one of the drinks the Delecato

— brandy, Kahlúa, ice cream; the other, the Dusty Road, was a blended mix of cherry Heering, orange curaçao, and lime juice. Neither recipe converted Zien into a sale.

But now this Kroc purveyed something that actually struck his fancy: an opportunity to buy into a newfangled variation on the hamburger craze — a twist on the traditional drive-in. The twenty-four-page blue-and-red prospectus he'd received in advance of Ray's visit laid out the details of this alluring business proposition.

McDonald's Speedee Service Drive-Ins: A sensation in California and Arizona. Do more volume . . . make more money the McDonald's way.

Zien had pored over the booklet several times. Included was a gaily illustrated copy of the simple ten-item menu, along with a number of photos depicting the unusual-looking restaurant, with cars and people gathered around its glowing, rainbow-like arches. Trade magazine clippings provided additional detail:

Here is a restaurant that permits a high food cost and a very low labor cost and a constant ring to the cash drawer.

This establishment promised a more efficient operation than the typical hamburger stand, minus the carhops — the polar opposite of the white tablecloths and linen Zien offered at the Criterion:

A merchandising trend through the country toward self-service was readily apparent in grocery stores, at drug stores, filling stations, etc. So the McDonald's brothers set to find out if the public was ready for a self-service drive-in . . . The service was lightning fast, the hot foods always piping hot, the cold drinks really cold, and an aggravating tipping problem was eliminated.

Zien knew this wasn't hype. He had seen it for himself, this shift toward speed, manifest in the lines of customers waiting at the nearby McDonald's in the growing suburb of Roseville. The "Speedee Service System" was a love note to twentieth-century progress: twenty-four hamburgers fried up at once; pre-cut buns delivered from the bakery and dressed with mustard and ketchup using a specially commissioned gadget; milk shakes whipped up in Multi-mixers and stored for ready retrieval; delectable golden French fries scooped up from a specially designed stainless steel heated box. Total elapsed time from order to pickup: twenty seconds. That was translating into $100,000 a year in profit for the brothers McDonald. Business was also brisk at Ray's very own McDonald's in the Chicago suburb of Des Plaines, Illinois, each month, mostly thanks to word of mouth and an occasional mailing or two to local residents. Just think what Zien could do with a stand if he actually got creative with the advertising. Radio was a medium untapped by any food service in the area; it wasn't appropriate, or even necessary, for the understated and already popular Criterion, but for this McDonald's . . . He could *hear* the possibilities.

His friends couldn't believe that a restaurateur of his caliber would even consider entering into such a venture. Hamburgers, served in paper wrappers! To Zien, the populist appeal of McDonald's offered tremendous potential on a wider scale. It didn't take a genius in mathematics to see that there was exponentially more demand for inexpensive family meals than there was for high-priced dining. Quick plus cheap equaled the backbone of the new American dream. A variety of players were jockeying for position in the national hamburger game, and he could buy into those, or try to replicate them himself, but something about this one felt right. Moreover, Zien felt simpatico with the work ethic these McDonald's people were demanding. This was no schlock operation. The pamphlet he was holding in his hands said as much.

It's the McDonald's System — simply amazing because it's amazingly simple, as you shall see.

When Ray Kroc walked into the Criterion restaurant, impeccably dressed in suit and tie, hair slicked back, nails manicured, he didn't look like a man who'd sweat over a French fryer for a living, or someone hatching a scheme to make it possible to get an inexpensive meal in Iowa that tasted the same as it did in Arizona. Nor did he seem panicked about the mountain of debt under which he was buried or the stress of his home life. He looked, rather, like he could be one of Zien's regular customers, one of the well-heeled legislators from up the street.

Ray's enthusiasm belied his years, almost fifty-five of them, and his myriad health issues. Neither his diabetes nor his arthritis was apparent to the outside observer; he moved so fast, in a whir, that men twenty years his junior were surprised to learn his age. When they found out, they marveled at his stamina. His poor hearing caused him to shout, which contributed to the domineering presence that offset his diminutive stature. Years of toiling around America as a traveling salesman had precisely tuned Ray's abundance of unwavering focus, confidence, and optimism, which hadn't waned even as his health had.

He'd been selling franchises for the McDonald brothers for two years now. There were thirty-four stores up and running, fourteen of them sold during Ray's tenure, including his own. Most boasted brisk sales and generated handsome monthly royalties. Every penny paid out by those franchises that wasn't sent to Dick and Mac was plowed right back into the McDonald's corporation, for office rent and scouting and salaries for the growing team Ray had hired to assist him. The Multimixer business remained his bread and butter.

The finances were less important to Ray than the product. By now, the blood in his veins had turned to ketchup. Day and night, Ray schemed improvements. Dreamy visions of golden fries and perfectly sliced buns floated across his closed eyelids. When he wasn't fantasizing about a test kitchen where full-time technicians could test products and tinker with preparation methods, he was obsessed with negotiating the best prices for bulk purchase in each region. The smaller details consumed him, as well: He'd quiz Dick and Mac on procedural matters like how to grill the buns so they were perfectly toasted; how to prepare onions in advance, because frying them to order slowed down operations; how to construct the burger so the ketchup didn't dribble off the side. Serving a good hamburger wasn't his only goal. He wanted to serve a *good-looking* burger. Dick and Mac would parry with suggestions of their own, eager to remain part of their growing, evolving masterpiece. How about golden Speedee awards, à la the Oscars, for the best employees? What about handing out candy lollipops shaped like their mascot to Girl Scout troops, orphanages, children's wards at the local hospital? That, they said, would provide the kind of goodwill and advertising in communities that money couldn't buy.

Each morning at seven, Ray would arrive to spend a few hours at his own store in Des Plaines, then catch the train into Chicago to the office he'd maintained at 221 North LaSalle for years now, in the hulking art deco skyscraper across from the Chicago River. He'd return to the store at five p.m. for a few hours more. He spent all day on the weekends there, too. He was perennially on the lookout for people as ambitious and as fastidious as he — people who believed in working hard, not just aiming for a quick buck, people who gave him that inexplicable, indefinable "funny bone feeling" of "trust and faith and confidence."

He'd already been burned. After he denied an operator in Urbana-Champaign the right to open more stores, the wily proprietors copycatted the McDonald's format to the letter in Peoria and plastered the name "Sandy's" on it. This infuriated Ray. One of the worst infractions would be committed by one of Ray's former golfing buddies. When Bob Dondanville opened his own McDonald's in California, he not only deigned to raise the hamburger price to eighteen cents from the signature fifteen, he also brazenly stood in the window of his store, chef's hat perched on his head, gaily carving roast beef for the customers. This sort of deviation was not acceptable. The point was to build a consistent dining experience from store to store. When a customer spotted the arches, he had to be sure what was on the menu. No enchiladas.

No variations on the theme.

Dondanville's ultimate nose-thumbing of the rules: He'd grown a beard. Ray despised facial hair with an all-consuming passion; he saw it as messy and unkempt, and for a suit-clad man with a manicure and a proclivity for plucking up trash from the parking lot of his store, sloppiness, real or perceived, was a heinous crime. For his rogue behavior, Dondanville would ultimately lose his franchise. The need for this kind of policing was exactly why Dick and Mac had offloaded the task.

As he tinkered to find the best possible allies, Ray believed he needed more of the likes of Sandy and Betty Agate. The Agates were a hardworking Jewish couple who'd long wanted the freedom of owning their own business. To save money toward that goal, and to flesh out her husband's income as a printing press operator, Betty had taken a job selling Bibles door-to-door. In that capacity, she found herself roaming the halls of the office building that housed Prince Castle Sales, now doing double duty as headquarters for McDonald's Systems, Inc. Instead of selling a copy of the good book, she herself bought into the gospel of quick-serve food. The McDonald's she and her husband opened forty miles north, in

Waukegan, was, as Ray liked to say, "cooking with gas."

Would-be operators were always shown the books on the Agates' operation to tantalize them about the possibilities. Drawing on a local naval training center, the Agates cleverly staffed up their crew from the military, ensuring the precise regimen of the operation would be dutifully followed. Right off the bat, they started raking in so much money that the cash registers couldn't hold it all; they'd had to stuff their earnings in paper bags to unobtrusively spirit the cash to the tiny house they'd rented behind the store. Soon enough, they'd earned so much that they upgraded to a palatial six-figure home. Profits were on track to exceed $250,000 a year.

But when Sandy Agate deigned to contract with Pepsi and not the Ray-approved carbonated beverage, Coca-Cola, he was sentenced to the doghouse. Such assertions of independence would not be tolerated. "The individual seeking to go into the McDonald's business must have respect and trust for the organization," Ray said, explaining his philosophy to the brothers. "Any other way would be building on a marshy foundation."

As for Jim Zien, Ray had reservations.

That he was Jewish was a plus. Ray explained to the brothers that he'd concluded from his dealings with the Agates that Jews worked hard and never rested on their laurels. (Gentiles, he'd discovered, did.) On the other hand, he didn't see such a refined man sweeping the floors or lording over the crew in the kitchen from starting time till close. Passive investors hoping to make a quick buck who hired outside help to run their stores were wrong for this game. It was hard to ride control of the operation unless you had an owner's total commitment to the McDonald's way, as interpreted and embellished by Ray. An investment of time was as critical as — more critical than — capital. Fastidious obsession over every detail. The hunger to succeed. The desire to be part of a larger whole. Those qualities, Ray felt, were rarely found in absentee owners or employees.

Maintaining consistent standards was a job unto itself. To help police and enforce the rules as more stores came online, Ray had brought a twenty-four-year-old college dropout named Fred Turner into the fold. He'd started out as a counterman at Ray's own McDonald's in Des Plaines, hoping to learn the operational ropes while he saved enough to start his own outpost of the franchise with a group of friends. Ray had been so impressed with the young man's dogged dedication to the minutiae of the business that he'd plucked him from behind the griddle to manage one of the stores. When he showed exemplary devotion to the rules there, Ray anointed him vice president of operations. Fred now shadowed Ray on sales calls to prospective franchisees and suppliers around the United States. This time together allowed a familial bond to forge between the two men, a bond already far warmer than the one Ray had ever had with his only child.

As long-suffering Ethel became increasingly frustrated with her husband's workaholic lifestyle, his reluctance to settle down, and his mortgaging of the family finances to underwrite his whimsical ideas, their daughter had sided with her mother, pained by her suffering. Almost as if to agitate her father, she'd run off and married a musician. Like his father before him, Ray felt a man with family responsibilities needed a steadier paycheck. The marriage fizzled after several years, anyway.

Home had not, for a long time now, been a welcoming, nurturing place for any of the Kroc family. But in Fred Turner, Ray had discovered the son he'd never had. Though the future was still riddled with question marks, Ray was already grooming him — literally as well as figuratively — as his eventual successor. He'd given the young man an exact replica of the vanity kit he always carried inside his suit jacket, a not-so-subtle hint that Fred's nose hairs needed attention. If Ray hadn't been so fond of him, he likely would have sacked him for his sloppiness.

All this time together provided a crash course for Fred in Ray's proclivities: his aversion to mess, his desire for Early Times, his abiding love of keyboards. The boss loved listening to live music, to comment on the performance, to trip down his own personal memory lane and share tales of his earlier days in the business. Oh, the exhausting fun he'd had playing live on the radio back when he was newly married and juggling his job as a paper cup salesman. How he'd loved entertaining the Prohibition crowds at the Silent Night in Florida before the raid, he told his younger charge nostalgically. Ray had regaled Fred more than once with the story of how he'd "discovered" the act that became Amos 'n' Andy — and how he played a riotous double piano with bandleader Harry Sosnik. He'd even confided about an even more illicit experience with his music, when, as a young man, he'd been dispatched to serenade what turned out to be a whorehouse. If only he had the pipes to match his technical skill, Ray would lament to his young confidant, he might have been a star. That's what he really wanted: to croon. Much to his chagrin, he could improvise a dazzling obbligato on the piano, but he confessed he couldn't sing " 'Come to Jesus' in the key of C."

That night in the Criterion, as the candles flickered, Joan slowed the tempo to play "Because of You," the love song that had made the singer Tony Bennett a star. The dining room's din mixed with the sound of the organ, though Ray struggled to let the music recede into the background. Sidetracking the reason for his visit, he demanded his host tell him more about this talented woman. She radiated a stage presence of the sort that set star talents apart from the merely skilled, and that intensified Ray's attraction. A lady musician with the perfect combination of skill and soul, possessed of glamorous good looks, too — it was perhaps the most alluring cocktail of qualities he could have imagined in a member of the opposite sex. Not wanting to scuttle a business deal, Zien walked Ray

Kroc over to introduce him. Ray found himself stunned by her blond beauty.

Never mind that Joan's husband had just arrived to take her home for the evening with their young daughter; that Ray himself had a wife back in the suburbs of Chicago; or that Ray was twenty-six years her senior.

On that fateful night, what mattered was the music. As the men retreated to their table to talk business, Joan picked up her cigarette, snuck a drag, and let her polished fingernails tickle the keys.

4
FIRST FRUITS

An unseasonable cold spell in St. Louis Park, Minnesota, couldn't dissuade angry citizens from swarming city council chambers on November 18, 1957. Locals were livid that elected officials had green-lit a permit for the construction of a burger stand near the high school after denying an earlier request to build it in a wealthier part of town. An out-of-state concern was behind this newcomer business to be built at the northwest corner of West Lake Street and Dakota Avenue — its ninety-third store, they bragged. The permit named one Jim Zien, along with his business partner and brother-in-law, Sim Heller, as owners and operators of the place called McDonald's. Lines of customers jamming a similar outfit with the same name up the road in nearby Roseville were cause for concern; no one wanted that kind of traffic here. The very word "drive-in" conjured up images of trash, loitering, scofflaws. Why was another needed so close by, and why had these outsiders zeroed in on this city?

The head of the St. Louis Park Chamber of Commerce, Art Meyers, angrily demanded the council revisit the case. "This deal smells to high heavens," he said. Lawmakers, he insisted, had "shoveled" the fast-food request through the planning commission, craftily engineering their way around loopholes so, in his estimation, "the people didn't have a chance in the world to know what was going on."

Apart from some consternation a few years earlier over a mosquito infestation that made it unbearable for children to play outside, there had hardly been a brouhaha like this in St. Louis Park since the turn of the century. That one had to do with food, too, and the dawn of industrial agriculture.

In 1899, an impresario named Frank Hutchinson Peavey set his sights on the community as the location of a grand technological experiment he'd cooked up with local architect and builder Charles F. Haglin — the construction of a mechanized silo soaring 125 feet high, composed from an untested, newfangled material: reinforced concrete. Capacity was 30,000 bushels, with a name to match its scale: the Peavey-Haglin

Experimental Grain Elevator. While square elevators made from wood allowed the efficient storage and retrieval of wheat, oats, rice, and corn — more efficient than delivering the old-fashioned way, in heavy bags — they also posed a vexing problem. One spark could light up tens of thousands of bushels of crop in an instant. Despite this potentially fatal flaw, the matrix of such elevators had established America, generally, and Minneapolis in particular, as a superpower in the emerging industrial agrarian landscape. Peavey himself was a catalyzing force in this development, a maestro of the grain trade. One by one, he'd persuaded hundreds of farmers, who'd once produced just enough crop for their own use, to plant surplus and sell it to him. He, in turn, brokered the goods to flour, feed, and cereal mills. The grain elevators in his sprawling network were strategically situated along railroad lines, making gathering and distribution that much more efficient. This gave him might aplenty, inspiring the nickname "The Elevator King."

For this latest idea, people believed the "king" had gone mad; that the concrete material would surely dampen and thus mold and spoil the crops; that the act of retrieval would cause a vacuum to form, leading to a perilous explosion. "Peavey's Folly," they mockingly called the towering structure. Undeterred, the elevator king filled it up and let it sit. A year later, with dramatic fanfare, Peavey decreed it was time to test his grand invention. Crowds gathered in St. Louis Park for the display, anticipating a conflagration. One did not occur. The concrete elevator not only worked — it worked flawlessly. The experiment was a success. The grain was fresh as could be and was excavated without a hitch. The grain elevator king now had a working prototype on his hands. Immediately, the Peavey-Haglin model became the industry standard.

Before the elevator king died an untimely death from pneumonia a few years later, he delivered a speech in which he uttered prophetic words that could have served as his epitaph: "To be successful we must change with conditions and accept them as they are today."

Twenty years into the new century, the French architect Le Corbusier waxed poetic about these structures that enabled the storage of basic food staples. The earliest of skyscrapers, he deemed them, the hallmark of the new American landscape — "the magnificent first fruits of the new age."

∎ ∎ ∎ ∎

The arrival of the first fruits of the fast-food age was now roiling the locals, who'd moved to St. Louis Park in the first place to escape the urban perils of the Twin Cities, close enough for work but far enough away that tranquility was within reach. A trickle of newcomers became a surge as World War II's end stuffed veterans' pockets via the GI bill, which not only paid for tuition but also offered low-interest mortgages to put the dream of owning a home within realistic reach. Developers turned plentiful lots of land into affordable homes. A six-million-dollar apartment complex boasting six hundred units debuted on former marshland. The area was seen as a welcoming haven for families, Jewish families, in particular, who faced postwar discrimination in other parts of town.

During the fall of 1957, what to do about this McDonald's dominated conversation in St. Louis Park. Citizens simply didn't buy Zien's argument that this newcomer restaurant would be a boon for their neighborhood. Menacing visions of scantily clad carhops carousing on nearby streets at all hours danced in their heads. The principal of the high school described how he was already battling a daily after-class loitering problem. Administrators at the nearby junior high chimed in with their fears of increased truancy. A citizen named Leo Schultz delivered a passionate speech to the council about the antisocial behavior inspired by this kind of establishment. Consumption of hamburgers, he asserted, interrupted the sacrosanct nightly family meal.

Alongside concern for the general breakdown of society and potential nutritional scourge, there were worries about the uptick of vehicular traffic the McDonald's was certain to bring to the already busy intersection. An earlier proposal to construct an office building on the site seemed a far more palatable nuisance now that the alternative proved to be a "monument of neon and tile" that planned to stay open twelve hours a day, late into the night. And what about the environmental impact of a hamburger stand? Who was to stem the tide of trash? Another potential scourge: the "towering, blinking monstrosity of a sign" with a footprint of twenty-seven feet by fourteen. Zien promised to dial it back should it prove "obnoxious."

Chamber president Meyers stepped up his opposition, even offering the city $5,000 of his own personal cash for the creation of a local library if they would do something else with the land. The editorial board of the *St. Louis Park Dispatch* concurred that the deal was a rotten one: "Council pulled the lever on the jackpot . . . and when the wheels stopped spinning, three lemons showed up."

The fact that the plot of land in question was situated near schools smack in the heart of a residential neighborhood populated with young families was exactly what made it so attractive to McDonald's. To reinforce the argument, corporate brass had been dispatched from Chicago — the company's newly hired manager of franchises, Donald Conley, a veteran World War II bomber pilot. He and Ray had first met back in 1954 at a restaurant trade show in Los Angeles, when Conley was selling fudge warmers and performing double duty as a pilot, flying the brightly decorated corporate plane called *The Flying Hot Cup*. Ray had even tried to lure Conley to join him on that fateful maiden visit to the desert when he went to call on the brothers McDonald. Conley believed Ray's franchise vision a bit "pie-in-the-sky," but he couldn't help but get swept up in the salesman's enthusiasm and vision. As a show of support, he'd even been in the crowd at the opening of Ray's

McDonald's in Des Plaines.

Ray didn't have to work too hard to convince him to join him now. For a modest $150 a week, he'd agreed to the job of assessing whether prospects had a chance of surviving in the business — then collecting their fees as quickly as possible, and spiriting the money into the company bank account to pay down some of the company's growing pile of bills.

To earn extra money, Conley moonlighted on the weekends as a flight instructor at the Palwaukee airport outside Chicago. Hanging around the airfield, he'd learned about a tiny used single-engine Cessna 195 for sale for the bargain price of $6,000. It was a financial stretch, but a tantalizing offer he found impossible to refuse. When he told his new boss about the purchase, Ray insisted that McDonald's take on the loan payments so the company could use the plane — and, of course, Conley's flight services. Driving and traveling by train to meet with real estate owners and prospective franchisees ate up precious time; the expedience of flight would give McDonald's a competitive advantage. From the skies, Ray and his team could more easily scout out communities ripe for the picking, as evidenced by the presence of churches, schools, clusters of houses, all indications of potential customers. Then they could swiftly swoop in to negotiate the best parcels of land on which to situate their restaurants. It also made dropping in to the Criterion restaurant in St. Paul that much easier.

Standing before the City Council in St. Louis Park, the prematurely silver-haired Conley confidently argued the McDonald's case in front of the fractured council. They should put right out of their heads the idea that this drive-in would attract a sketchy crowd. There was no difference, he told them, between McDonald's and squeaky-clean institutions like the Girl Scouts, the YMCA, and Sunday school. The store would never install jukeboxes, pinball machines, or cigarette dispensers (which meant forgoing revenue, but diminished the likelihood of teenage shenanigans). There would be no carhops, no female staff at all, and litter would not be a concern: McDonald's stands were as pristine as operating rooms, and the staff was required to militantly scout the premises and surrounding area for trash and hasten its removal. Conley's explanation of the economics of the business perked up the ears of the council. Just because a typical meal at McDonald's cost only sixty cents didn't mean this was a slack, low-rent operation that served crummy food. Only quality ingredients purchased from local suppliers were used. Based on figures from other locations, the place was likely to generate an eye-popping $200,000 a year in sales, translating into a generous tax base for the city. This stupendous math didn't add up for several doubting-Thomas council members: "If he does that much business," one of them marveled, "we ought to open a municipal drive-in. Or else there will be another request for a similar permit in here, and it will be mine!" Another shook his head in disbelief. "If he serves a thousand meals a day, I'll eat the whole building."

As the dispute dragged on amid council indecision, the calendar clicked over to the year 1958. What finally tipped the outcome in favor of the new franchise was municipal interest in the city's reputation as a good place to conduct business. St. Louis Park couldn't afford to be seen as an unfriendly location that capriciously awarded and rescinded permits. At last, McDonald's could dig its shovels into the ground at the corner of Lake Street and get to work.

Six months later, on June 12, 1958, Zien and company were ready to raise the curtain on store number ninety-three. Don Conley flew Ray and Fred Turner to town from Chicago for the ribbon cutting. The lines never subsided that weekend, remaining two-deep until closing time on Sunday. In just four days, the restaurant rang up $23,000 in sales — twice what had been projected.

Overnight, Jim Zien and McDonald's morphed from villains to local heroes. Even the pricey, large-footprint neon out front rated a mention in the paper: "If you've never seen a sign worth this much mazuma, drop out that way, and enjoy some good food at the same time. His twenty employees will be happy to see you!"

Chief among those happy employees was Rollie Smith, husband of Joan. Zien had hired him to train as manager so that he himself didn't have to oversee the day-to-day. To get Zien and his brother-in-law on board, Ray had tabled his disdain of absentee owners. The long delay in the start of construction had been a nuisance for all parties, but it had proven to be a life-changing diversion personally for the Smiths and for Ray. Between the protracted debate that delayed the store's opening, and an easy commute thanks to the company Cessna, Ray had a ready-made excuse to drop into town — to stop by the Criterion to discuss business, and to frequently check in on that blond beauty.

Small talk gave way to duets in the Criterion after-hours lounge, a chance for Ray to show off his own proficiency on the keyboard. Their shared talent for music opened up a door to deeper intimacies. Ray could tell Joan what Ethel had no interest in hearing, his hopes and dreams and grand plans for the future of this company on which he'd staked his entire future. He was taken by how intently this new woman listened.

One afternoon, he'd boldly whisked her off to see the St. Paul Saints — their first "date," her first baseball game — in order to share his passion for the sport he'd adored since childhood. He arrived in a suit, as always, as if he were primed to negotiate a business deal, not as if he were about to spend two hours cheering a minor league ball team as they tramped in the mud after a rainstorm. Despite the weather, she later told a reporter, she'd been sure to wear her best dress and spike heels. She made a strong impression on this man, she knew, and she didn't want to dash the flame. They both were well aware of the danger in seeing each other. Though neither was particularly religious, each had been raised to believe in the sanctity of marriage. And yet, their attraction to each other had been instantaneous.

Joan wasn't prepared for sartorial Ray's instant transformation at the ballpark from smooth businessman to bombastic fan. "Go home, your mother's calling," he'd shouted at the opposing team's pitcher. It was a side of him she'd never seen before, a different, playful spirit from the one that erupted behind the keyboard. There was much to discover about this intriguing man.

Meanwhile, Rollie worked backbreaking twelve-hour days to make this new store a success. His ulterior motive: to prove his mettle as a future franchisee. Her husband's involvement with the company gave Ray another ruse by which to check in with Joan, by telephone. The mere sound of her voice sent chills of pleasure up and down his spine.

The winter of 1959 was proving to be the most exciting and frustrating time of Max Cooper's life. An invention called videotape had made possible his dream of bringing baseball and the boys of summer to television in the frosty off-season. After stints writing comedy and, later, radio scripts during World War II, Cooper had made a living largely as a press agent, representing the

Chicago jazz club the Blue Note and promoting movies and such around town. Another of his clients was the producer of the very first televised programs featuring bowling and golf. Cooper dreamed of becoming a producer himself. He was recovering from the recent failure of a big idea, a pinup magazine he'd created especially for the black man. *Duke,* he'd called it, after the great jazz player.

Television offered fresh possibilities. In just a decade of widespread existence, it had become an important medium for the delivery of America's favorite pastime to the crowds. Broadcast baseball games were consistently among the best-rated shows. The trouble was winter, when the sport went on hiatus. That's where balmy Cuba figured in. The four teams there routinely enlisted American players to play during the fallow winter months in the United States. Cooper knew fans would eagerly follow those familiar players while they themselves were holed up indoors. Beaming a game live from another country was an impossible technological proposition, but in this newfangled videotape, Cooper had a secret agent that allowed him to achieve the next best thing to a live broadcast.

After confabbing with the Cuban baseball

commissioner, Arturo Bengochea, Cooper negotiated a deal to bring his crew of twelve, including five cameramen and veteran baseball announcer Al Helfer, into the country. Then he got his hands on a couple of the very first, very pricey video recorders — $50,000 apiece. Games at Havana's Gran Stadium would be recorded live to tape. Back at the offices of the Cuban television station, local women were paid twenty-six dollars a week to painstakingly splice hundreds of pieces of videotape in order for the game to run a precise seventy-two minutes. Performing the postproduction locally saved Cooper a bundle. Making just one edit back in the States would have cost seventy-five dollars. Announcer Helfer then watched the show and scripted and recorded the play-by-play. *Winter Baseball,* Cooper called the series. Nearly a dozen stations around the United States signed on to carry the program, which was shipped to each subscriber by post, arriving just in time for airing to the baseball-starved American public on Saturday night. Viewers were wowed by the vision of the boys of summer on the field in the throes of winter, replete with quaint, localized touches, like a hand-operated scoreboard, maneuvered by a comely Cuban fashion model.

There was only one problem with Max Cooper's plan. His name was Fidel Castro. The magnetic young leader had recently risen to power after overthrowing Cuba's dictator, Fulgencio Batista. When Castro, who'd played the game as a college student, asked if he might throw out the first ball, Cooper had naturally consented, and had happily posed for a photo with his host. Flattery would get him everywhere; he deployed his pricey equipment to record the new leader's five-hour speeches. But as Castro's long-winded talks became increasingly tinged with anti-American rhetoric, tensions mounted. Suddenly, anything related to Cuba was equated with politics. Even baseball. Cooper's great idea struck out after just one season — and Castro soon after banned not just *Winter Baseball,* but all professional sports.

Back on the ground in Chicago, two of Cooper's associates had been minding his bread-and-butter business of public relations: Ben Burns, the now former editor of the black girlie magazine, and Al Golin, a young former salesman. The art of public relations required different finesse than advertising. PR men were paid to prod and coerce journalists to write stories about their clients, crafting messages and massaging facts to support their agendas. There was risk in this practice of "placing stories," since there was no way to guarantee a reporter would write up the message the way you wished, but it was worth it to try, especially since the public was more likely to trust what a journalist said than believe a paid claim.

With the boss otherwise engaged and eager to drum up new work, Burns had spotted an ad in a neighborhood newspaper for a new hamburger stand just outside the city in Des Plaines. A cold call on the telephone led to an invitation to stop by the office at 221 North LaSalle. Ray regaled Burns and Golin with his passion for hamburgers. They, in turn, regaled him with the power and potential of publicity. The men left the towering office building along the Chicago River dazed by this new client who'd committed to paying them $500 a month. In exchange, the press agents promised to work diligently to get the word out about Ray and his growing flock of franchisees. It seemed a luxurious commitment for a cash-strapped business, but it was cheaper than advertising, and Ray believed press coverage could help put McDonald's — and him — on the map and to stand out in an increasingly crowded field. Surely other hamburger concerns wouldn't be so wily. A publicity strategy could also help counter the combative reception they were receiving in other places as they had in St. Louis Park. An out-of-state corporation invading the local business landscape was an unwelcome event in many communities. The newly enlisted PR team crafted ready answers to the complaints. Arches! Speedee! Family! There were endless creative possibilities.

Clacking typewriters provided the sound track at the busy newsroom of the Associated Press at 50 Rockefeller Plaza in New York City. A bank of Teletype machines added to the noise, belching out tufts of paper on which the latest news was etched. The noisy din masked the sound of the high heels worn by the pretty young secretary who led Ray Kroc into the fray of the newsroom. Ray didn't understand how anyone could damned well think in this environment.

The PR team had been working to score an audience with the all-powerful news wire service for months. They needed an impressive "hit," a major placement that would justify their cost to Harry Sonneborn, the finicky financial wizard Ray had hired, who was watching every bill. The problem wasn't that the price Ray had agreed to pay for PR services was the exact sum Harry, a skilled executive, had agreed to take as salary. The issue was that the company was on a rapid descent into bankruptcy, and cost cutting was necessary to survival. The franchise agreement Ray had signed with the brothers just didn't add up to a sustainable business. Their chain now boasted 125 hamburger stands that had racked up close to $4 million in sales, and yet McDonald's and Ray were drowning in debt. The 1.4 percent portion of the royalty that stores sent to corporate simply didn't cover the bills. An emergency switch had been made from weekly to bimonthly payroll to stem the bleeding cash flow; a note posted on the corporate bulletin board offered a loan of fifteen bucks from petty cash to anyone strapped by the new schedule. A fresh and urgent burden had appeared. A builder had just defaulted on the construction of nine new stores, leaving the McDonald's corporation on the hook for at least half a million dollars — money the cash-strapped start-up didn't have.

Cooper's team had been working hard to earn their monthly retainer. Getting attention for a visiting celebrity was like shooting fish in a barrel. Getting it for the chief of a fifteen-cent hamburger restaurant was proving a bit trickier. There were dozens of them, variations on a theme. So far, Cooper and his men had managed to get the McDonald's name dropped in a handful of the important Chicago newspaper columns, attached to light, pithy human interest squibs:

A University of Omaha student, an heir to the Zenith millions, worked for $1.10 an hour to "make a little money" at an Omaha McDonald drive-in. The manager said, "Stormy would drive up in his custom designed car, park it next to my battered old Chevy, and then come in and work . . . for me."

The ultimate hit for any headline seeker was a mention by the man Ray and his entourage were here to see, the Pulitzer Prize–winning World War II correspondent turned opinion maker Hal Boyle. Boyle's wildly popular column ran in seven hundred papers around the nation, making him more widely read than any other journalist. A mere mention by Boyle was practically a guarantee that an avalanche of other press and, along with it, public interest would follow.

The celebrated, prolific newsman had

agreed to a lunch meeting, if only to get these flacks to stop hounding him. With that, Ray had been coerced into a trip to the Big Apple. While he loved appearing center stage, being the front man, he felt anything other than a call on a McDonald's, or prospective franchisees, or suppliers, was a waste of his time and money. Besides, with what little time he had for distraction, he'd rather take a trip to St. Paul, where he could indulge in the guilty pleasure of seeing and talking to that blond beauty with whom he was smitten.

The meeting with Boyle almost fell through. The columnist had forgotten another, more pressing commitment. In an instant, the planned lunch was cancelled. An alternative morning drop-in meeting at the AP offices was proposed. Bringing Ray into the newsroom might mean he'd get short shrift, but it was better than incurring his wrath for a wasted trip and altogether missing the chance of an audience with the great Hal Boyle.

Boyle was accustomed to speaking to brave soldiers on the battlefield or the generals who commanded the troops. Filling five columns a week could be a chore. Maybe this Kroc fellow had something relevant to say. America had gone mad,

Boyle would begin his story, for quick, casual meals like pizza and burgers.

Ray sniffed as the receptionist marched them to the venerable reporter's earthquake of a desk, the kind of disorganized mess that would, back at corporate headquarters or, God forbid, one of the stores, send Ray into paroxysms of ranting anger. Fred Turner had recently spotted the fanatically immaculate boss cleaning the holes of a mop wringer with a toothbrush. The PR men bristled at the sight before them, fearing the clutter might incite a Ray eruption, as it would, without question, on home turf. They were counting on this interview to come off perfectly. If Ray would just turn on the charming raconteur half of his personality and keep the hotheaded side closeted for a half hour or so, Boyle would write a great story, the McDonald's fortunes would soar, and their retainer would be assured.

Boyle absentmindedly shoved aside a stack of papers on a chair to make room for his guest; Ray sniffed, choosing to perch on his host's desk.

The reporter fired his first salvo: What was the story with these fifteen-cent hamburgers?

The diminutive Ray smiled his wily smile

122

and took a breath. He spoke even louder than usual, so his story didn't get lost in the newsroom noise.

"I put the hamburger on the assembly line," he declared, taking ownership of the brothers' efficient choreography. Reporters at surrounding desks slowed their typing so they could eavesdrop as this visitor described his transformation from dropout to cup salesman to savior of the hamburger operation in the desert. Ray didn't need PR coaching to remind him to spout his usual bluster. It was far more alluring to sound like the rescuer of this sleepy joint than the reality, that he had pressed the McDonald brothers for the right to work with them because *he* was desperate for a lucky break. McDonald's was more than a restaurant, he told Boyle. It was a vital part of the *community,* as virtuous and essential a presence as the Scouts, he said, repeating the refrain Conley used to defend their honor. And just look at the cross section of men he'd launched into the ultimate American dream of small business ownership: retired doctors, dentists, and navy commanders. A former Linotype operator. A former schoolteacher. One hundred million hamburgers a year, and counting. Sixty new restaurants in twenty-five states were under construction.

The growth was phenomenal.

What he didn't let on was that the corporation could implode at any moment, and all the individual McDonald's stores would be left to fend for themselves. They might change their names or their menus, but at least they'd have a going concern. Ray, though, would be left in the dust. Ever the salesman, he wasn't going to let the impending dire prognosis for the corporation get in the way of a good story.

Boyle scribbled away. The numbers were a compelling hook. The PR men were excited; the old war correspondent seemed to be getting the gist of it. The other reporters who'd gathered appeared to be calculating the math, too.

By the time Boyle declared the end of the interview, an hour and a half had elapsed.

His column soon ran across the nation, accompanied by breathless headlines that anointed Ray a millionaire, when in fact he barely had two nickels to rub together: "He's Getting Rich on Hamburgers" and "$25 Million in Lowly Hamburger" and "Burger King Keeps Making Huge Fortune."

The behind-the-scenes economic reality of McDonald's didn't matter to Boyle or to the newspaper-reading public. The story did the trick Cooper's team had hoped it would. Boyle's column in 1959 led to a deluge of calls and letters to 221 North LaSalle from potential franchisees eager to hitch a ride with this man named Ray Kroc — to help him with his vision of building golden arches and dispensing hamburgers across the land.

5
WRETCHED CITY

YOU MUST BE A PERFECTIONIST.

Bold, declarative statements punctuated the bare-boned logistics conveyed in the saffron-colored manual Joan held in her hands. As far as Ray was concerned, McDonald's wasn't a hamburger restaurant — it was a religion. If that was the case, this spiral-bound opus was the Bible, and Joan and Rollie Smith were converts:

> Your parking lot — as seen by your customers — is to McDonald's what the lobby is to the Waldorf. THE OUTSIDE MUST BE GROOMED AND MANICURED AT LEAST EVERY HOUR.

A luxurious New York City hotel seemed about as far away as Mars from the perch where Joan sat — a desk tucked behind the walk-in coolers in the back of a newly constructed set of arches on West Main

Street in Rapid City, South Dakota. The Rapid Creek that gave the city its name flowed adjacent to the property that had been acquired for this store. On the tracks across the street, the passing railroad poured out a plaintive wail. From the park erected to celebrate prehistoric creatures up on the crest of Skyline Drive, an enormous bright-green concrete statue of a brontosaurus loomed over the city — a shrine, of sorts, to this area's long-ago inhabitants.

A half hour's drive south of here, another far larger curiosity, this one a monument to democracy, soared high on the side of a mountain — four presidential faces immortalized, larger than life, in granite. The new hit thriller *North by Northwest,* from the master of suspense, director Alfred Hitchcock, featured a heart-thumping chase scene around this Mount Rushmore. The entire film had been inspired by Hitch's vision of an actor crawling all over Abraham Lincoln's eyebrow. Restrictions by the skittish National Park Service had dashed his dream. Instead, he had to settle for dispatching movie stars Cary Grant and Eva Marie Saint for a climb over a facsimile erected on a Hollywood back lot. Still, flocks of tourists arrived at the real mountain, querying park rangers for clues to where the action had taken place. It was suddenly an exciting place to visit. Perhaps traffic at this monument and at the dino park would translate into business for Joan and Rollie's McDonald's.

As for the cleanliness expected of owners, outlined with military precision in the manual, Joan needed little reminder. Rollie had himself been indoctrinated over the last year in his job as manager in St. Louis Park. There were five pages alone on how to clean stainless steel — more space, even, than was committed to the sacrosanct blueprint for the showpiece spuds in the chapter "The Curing and Frying of French Fry Potatoes." Rollie dutifully mimicked the manual's instructions and snapped up errant trash when he left work in St. Louis Park at the end of his shift.

Ray's attention to detail, his ambition, and his natty dress had left a deep impression on Joan, too. Her sister's husband was working now at Zien's McDonald's, hoping to rate a store of his own. Ray Kroc appeared to be the family savior. She knew from how intently he looked at her when they were together that if she wanted, he would save her personally, too. She also knew if she let him, the consequences would be steep.

For the moment, she was the wife of a

newly minted McDonald's owner-operator, focused on her mission to help Rollie carve out his own empire here in these wide-open Black Hills. They had moved into a spacious home in the South Canyon neighborhood at the corner of 38th and St. Louis Streets, a quick mile-and-a-half drive from the store. The split-level house was just a few years old and, at 1,600 square feet, larger than any place the Smiths had lived in their dozen years of marriage. In what little downtime Rollie would have, he looked forward to dipping a fishing rod into Lime Creek, the cold, gushing stream that ran right in front and imbued this suburb with a countrified feel. Maybe he'd get lucky and snare a rainbow trout.

For his hard work managing the St. Louis Park store back in Minnesota, Rollie had earned a cash bonus of $12,000. It was an astronomical sum, double what he'd taken home from his work on the railroad the year before — more money than he and Joan could ever have imagined in their possession at one time. They plowed this windfall right back into its source as a deposit on their new business. Zien served as silent partner, pitching in the difference in the start-up costs necessary to build out the restaurant and get Rapid City up and running.

The cost of the move had aggravated their usual strapped-for-cash finances, and the Smiths had arrived in town flat broke. A nice lady Joan met on arrival invited her to lunch — there were so many nice ladies in a place like Rapid City — and when it came time to pay, Joan dug into her purse and displayed for her new friend all the money she had in the world: one dollar and fifty-six cents. At least once the store opened, Joan said as she shrugged, her family would have a steady source of income, and, hopefully, wealth.

Such motivation propelled the Smiths as they plunged into the task of establishing McDonald's store number 223, the first in the state of South Dakota. Would-be franchisees who didn't own their own land typically had to relocate where the corporation had found lots to develop. Allentown, Pennsylvania, had been the other option presented to Rollie and Joan, but they'd chosen Rapid City for the proximity to each of their families. Rollie was a Montana boy at heart, and this situated him closer to his roots. For the inconvenience of moving, and the required elbow grease, getting to own a McDonald's was seen by many as the equivalent of being handed a winning lottery ticket. Ray's sister, Lorraine, had recently set up shop in Lafayette, Indiana, and in their first month of operations, despite inclement weather, they'd taken in $22,000. They were, Ray had told the brothers, happy as a couple of kittens.

If the sacrifice meant her family wouldn't have to fret about food or finances anymore, Joan felt the upheaval a worthy inconvenience. People here were welcoming enough, in that polite but reserved way midwesterners acknowledged newcomers. The born-and-bred locals were accustomed to outsiders from all over the world arriving for short- or long-term stints in and around the air force base.

Joan strategized her debut. If they made friends over there, perhaps she could play at the Captain's Club. Or up at the Arrowhead Country Club, which Rollie longed to join so he could tackle the golf course. The Canyon Lake Club was another venue where live music could be heard. Joan had already introduced herself down at Plummer's Piano and Organ, and the wife of the shop owner was so taken with her playing that she'd signed on with Joan for lessons. Her music had always opened doors. Look at how she'd met Rollie — and Ray. She loved that just by sitting at the keyboard, she had the power to make people laugh or cry. Or fall in love.

From up on that hillside at the dinosaur park, Joan could gaze at the blankness of the landscape for miles and miles and miles and consider her new home. A greyhound racetrack sat out near the base, and a few drive-in movies as well as saloons were scattered around downtown along with a few upscale nightclubs and dance halls. About the most intriguing part of Rapid, as the locals shorthanded the name of their town, seemed to be the presence of ghosts in the fancy Alex Johnson Hotel on Sixth Street. That, and the local artist possessed with sculpting a mountain, just seventeen miles from Rushmore, into the likeness of a Native American chief. Joan would have to search to find her place here.

Aside from her lack of money, time was in short supply. Crewing up the store was the next order of business. The only women allowed to work at McDonald's were the wives of owners, who were encouraged, if not expected, to assist their husbands with behind-the-scenes tasks — scheduling, personnel, and ordering food and supplies. Particularly since his own wife had refused to have anything to do with his business,

Ray emphasized the importance of a spouse's buy-in and support of the hard work it would take for the restaurant to succeed. Even wives, however, weren't allowed to perform front-of-counter work.

Finding clean, well-mannered young military men or students from the South Dakota School of Mines looking to earn seventy-five cents an hour was a cinch. Rollie and Joan set about training the men so they could nimbly move from grilling burgers to peeling and curing potatoes and frying them up to scooping ice cream and operating the Multimixers to scrubbing every inch of the place on a rigid schedule. The ability to perform each task kept everyone in synch and made the rhythm of the work flow smoothly.

It was a proven system. Ray's charge Fred Turner had been compiling and perfecting the manual for several years now. The confidential "Bible" had grown to eighty-four pages, which included forms for calculating inventory, cash on hand, work schedules, and monthly royalty payments — precise, paint-by-numbers directions provided for every facet of the operation.

The scolding voice of Ray leaped off the page:

Anyone can make and sell a hamburger — but only you can sell the atmosphere, wholesomeness, quality, cleanliness, speed of service, courtesy and dozens of other intangibles which McDonald's offers.

It was critical that the finest food be purchased. That meant lean meat: "No hearts, lungs, dyes or preservatives." Buns were to be ordered up from a local baker who used Ecko-brand pans number 7524 — not a cluster bun, "sliced clear, not hinged." The crucial potatoes were to be delivered weekly. An operator could expect to use three to ten hundred-pound sacks per day. When the spud of choice, the Idaho Burbank russet, was out of season, it was acceptable to sub out California white, Oregon or Washington russets. Joan placed her order with the local produce supplier, Fred Kuypers, who was certain this woman on the other end of the phone must be loopy. What could a new establishment, a drive-in place, possibly need with a *thousand* pounds of potatoes? When he arrived on West Main Street with just a one hundred-pound sack, Joan corrected him. He returned to fill the basement with every last potato in his warehouse, and berated this novice for buying so much produce it would surely rot.

When doors opened for business on West Main Street, she happily proved him wrong. The entire order was used up within the first week. The absence of carhops was hardly a deterrent for customers who knew they could get that kind of service at the other area drive-ins, like the Snow White or KP's. McDonald's was more for families, anyhow — and *its* parking lot was paved. "Two hamburgers, two sodas, and two shoes," the locals called out their orders. Already, Rollie's regulars had a shorthand for the fries. He thought it amusing enough that he sent it in, proudly, as an item of note for the newly launched McDonald's operators' newsletter.

The Smiths didn't have to work too hard to get noticed in Rapid. Rollie quickly became known as the local "Mr. McDonald's," the tall, handsome, affable face of this new business who sternly policed his workers in order to keep up with corporate standards. Joan was his beautiful young wife, the vivacious blond piano player who'd have a cigarette in one hand and a martini in the other when kids came over to play after school, but who'd also dutifully take her daughter to services at Trinity Lutheran Church downtown. Perhaps she was a bit more outgoing than the typically reserved locals would have liked, but big-city people were like that, they supposed. Locals came to consider these newcomers fun-loving — an ideal couple, really. One prominent businessman heard them sneak into his swimming pool one night to go skinny-dipping, and he let them be.

Tongues wagged whenever the diminutive chief of McDonald's arrived from Chicago at Rapid City Airport on his private plane emblazoned with the company logo. He'd been spotted in town having dinner with Joan and Rollie, and gossips observed scornfully that Joan seemed to lean in across the table toward her husband's boss a bit too suggestively. Every so often, she'd impose on a friend to mind her daughter for a few days, offering up a vague excuse with a wink for her need to get out of town — without her husband. The friend couldn't help but wonder: Was it to see Ray? What, if anything, was going on between them?

Business was so good on Main Street, permission was granted within a year for Rollie to open another restaurant, on the south side, just a bit east off Eighth Street near the putt-putt golf and the main thoroughfare that led tourists to Rushmore. As the dutiful spouse, Joan would drive out to check on the construction site each day.

Despite how entrenched she was with Rollie, despite the friendships they formed with officers and their wives from the air force base, despite her occasional piano gigs, which yielded admiration of her skillful technique, Joan couldn't fathom a future here. The wind in the winter whipped colder, the summer humidity a bit more intensely than back home. The locals could shorthand it "Rapid," but she developed her own nickname for the place: "Wretched City."

Ray Kroc offered the promise of escape to another, dynamic world. He was so charming, and he played piano so well. Ray, she believed, was her knight in shining armor. And Ray was desperate to make this blond beauty with so much pluck and charm his wife. The connection between them had been instantaneous. Each time they'd talked since that night, they'd grown closer, and despite the fact that they were married to other people, he was certain of his love. He kept asking for her hand in marriage, and she kept stalling, saying she needed more time.

In April 1961, she said yes.

The complexity of his personal life continued to be just a fraction of the trouble facing Ray. The potentially fatal cracks in the company's infrastructure deepened. Sales at individual stores were booming, with franchisees continuing to rake in phenomenal sums, an average of more than $17,000 each store, per month, in the summer. And yet the numbers just didn't compute. With the expense of scouting locations, building out stores to local code, renting the extra space necessary to accommodate employees at 221 North LaSalle, and paying staff salaries, the corporate net income totaled half what it was the previous year, a paltry $12,000. Banks were wary of lending to the business, given its puny books and prospects. There was no way around it: McDonald's, the corporation, was on a precipitous march toward bankruptcy. The elevator operator at headquarters who gaily declared, upon arriving at the McDonald's floor, "Hamburger Heaven," had no idea how close the company was to rising to the great hereafter.

Ray's personal financial situation was just as precarious. He was leveraged to the hilt, and he still wasn't paying himself a penny for the new venture. He and his longtime secretary, June Martino, still relied on their income from Prince Castle Sales. The tall, plucky, blue-eyed June had been an indispensible and generous fixture in the office for years now, since back when Ray first started selling Multimixers. The PR team had parlayed the secretary's unusual résumé into a newspaper story, where she was celebrated for being as average as "an Eskimo in a hothouse." She'd been a secret shopper for the department store Montgomery Ward, and secretary to meat purveyor Oscar Mayer, whose German heritage she shared. She'd met her husband, Louis, an engineer, when they both studied electronics. During World War II, she'd patriotically signed on to test radar systems and troubleshoot airplane radio systems as part of the Women's Army Corps. Together, they'd launched a heating and contracting business, where she was pressed into service as needed, wiring chicken coops or performing feats of plumbing.

When her parents became ill, their medical treatments ultimately tapped out the family finances, and June was so desperate to find a job, she'd marched into an employment agency and announced: "I am broke. I need work. Give me the first job you have. I will be an acrobat if you want." Her proficiency as a figurative juggler was evident to Ray within moments of their meeting. He hired her on the spot.

The encouragement Mr. Multimixer didn't receive at home from Ethel rained down in abundance at the office from June. When Ray first signed on to serve as franchise agent for the McDonald brothers, it was June he called with a report from San Bernardino. "Let's go for it," she'd responded enthusiastically. For all her practicality, June had a predilection for the mystic. She'd never forgotten the prediction her boss had told her he'd received as a four-year-old from a phrenologist, a soothsayer who divined a person's future by "reading" the bumps on their head. His assessment of young Ray was that he'd find success in the food business after age fifty. (He was, when he met Dick and Mac, age fifty-two.) She was more than merely supportive about jumping into this alliance with the McDonald brothers. She bankrolled it, taking out a personal loan and adding a hundred dollars' cash from her own purse to help Ray incorporate McDonald's Systems, Inc. The long shot of a restaurant concern taking off in any measurable way didn't daunt her as she toiled alongside her boss for hours on end. She and her husband signed on early as franchisees, opening a store in the suburb of Glen Ellyn, Illinois. And as the corporation sputtered along, June stepped into another, unofficial role, as den mother. She'd patiently counsel the growing staff, wiping their tears after botched love affairs or wrath-filled encounters with Ray, welcoming them into her home in times of personal crisis and proving to be resourceful in the face of any challenge. When she mistakenly ordered sandwiches filled with meat for a company meeting on a Friday, forgetting that the mostly Catholic staff couldn't indulge, she boldly placed an urgent call to the cardinal's office to request special dispensation. She wasn't Catholic herself; she simply couldn't bear to waste the food.

For her dedication and relentless optimism and for forsaking her own family in service of the company good — not to mention her navigation of his temper, even when it was directed at her — Ray rewarded June 10 percent of McDonald's stock. And though that seemed a grand display of generosity, he pointed out that a Chicago Transit Authority subway token held more value.

While June was the soul of the operation, the next hire Ray had made proved to be the brains of it. The lanky thirty-nine-year-old Harry Sonneborn, who, in Ray's estimation, resembled Abe Lincoln, had left his job as vice president at the chain of six hundred Tastee Freez stores over a dispute with the company's owner. Before that, he'd worked in a garment business that made men's slacks. An orphan raised in New York City by an adoptive family of Orthodox Jews, Harry had initially bristled at the idea of approaching Ray. Word swirled in the restaurant trade that Ray was anti-Semitic. Harry was assured Ray's salty speech was peppered with epithets directed at all races, religions, and creeds, including his own Christian faith and Bohemian heritage. Despite his misgivings, Harry arranged an interview.

The men bonded over their obsessive passion for the mechanics of franchising. Ray was far too overextended to pay such an experienced executive a reasonable salary, but Harry agreed to work for a pittance, eager to put some ideas to the test that he'd never got to try in the ice cream trade. The true rewards would come later. Ray loved this mentality, too. Money, he believed, was secondary to passion for the work. It proved to be a good and necessary pairing. Harry offset Ray's bluster with a sober appreciation and respect for fundamentals like banking, mortgages, and finance. To Harry, the food that was served was of little consequence. The persuasive power of the balance sheet was the essence of business. To right the sinking ship that was McDonald's would take much more than attention to details like the taste of the pickle and the size of a dollop of ketchup that consumed Ray's every synapse. Harry had something else up his sleeve.

The idea of enlisting an army of accomplices willing to pay for the privilege of assisting an ambitious entrepreneur in fanning out his creation across the nation had hardly begun with the race to franchise McDonald's, or even fast food. Its modern roots sprouted in the mid-1800s, with an indispensible household invention — the sewing machine. At a time when most clothing was still stitched and mended by hand, a man named Isaac Singer concocted a nine-hundred-stitch-a-minute sewing machine that was nothing short of revolutionary. Every homemaker coveted one of these efficient wonders, and Singer made ownership possible even for those who couldn't hack the steep $120 purchase price. He set up a national network of distributors who paid a fee to Singer for the right to sell the machines. Local buyers, in turn, paid them off, a dollar a month. When repairs were needed, the franchisee was sure to get their business.

Franchise ownership was a compelling conceit for the would-be businessman (and it was, more often than not, a man) industrious enough to want more than to punch a clock, but not necessarily confident enough or inventive enough (or wealthy enough) to launch a business entirely from scratch. Consumers were attracted to them for different reasons. As trains, then roads, broke down geographic barriers and allowed for seamless flow from one community to another, the public began to put stock in the cachet of a recognizable brand, trumping the unreliable unknown of a local merchant. The franchise model was deployed to distribute all manner of products and services: Coca-Cola used it to get its formula to local manufacturers, who brewed, bottled, and distributed the syrupy drink. Holiday Inn used it to spread its chain of consistently clean motel rooms where families were welcomed. Henry Ford used franchising to build a network of outposts at which his vehicles could be sold. Howard Johnson had been selling the rights to his orange-roofed ice cream stands since 1935. Root-beer stands called A&W swept the middle and the western states, with 171 in operation by 1933.

Ray and Harry could have opted to charge franchisees a higher royalty, license entire territories to wealthy groups of investors, or, as other chains had, aim to sell out to a larger corporation. They could supply the food to stores and skim a percentage of the cost off the top. Were they to do that, they'd have to create a complicated web of suppliers, who'd inevitably expect kickbacks, and the quality of the food would be lowered. In Ray's estimation, most of the food the competition sold was garbage. He sniffed at the frozen hamburgers with onions ground right into the meat and frozen pre-blanched potatoes and milk shakes made from mixes that other stands deigned to offer.

Harry offered up the perfect solution: McDonald's should own its real estate. He believed that far more valuable than what a franchise sold was the land on which those sales occurred. Given its financial situation, though, McDonald's, the corporation, struggled to keep the lights on. Investing in property was an impossibility. Harry calculated the perfect way to skirt that problem. Landowners eager to cash in on the great suburban migration were persuaded to sell or lease their unused property to a subsidiary Harry created called Franchise Realty. New franchisees eager to get in on the Mc-

Donald's game would, in turn, plunk down a $7,500 security deposit. Harry would use that money to make the down payment on the land and for construction on the restaurant. Once it was opened, the franchisee would pay a premium rent to McDonald's, a percentage of sales, giving the company additional income. It was the classic business fix: Use other people's money to build your empire.

In his role as Franchise Realty's president, Harry hit the skies with a team of five other scouts, but not until pilot Conley upgraded from a single-engine plane to a less risky ride. Logging over a hundred hours a month in the air, Harry paid call after call in search of new locations and to court banks and other willing coconspirators.

Now, along with its delicious food from scratch, McDonald's would be distinguished by its unbeatable asset: a growing network of prime properties in desirable locations. This held tremendous appeal to prospective lenders.

For concocting this ingenious plan, Ray rewarded Harry with twice the stock he'd gifted June, a whopping 20 percent. That left Ray with 70 percent. Collectively, it was worth as much as fistfuls of Monopoly money.

Harry remained as emotionally invested in the success of the company as Ray. When that builder had run off in 1959 and left them on the hook for half a million dollars and the implosion of McDonald's seemed a certainty, Harry was so despondent he contemplated suicide. But by turning to various suppliers of paper goods and buns and the like — people eager to see their customer survive — he'd managed to quickly raise $125,000 in cash. The immediate infusion kept the hand of doom at bay, but it still hovered ominously overhead.

With the help of two former IRS accountants June had brought into the fold, Harry creatively fiddled with McDonald's books, understating the corporation's expenses and overstating earnings in order to show a profit. "Development accounting," he called it. The numbers in this rosier balance sheet painted a picture of the company's future that was far more compelling to potential lenders. Finally, in a hotshot young finance wizard named Fred Fedeli he found a risk-taking banker who had a gut feeling there might be something to this drive-in with the real estate plan. In exchange for a $1.5 million cash infusion, Fedeli demanded a 22.5 percent chunk of the company's stock. Ray balked at the terms, but Harry convinced him that without this money, not only would the stock continue to be worthless, the entire business would be as well.

As part of the lifesaving agreement and to bolster confidence among the banking types, Franchise Realty was folded into McDonald's, and the money-minded Harry replaced Ray in the role of president and chief executive of the new, combined company. For the first time, in his new capacity as chairman, Ray was able to pay himself a salary.

This would come in handy as he set about addressing his personal life.

There was hardly a person in Rapid who wasn't surprised — or scandalized — when Rollie's vivacious wife and the McDonald's boss left their spouses to start a new life together. Despite Ray's wobbly finances, a house was secured for him to move into with Joan in Woodland Hills, a wide-open enclave in Los Angeles County, nearly thirty miles north of the bustle of the city's downtown. The home conveniently offered a view (with the aid of binoculars) of the local McDonald's on a street down below. With Harry handling day-to-day operations, Ray would be content to settle into his role as chairman from the satellite office he'd started for the company in the golden west with the woman he loved by his side.

In an attempt to soften the blow of the family upheaval, Joan's now fourteen-year-old daughter, Linda, was whisked off in the corporate plane and treated to trips to Chicago and California, where she toured the private school for girls, Westlake. She'd been enrolled there for the fall. She'd met Ray at the Criterion, and she knew he was important from the reverence with which his name had been spoken in their household. All of a sudden, he was to become her stepfather.

Before they could settle into their new lives, Ray and Joan first had to establish temporary residence in Las Vegas, a place where no-fault divorces could be obtained quickly. They'd just need to wait out the requisite six weeks before they could be free to legitimize their relationship in the eyes of the law and social convention. Five weeks into their stay, Joan backed out of the engagement. Was there something she learned about Ray in those five intense weeks of togetherness that made her change her mind? Or was she caving, as she said years later, to the pressure from her family? Joan's mother had registered her stern displeasure with her abandonment of Rollie. As for Joan's daughter, the wooing seemed to have fallen flat. "If you marry him," Linda advised Joan, "forget that you have a daughter."

And so Joan returned to Rollie, the vast Black Hills, and Wretched City.

"Will you state your name, please?"
"Ethel Janet Kroc."

A sense of resignation choked the weary voice of Ray's soon to be ex-wife as she took the stand in Cook County Court in Chicago. At this stage, the appearance was purely a formality. In moments, the door would be shut on nearly forty years of marriage. The news that Ray planned to leave had been transmitted to Ethel secondhand. She'd been visiting Pensacola, Florida, to help care for her ailing mother, who lived there with her sister Mae. Mae and her husband had seized the opportunity to launch McDonald's in the Panhandle. Their first two stores were consistently among the top producers. Ray had flown in on the company plane for the day, as much to check in on operations as to see his wife. He took his brother-in-law out for a ride, and on the way informed him that he was going to file for divorce. Before Ethel returned to Arlington Heights, he'd moved out of the house and off to California with Joan. Except for his clothing, he'd left everything behind — even his beloved natural wood Steger and Sons mid-grand piano.

Joan's sudden departure from Woodland Hills didn't squelch Ray's intention of ending his marriage. It was time to get out. "Dry rot" had long been creeping in and strangling their relationship. Having already established a residence and an office out west made the break easier. Ray would just take a room at the Whitehall Hotel on his visits to Chicago. The oak-paneled private club there was one of his favorite haunts in the city.

"During the time you lived together as husband and wife, did you treat him as a good, true and faithful wife?" quizzed Ethel's attorney, Norman Becker.

"Yes I was," said Ethel.

"Calling your attention to on or about April seventh, 1961, did you leave your husband or did he leave you?"

"He left me."

"Did you give him any cause or reason for leaving you?"

The answer, to Ethel, was no. But to Ray, Ethel's mounting distress with his ambition

151

had been responsible for layering the bricks of the wall that rose between them. Of course, there was also the fact that he'd fallen in love with Joan.

To serve as witnesses to her character, Ethel's sister Mae was joined by Ray's sister, Lorraine, whose McDonald's in Lafayette was experiencing a steady rise in sales each day. These two women knew each half of the couple well. They'd witnessed Ethel's suffering. How sad and ironic it was that *her* family had been destroyed by this business, while each of theirs had prospered because of it. Each woman concurred, under oath, that Ray's wife had been a good spouse and that she had, indeed, given her husband "no cause or reason" for leaving.

To buy his freedom, Ray signed over their home and all its contents, as well as their Lincoln Continental, and agreed to pay $30,000 a year in alimony. To finance the settlement and attorneys' fees, Ray sold the one asset he had that was worth anything — Prince Castle Sales, the distribution company he'd formed from which to sell the Multimixers. A team of his employees bought him out for $150,000 — with cash they got after Ray cosigned a loan arranged by Harry. They were, after all, cash-poor themselves.

"Your husband has also agreed in the event of his decease, he will make an irrevocable will, whereby your daughter, Marilyn Barg, is to receive one-third of his net estate, you understand this?"

"Yes."

Ethel most certainly understood. She'd pressed for this provision. She was deeply worried for her daughter, Marilyn, nicknamed Lynn. At age thirty-six, divorced and now remarried, Lynn was struggling to make it as a singer. She was struggling with alcohol, too. Ethel wanted to know that her only child would have the promise of a safety net. Even though their relationship was frosty, and even if, at the moment, he had more debt than money in the bank, at least Ray would be obligated to provide for their daughter if anything were to happen to Ethel.

The headline in the news in the aftermath of the divorce decree cinched a humiliating finale: "Loses Kroc, Wins Pot." To keep her newly single daughter company, Ethel's mother returned to Illinois to live with her in the house on Ironwood Drive. Though Ray was gone, his presence loomed large in all that he'd left behind: the furniture he liked to acquire at estate sales, which allowed him to get much nicer quality than he could otherwise afford. The splurge purchase of twin lamps featuring sculptures of the emperor and empress of Japan. The monogrammed mink stole from Lobich Brothers Furriers. She could stuff the photos from their occasional vacations — snapshots of happier times — into a drawer, but she couldn't entirely shelve the good memories. Or, for that matter, the bad.

There was one artifact remaining that she couldn't bear to keep underfoot: that piano, a constant reminder of those carefree days long ago at Paw-Paw Lake, when she'd first fallen for Ray. It was one thing, before McDonald's, that had made him so happy. How long had it been since he'd even made time to play?

She was sentimental enough to want to keep the instrument in the family, but she had no desire to have to look at it day in, day out. Its very presence left a tiny glimmer of hope that he might, one day, return to take a seat at its upholstered bench and serenade her with beautiful music.

Ethel called the movers to crate it up and ship it south, to her sister's house in Florida.

Liberated from his unhappy marriage, Ray set about obtaining an equally important divorce, this one from the brothers Mc-

154

Donald. It proved an even costlier separation. Seven years into the partnership, long-simmering resentments had boiled over. Ray had been working hard, for free, leveraged six ways to Sunday, while the brothers received a handsome monthly check as part of their agreement. In 1960 alone, their slice of the royalty topped $189,000 — and that didn't factor in the $100,000 income they were earning from their own store, the original McDonald's.

Despite their grand income, the brothers were beginning to feel frozen out of the business that carried their name. They'd kept up a brisk communication with Ray via Dictaphone tapes, recorded monologues dispatched through the mail, chock-full of ideas and updates and punctuated with silly, slightly off-color jokes. It made for a one-sided virtual water cooler, offering an exchange more vibrant than a letter, but without the capacity for real-time interaction that was possible in a phone call. This distance from corporate headquarters was taking a toll. Their input was usually dismissed.

Particularly irksome was a promotional photo of Ray, June, Harry, Don, and Fred standing before an enormous cake gaily decorated with the words "Happy Fifth Anniversary Ray Kroc's McDonald's." McDonald's had been around for far more than five years, and it most certainly wasn't *Ray's*. The increasing drumbeat of press that exalted Ray as "the founder," and placed the location of the very first store in Des Plaines, Illinois, seemed to erase Dick and Mac, and the original store in San Berdoo, from history.

It wasn't just that the working relationship was uncomfortable. As far as outside investors were concerned, it was risky. Prospective lenders analyzing the contract feared that the whim of the brothers could leave the corporation on the hook at a moment's notice. After all, their deal stipulated that they had final say and complete control of all the stores. Ray was legally obligated to get any change made to original blueprints okayed in writing, like the addition of a basement for a boiler, necessary in locations where winter was a factor. Dick and Mac had given verbal okays, but, on the advice of their lawyer, never written ones. They'd refused Ray's demand, delivered via telegram, that they give him more control.

Severing ties seemed to make the most sense for the sake of the corporation's long-term future. Ray and Harry asked Dick and Mac to name their price to walk away from the business they'd created. The brothers had a new idea, anyway, for a series of sparkling clean, efficient low-budget motels, spread across the country every four hundred miles or so. Bagpipers, they imagined, would serenade the customers to their rooms adorned with murals of the Scottish Highlands. They had even chosen a name: A Wee Bit O' Scotland.

They deliberated and delivered their verdict. They'd sign over total control of their creation, including their name and their monthly royalty, to Ray — in exchange for a one-time cash payment of $2.7 million. After taxes, that would leave them each a million dollars — exactly what they'd aspired to amass when they first arrived in the West. After thirty years of working seven days a week, they felt they'd earned it.

Ray didn't give a damn what they thought they deserved or what they intended to do next. Raising that kind of money was unfathomable.

"Where am I going to get 2.7 million dollars?" he demanded angrily.

Dick didn't give a damn, either. "Well," he responded, "that's not our problem. That's *your* problem."

Financing, he told Ray, was out of the question. The brothers McDonald wanted the entire payment at once, and if that wasn't possible, they'd be happy to continue with the agreement as it was, collecting the 0.5 percent royalty due them. Ray knew that until he rid himself of the albatross of Dick and Mac, the company was in a straitjacket.

In search of a source for this pot of gold, the beleaguered Harry flew to New York to appeal to a group of a dozen institutional investors. He was primed to deliver his speech: "The only reason we sell fifteen-cent hamburgers," he told them, "is because they are the greatest producer of revenue from which our tenants can pay us rent." Hiding his nerves once his monologue was done, Harry excused himself to use the restroom while the men deliberated his request. Their answer would determine the fate of McDonald's. Without this cash infusion to pay off the brothers, Harry didn't know what he'd do. As he stood at the urinal, one of the executives joined him and casually let slip that the deal had been approved. By the end of 1961, Dick and Mac had their checks in hand — and now, McDonald's belonged, outright, to Ray, Harry, June, and a cadre of intrepid investors making a bold gamble. Among the insiders, the financial saviors became reverentially known as "the Twelve Apostles."

Ray hadn't seen the last of San Berdoo. When Dick and Mac informed him that they had no intention of turning over their original store as part of the buyout, he exploded in a rage, ranting and raving that he hated their guts. To comply with tax law, the brothers took down their arches and obliterated their family name, renaming the hamburger place that had made them millionaires the Big M. They left the business in the hands of their longtime employees and bought a house in Palm Springs.

On the warpath for revenge, Ray flew to the desert, bought a parcel of land a block away from the hamburger stand that had captivated him and changed his life, and built his own McDonald's, arches and all. For the rest of his days, he maintained with pride that he'd run the brothers out of business. Dick, when asked, recounted the story a bit less dramatically; they'd sold the Big M, the original McDonald's, after a few years when Mac became ill, dashing their motel dream, and settled full-time into retirement.

Having lost the woman he adored, and having come close to losing the company in which he'd invested every fiber of his being, Ray quivered like a lovesick schoolboy, pouring out his heart and soul to the man who had become his best friend, Art Trygg. Trygg worked at Ray's country club, and had confessed as they became closer that he had a checkered past — he'd done time in the state penitentiary for armed robbery. That didn't squelch the friendship; indeed, Ray said, he preferred the honesty. (He toned down Trygg's charges when he wrote about him in his memoir, saying that his friend had been busted for driving a beer truck, not for the armed robbery that had actually landed him in prison.) Trygg loyally served Ray as his valet and chauffeur, keeping watch over him when he was out on the town. Ray also put him in charge of the upbeat monthly McDonald's newsletter, *McDonald's: The Drive-in with the Golden Arches.* The house organ was intended to excite existing owners with the growth of the company and to soothe the frayed nerves of franchisees who'd plunked down their fees and were enduring long waits, up to a year, for their store to be ready for business.

The night Ray lopped off the top of his left middle finger in his car door, Trygg dutifully ferried him and the detached joint to Henrotin Hospital, then wrote up the incident for the newsletter. (Reattachment surgery failed, leaving Ray with a stubby middle finger.) The lonely hamburger king even enticed his friend to join him out in California. Though he was relieved to be unencumbered by Ethel, he hated being a bachelor. Not being married made him feel incomplete.

Over the next two years, Joan would steel herself to defy her mother's disapproval, her daughter's threats, and her husband's sadness. She was finally prepared, in the face of all the pressure and shame, to escape Wretched City, and marry Ray, once and for all.

There was only one problem with her plan: the new woman in Ray's life.

6
THE J AND R DOUBLE ARCH RANCH

No one who met Jane Dobbins would ever guess she'd been born in a logging community in the state of Washington. A rarefied whiff of glamour and refinement enveloped everything about the petite, elegant beauty: her golden blond hair, her stylish dress, her resemblance to Doris Day. Her visits home to her native Walla Walla left her relatives spellbound. Their beloved Jane, it seemed, had taken a magic-carpet ride into a fairy-tale life.

The tug toward something greater must have been innate. She divorced her first husband because she couldn't fathom living the rest of her days in the Pacific Northwest. Her second husband met a tragic, untimely end in a car crash in Utah. The third man she married, Vic Green, had an exciting career, working for Walt Disney as an imagineer. Green was trusted with activating Disney's vision of an amusement park ride inspired by the famed animator's visit to the majestic Swiss mountain the Matterhorn. As for Jane, her engaging and accommodating personality lent itself to her work as a secretary to the stars. The actors John Wayne and Walter Pidgeon had been among her employers.

Divorced from Green at age fifty for unspecified reasons, Jane arrived on the southern California dinner party circuit, where a mutual friend introduced her to a new man in town, a man who, coincidentally, had briefly been a cohort of Disney's long ago near the end of World War I. Immediately, Ray was swept up by Jane's "sweet disposition." The night after they'd met, he invited her for dinner, did so for the next two days as well, and two weeks later, on February 23, 1963, they were married in Palm Springs, California — just miles from the birthplace of the business that comprised Ray's entire reason for being. That his bride had been married three times didn't disturb Ray. That Ray ran a burgeoning empire of fifteen-cent *hamburger stands,* a downscale pursuit for a woman who traveled in such refined circles, not to mention that that empire was teetering precipitously on the brink of failure, didn't stop Jane from falling for the dapper and confident raconteur. He confessed to his new love that there had been an earlier paramour. She'd left him, he told her, because he wasn't wealthy enough. To erase the remaining trace of Joan, Ray traded in the ill-fated Woodland Hills home for one in Beverly Hills, closer to the social swirl and shopping his new lady, Jane, preferred.

His glamorous new companion matched his new California life. She was far more worldly and refined than Ethel, a brighter light who could hold her own with witty small talk at cocktail parties, mingling with ease. Even June Martino had given the thumbs-up, conspiring with Jane at a company Christmas gathering in Chicago when the new bride asked for wisdom on navigating the tensions and politics of the corporate landscape that occupied Ray's every breath.

Though Ray was installed in an office thousands of miles away from corporate headquarters, he and Harry were increasingly at odds over the direction of the company whose rescue Harry had masterminded. Ray's desire to aggressively ramp up McDonald's over the next decade by four hundred stores a year didn't square with Harry's more conservative plans for half that. Ray was pushing for the corporation to buy out some franchisees, so they'd at least have stores under their control to fall back on if the corporation fell apart. Harry disagreed with the strategy. There were conflicts over personnel: Ray had promoted Fred Turner to vice president, and Harry had installed his own man at an equal rank. And the fiscally prudent Harry wanted to take the company public, the ultimate triumph for a serious businessman, while Ray was wary of that path. He wasn't keen on having to live by Wall Street's rules and regulations. Harry believed selling stock was the only chance they'd get to personally cash in on their hard work.

Though Ray would religiously devour the morning sales reports for each store — paying particular attention to the numbers from Rapid City, where Rollie was still at the helm — he continued to find the nuts and bolts and rules and regulations of the financial world of no interest. Those "codfish aristocrats," he sniffed, knew nothing about real work. He preferred his role as chairman-salesman, swooping in to police the parking lots for trash and micromanaging the presentation of food by the hourly workers, confabbing with the franchisees on whose backs the business had been built. They revered him.

With a swagger, he liked to dangle the carrot of a franchise to select associates and friends. To make it possible for some of Jane's family to get in on the game, Ray waived the required cash deposit, which had risen to $15,000. Harry was not only angry about this bush-league transgression; he worked to block it, calling on the corporate lawyers to support his resistance. Everything needed to be aboveboard, by the book, so that the ledgers were as bulletproof and defensible as possible. Ray harrumphed and managed to front the necessary deposit money to the relatives himself.

Though his permanent address was now on the West Coast, Ray's physical distance from 221 North LaSalle hardly meant he was invisible. When he'd phone to talk to his protégé, Fred, the sound of his voice projected so loudly, cascading into the halls, it was as if he was right there on the twentieth floor in Chicago.

Since he was an eager twenty-five-year-old employee in a sea of fortysomethings, Willard Scott seemed to be the logical choice among his colleagues at WRC in Washington, D.C., to play the televised role of an affable, goofy clown. Already he co-hosted a popular daily half-hour radio show called *The Joy Boys,* and was costar, on television, of a program called *Afternoon,* with a supporting cast that included teen-age puppeteer Jim Henson and the lovably moppy creatures he called the Muppets. Scott's friendly voice lent an upbeat, enthusiastic tone to comedic bits as well as local advertisers, such as:

McDonald's Drive-in keeps growing, my friend.

For fifteen cents you get the most delicious burger you've ever tasted in your whole life on a bun, 100% pure beef, and . . . aged Idaho potatoes all French fried up so good and crisp and crunchy golden brown and gooey goo.

Reading a McDonald's ad out loud on the radio was just the start of his association with the company. Like dozens of other stations, WRC had purchased a license to the franchised television character Bozo the Clown. Bozo's cheerful likeness had already motivated the sales of a million sing-along songbooks that helped kids learn to read. Now, local television outlets were being given the chance to cash in on the popularity of the character. For their fee, stations got a script that a locally cast talent brought to life in front of a live studio audience —

the televised equivalent of a hamburger franchise.

To prepare him for the role, Scott, three days a newlywed, was shipped off to Hollywood and enrolled in "clown school," where he was indoctrinated in the ways of Bozo — how to talk, proper technique for suiting up in the requisite blue costume with giant frilly white bib, tips on applying the pancake makeup over every inch of his face, and how to top off the look with a wild, orange-haired wig. He improvised his own dramatic flourish, swinging into the studio on a rope from the wings, rousing the thrilled children into a frenzy.

This same studio had provided the backdrop for a very different media event: the first-ever televised presidential debate between Nixon and Kennedy. The child of the winner of that election counted herself among Bozo's fans. Performing at First Daughter Caroline Kennedy's birthday party at the White House was a thrill, but it didn't offset the exhaustion of the other public appearances he was required to make in character in addition to doing the live show. When a local McDonald's franchisee commissioned the clown to drive his signature fringed surrey into one of their stores' parking lots, so many thousands of people gathered that roads were shut down and police dispatched crowd control. There was something about the combination of hamburgers and Bozo, Scott observed, that was irresistible to kids.

And kids were irresistible to McDonald's. Fortunately for the hamburger chain, many parents in this new era of well-to-do indulgence were loath to refuse their children's request to eat there. Ads targeting after-school programs became a prime target of local franchisees. Vigilance in ensuring that the stores remained as family-friendly as possible continued to be a top priority.

Few people in the company's constellation needed to be convinced of the power of advertising or public relations. The mantra "Early to bed, early to rise, advertise, advertise, advertise" was practiced with devotion by franchisees. In Minnesota, Jim Zien had done well with the catchy radio jingle he'd commissioned:

Forty-five cents for a three course meal.
Sounds to me like that's a steal.

Zien had convinced the other franchisee in Roseville to pool funds, which allowed them to double their ad buy, a model that McDonald's would soon mimic on a na-

tional scale. Because of this sort of experi-
mentation, store sales were soaring and
royalties paid to the corporation had multi-
plied sixfold in the first three years of the
1960s. All across the country, ads were being amplified by manufactured goodwill,
like free hamburger giveaways to schools
and sponsorship of teams and carnivals for
orphans subsidized by local franchisees. In
1960 alone, the PR firm had sent out close
to five thousand press releases, estimating
the "McDonald's message" had reached
forty-six million Americans. The impact of
such appeals was incalculable in distinguish-
ing the drive-ins from other burgeoning
chains, like Henry's and Hardee's and Red
Barn and Royal Castle.

And it provided powerful fodder as Harry
made the rounds of finance partners to line
up the initial public offering. Financial
analysts might be skeptical about the fifteen-
cent hamburger game, but they were dazzled
by this company's skilled use of mass media.
This made the difference between a locally
operated hamburger "joint" and a brand
that could conquer the universe — or, at
least, fly high on the stock market.

WRC management cancelled the Bozo
show in 1962, and the local McDonald's
franchisees, given their dependence on the

clown as marketing tool, were frantic. Scott took it upon himself to invent a variation on the theme. He topped his head with a cardboard takeout tray and covered his nose with a McDonald's cup, giving birth to the world's "newest and most hamburger-eatingest clown." A local ad agency proposed calling this new character "Archie McDonald." But that happened to be the name of a local sportscaster. Willard, in a pinch, rhymed an alternative — "Ronald" — and began making appearances under that name. A half million dollars' worth of ads featuring the happy clown caused sales at the stores in the region to skyrocket 30 percent. For a brief time, the new character even rated his very own TV show.

Ronald McDonald became such a hit in Washington, D.C., that the local franchisee offered up the character to corporate, for free, in the spirit of helping their fellow operators. Getting the mascot out there in other cities would hammer home the message that McDonald's was a national phenomenon. Besides, the original McDonald's mascot needed updating. The Speedee character invented by Dick and Mac had never translated from signs outside the stores and print ads, not to mention its identity crisis. Was he a chef or an animated hamburger? Worse, people confused it with *another* Speedy — an anthropomorphized tablet that advertised Alka-Seltzer.

That tricky problem didn't convince the new corporate marketing man to give the clown a try, though. PR agent Max Cooper was so dazzled by his client that he'd left his firm in the hands of Al Golin so that he could take a job in-house as the company's first marketing director. (Ben Burns returned to journalism, confessing that PR flacking had never been a good fit for him.) Urban sophisticate that he was, Cooper pooh-poohed the use of the character. But then Ray persuaded Harry to buy up the franchisee's sixteen stores, and they inherited Ronald anyway.

The escalating conflict in Vietnam, increased defense spending to fight it, cuts in income taxes, a looming steel strike, and President Johnson's gallbladder surgery all contributed to a roller-coastering stock market in 1965. It spiked, then crashed, and before it recovered, even the Federal Reserve Board chairman hinted at the perilous parallels of the market to the doomsday crash of 1929. Amid this dramatic backdrop, Harry was poised and ready for the stock market debut of McDonald's, the first time a fast-food concern had gone public. Ray called them "hamburger stands," but Harry preferred the more august description of their business as "drive-in self-service restaurants." The risk-averse financial types tabled their reservations about buying into the chain on April 21, 1965, when shares began to trade on the over-the-counter market. A single share of stock debuted in the initial public offering at $22.50 and, by the end of the day, had zoomed up to $30. By the end of the week, it had reached $36. Investors who had never heard of McDonald's were scrambling to buy in, certain that they'd turn around and sell their shares for a profit the next day. It was a repeat of the Florida land grab, except that this time, Ray was the biggest winner.

Just how big was almost impossible to grasp. In an instant, he, Harry, and June morphed from underpaid executives at a faltering chain of hamburger stands to multimillionaires at the helm of Wall Street's darling: Ray, age sixty-three, suddenly found himself with $3 million in cash and a net worth on paper of over $33 million. Harry's 20 percent stake meant he was now worth close to $10 million. June, with her 10 percent ownership, found herself with a little over $5 million in stock in her possession. She was so proud and dazzled by these numbers that she suggested posting the daily closing stock price at the counter of each store. Not that the average McDonald's customer — the average American — held individual stocks themselves, much less followed the markets.

The offices the elevator man referred to as "Hamburger Heaven" were now imbued with a new patina of legitimacy. Harry celebrated by redecorating and, as a connoisseur of fine art, even bought a Renoir to hang on the wall.

The stock's sensational ascent continued. By the end of the year, the price of a share had more than doubled, to $49. Not long after, the stock split, three shares to two. In July 1966, Harry pushed to move the McDonald's listing to the more prestigious New York Stock Exchange. For dramatic flourish, he had burgers sent onto the trading floor and posed for photos with the exchange president as they hungrily chomped them down. Real estate and creative financing were the backbone of the business, but Harry had finally learned the power of clever messaging.

While McDonald's was being heralded for orchestrating "the greatest growth in the history of the restaurant business," Ray, befuddled by the business of high finance and still peeved at Harry, was off with Jane on a six-week cruise. He brought along notebooks to jot down his not-so-meteoric rise from cup salesman to burger king. Perhaps it would be fodder for a memoir someday.

They'd soon take another vacation in California that would expand their horizons even more.

Happy Canyon Road twists and ribbons past an endless procession of majestic white oaks and digger pines in the rolling hills of the Santa Ynez Valley until it delivers the traveler to the entrance of the Los Padres National Forest. Area lore has it that this narrow stretch earned its name during Prohibition, as home to the spot where locals could buy alcohol. This rustic region off an old stagecoach route northeast of Santa Barbara was famous for its cattle and horse ranches, and a curious facsimile of a Danish village called Solvang, Danish for "sunny fields," where windmills tilted in the breeze and the sweet scent of freshly baked strudel wafted from bakeries that looked plucked straight from Scandinavia. Up the road, the tourist-friendly Pea Soup Andersen's purveyed three-quarters of a million bowls of the elixir each year to travelers heading between San Francisco and Los Angeles.

When the newly mega-rich Ray and Jane arrived at the hotel at the posh ten-thousand-acre Alisal Ranch for some rest and relaxation, it was only natural Ray would be drawn to the piano in the lounge. While contemplating his newfound fortune, he joined the on-duty pianist for some casual duets. Flush with more cash than he could ever have imagined, and intoxicated by the landscape, Ray couldn't resist when he learned of a 210-acre ranch for sale. He called his lawyer and told him to buy it — and to pay the asking price of $600,000 — no negotiation. Jane explained to her relatives that her husband had hit the jackpot. Money was no object, and it never would be again.

To mark the territory, three flags were hoisted up flagpoles at the entrance to the property: the stars and stripes, the California state flag, and a third that proudly displayed the distinctive McDonald's "M" formed by golden arches. Cows of many colors roamed serenely amid Arabian horses and golden retrievers, as Ray had the land built out to his specifications. He dubbed the place "The J and R Double Arch

Ranch."

The name reflected his dual vision for the property. The ranch would serve not only as a personal refuge for him and the Mrs., but as a corporate retreat — a reward, perhaps, to the best employees. There was little division between his personal and professional life, anyhow. A sprawling property in cattle country meant McDonald's could now conduct experiments involving the key ingredient for McDonald's food: beef.

June's husband, Louis, had already established another research facility for the company, in Addison, Illinois, where he and a team of engineers tested new equipment with which to expedite cooking. As the chain continued to multiply in size, centralized mass production of food — the prefab food Ray dismissed as garbage — was becoming necessary to ensure continuity. Making fries using Mac's formula, store by store, was a time-consuming burden. Just gathering enough of the necessary potatoes year-round required deals with 175 different farms — not to mention the elaborate curing process necessary to achieve the desired crispy result. To ease the burden and ensure consistency from store to store, Ray commissioned a frozen French fry from a food scientist turned franchisee in Wisconsin, Edward Traisman. He had under his belt another indispensible invention, a bright yellow cheese sauce in a jar with an improbably long shelf life, Cheez Whiz. With a coinventor, Traisman had patented his frozen fry formula, which was currently being rolled out to the stores. Even the Multimixer, the staple device that had sustained Ray's existence for decades, was being phased out at McDonald's in favor of milk shake mix. Employees couldn't be trusted to reliably measure and prepare shakes the old way.

Convincing critics that McDonald's food was top quality had been hard enough when it was made from the freshest local ingredients. These new developments raised the eyebrows of nutritionists ever more skeptically. What was the fat content of those hamburgers? What about those fries? What impact did this food, much less all those commercial messages, have on kids? Having the hot stock on Wall Street made them rich, but with it came the downside of increased public scrutiny and criticism, which Ray dismissed as bunk. "What do all those nutritionists and college professors . . . know?" he would say. "How many jobs have they ever created?" It became clear to Ray's advisors that their founding chairman couldn't be held to the press simply as an example of a man who made it rich after years of uncertain toil. He had to be rich, and benevolent, too. And so, the goodwill PR strategy deployed so efficiently on a local level was put to use in service of the boss. Ray began strategically and publicly gifting slices of his new fortune to charitable concerns, usually ones focused on children, zoos and hospitals and planetariums. To further maximize the benefits of the ranch as a tax deduction, his advisors suggested that Ray start a formal foundation, to be headquartered on the property's grounds.

As its chief, Ray turned to his only brother, Bob. The two men had hardly talked in years. Though Ray had twice dropped out of high school, Bob had earned a bachelor's and a master's from Oberlin College, and a PhD in zoology and physiology from the University of Wisconsin. He'd taught for a while at Indiana University, and then shifted from academia to the more lucrative pharmaceutical business. While his brother was concerned with matters like finding the perfect portable dessert to serve at his chain of drive-ins, Bob was directing the physiology department at Warner Lambert, leading teams that developed pioneering drugs involving the hormone relaxin. There was a common trait in their genetic matter: fastidiousness. Once, Bob had dispatched a polite, typewritten missive to his favorite shoemaker, Allen-Edmonds, asking what to do about the stains metal eyelets made in his white buckskins. In short order, he'd be dashing off a letter to anyone who neglected to capitalize the word "The" when referring to the foundation.

Ray indeed gave his brother carte blanche in how he'd dispense the money he'd earmarked to help humanity's greater good. That he was giving was more important than to what. Bob took his assignment seriously, plunging into due diligence with scientific precision and zeal, quizzing leaders at other foundations about the particulars of philanthropy and researching how other enormously wealthy families, like the Rockefellers and Astors, had decided to gift their fortunes. He concluded that the best way to spend the funds in The Ray A. Kroc Foundation was on medical research around diseases that plagued their family. Since diabetes and arthritis had impacted Ray, Bob focused on funding research and convening conferences of scientists involved with those diseases, and then expanded to include the study of multiple sclerosis, with which their sister, Lorraine, had been diagnosed.

The scholarly, scientific nature of the work was so impressive that soon Bob was fending off overtures from the PR men, who were inquiring about how they might co-opt Ray's philanthropic work as a promotional tool for McDonald's. Brother Bob pushed back, warning against the pitfalls of Ray's personal foundation seeming like some sort of "tax loophole" for his business. It wasn't right, Bob believed, to use Ray's charitable contributions in such a way. Besides, he added, "we are constantly trying to avoid the McDonald's label." This was Ray's charity, not the company's.

The locals watched the unfolding action on this serene stretch of Happy Canyon Road with curious amusement. Their whispered fears soon became neighborhood legend: This McDonald's man planned to build a structure on the highest point of the property that would resemble a gigantic hamburger. In the fall of 1968, the upscale design magazine *Architectural Digest* took those who didn't rate an invitation inside with a fourteen-page spread that showed off some of the unique features of the J and R Double Arch Ranch: An elegantly appointed fifteen-room guest lodge. A state-of-the-art cattle barn boasting air-conditioning, piped-in music, and automatic sanitation. A dining room that could seat a hundred and be easily converted for use as a ballroom or movie theater. Custom-made chandeliers. In the 3,500-square-foot living room, a 28-foot faux fur sofa created a conversation pit in front of a fireplace constructed from a hundred tons of native stone. A buffet-style kitchen allowed guests to serve themselves from available snacks at any time of day. The grounds featured two helicopter pads and an equal number of swimming pools. Entry doors hand-carved by a local artist lent a hint of erudition to the place, with panels that featured abstractions of cells, chromosomes, and Einstein's famous equation, $e = MC^2$ — a design flourish that only scientist Bob could have dreamed up.

But the ultimate feature of the ranch was Ray's pride and joy, the automated bar, a functional work of art, boasting an icemaker and twelve spigots that allowed guests round-the-clock access to an endless flow of beverages, including, of course, Early Times, as well as gin and vodka, all dispensed handily in 1.5-ounce shots at "the touch of a glass." Those glasses came from Tiffany, courtesy of Waddy Pratt, McDonald's grateful supplier of Coca-Cola. The bar was a perfect contraption for the glamorous parties Ray and Jane convened on the ranch grounds.

Despite the luxurious finishes on his exquisite property, the beautiful wife, the public acclaim, the limitless pools of cash, the pleasure in having made so many other people rich — despite the delight in giving money away and the accolades that followed, and despite his acclaim in the media as a kingmaker and captain of industry — Ray's heart remained bereft. He tried his hand at entering the upscale restaurant market with two fancy burger places in Beverly Hills and Chicago, dubbed, with an exotic twist on his name, Ramon's. His bids to buy Baskin-Robbins, Taco Bell, and Marie Callender's bakeries failed, as did his sandwich creation of pineapple on a bun called the Hula Burger. He tinkered with a new project named for his wife — Jane Dobbins Pie Shops — hiring as its chief renowned pastry chef Boston Strause, innovator of the graham cracker crust and chiffon pie. (Another fizzle.) He seriously entertained the idea of building an amusement park, and even offered the actor Fess Parker $50 million to buy into one he had planned. (After Parker's lawyer interfered,

Ray killed the deal.)

His marriage was fine enough, but life with Jane lacked luster. He'd bought her a convertible and she'd wondered why it must have the golden arches logo, already ubiquitous in their lives, affixed to its bumper. Ray erupted in a fury. Jane just didn't love the business the way he did. Even worse, Ray swallowed bitterly, he just didn't love Jane the way he loved Joan.

Once, Joan even called to ask if he was happy. "Yes," he blurted out, and hung up the phone.

But the truth was that he'd never stopped loving her, and knew he never would.

Though her official title after the McDonald's public offering had become treasurer, June Martino found herself, in the two years since she'd become a multimillionaire, just as frequently inhabiting her unofficial role as the company's vice president of equilibrium. The scrappy start-up days were history, when the devoted triumvirate of Ray, Harry, and June would talk shop for hours on end in Ray's living room in Arlington Heights. They'd been so close then. In those early years, they'd collectively bought a beer garden on Chicago's South Side, called Hottinger's, and all pitched in to run it. There'd never been any doubt that they were marching together toward the same goal, and that each was making an important contribution to achieve it. The doubts had to do not with one another, but with whether McDonald's would survive.

Now, the nail-biting revolved around the deepening fissure between Harry and Ray. The two men were at such odds they wouldn't even speak to each other. To communicate, they relied on their trusted colleague with finesse for smoothing ruffled feathers and a natural aptitude for seeing all sides of an argument — especially involving two men she admired equally.

In his capacity as president and chief executive of the corporation he'd taken public, Harry began stepping onto the public stage he once happily ceded to Ray. As president of a business that revolved around "arches," he'd been invited to appear in St. Louis at the groundbreaking ceremony for the 630-foot stainless steel sculpture, about to get under way, known as the Gateway Arch. Inspired by the tremendous success of local advertising, he signed off on the company's national debut, a $75,000 sponsorship of the vaunted Macy's Thanksgiving Day Parade, hosted by Betty White and Lorne Greene. Max Cooper tabled his disdain of Ronald McDonald and pushed to deploy him, but Harry vetoed the idea of making the company's national television debut with a clown. Instead, a high school band from New Jersey was enlisted to carry an enormous drum wrapped with the company logo, never mind that displaying logos was in strict defiance of the parade's rules. For the first time, franchisees were asked to contribute to a national fund, a crucial step in brand building. Harry loved the fanfare and the results so much that he authorized spending $170,000 for a McDonald's ad to run in the debut Super Bowl a few months later, which came with an added bonus of a few extra spots to run on Saturday morning cartoons — the better to appeal to those crucial customers, children.

By the next Thanksgiving, Max Cooper had prevailed and casting began for the role of Ronald McDonald. Willard Scott was deemed unfit to take his big idea national. Instead, a veteran circus clown named Michael Polakovs made his debut in the part in a taped commercial. Soon enough, fifty Ronalds would be cast to fan out across the nation. The PR team kicked into high gear to promote their arrival.

■ ■ ■ ■

Fierce battles erupted as Ray and Harry clashed over whether to raise the price of a hamburger from its long-standing fifteen cents to eighteen (Ray was in favor, and Harry opposed) and how many new stores to add (Ray favored an aggressive growth strategy, while Harry pushed for measured, deliberate expansion). Ray felt Harry cared too much about catering to the financial set, while his own concern was in bolstering the reach of his product by opening more stores. As the standoff intensified, it was only natural that the now three floors' worth of employees at 221 North LaSalle would take sides with one man or the other. Regardless of President Harry's title, financial acumen, and supporters in the corporate boardroom, it was also only natural that with Ray's controlling stock, it was he who would prevail. There wasn't enough room for the two of them anymore. And so, the man who saved the business from almost certain oblivion and then catapulted it to unimagined heights succumbed and tendered his resignation. Ray promised him a severance of $100,000 a year.

Because he knew Ray was unconcerned

about Wall Street, Harry feared he would proceed to run the company into the ground. So the outgoing president sold what stock he had remaining, cashing out with about twelve million dollars. He picked up and moved full-time to a 14,000-square-foot estate he built for his second wife, Aloyis, in her home state of Alabama, where he indulged his passion for collecting historic signatures (of such varied figures as George Washington and Adolf Hitler), original historic documents (a formidable collection of state constitutions), and jade. For his passionate involvement in historic preservation, Lincoln College in Illinois awarded him an honorary degree of humane letters in June 1968. Though his severance checks continued, Harry confessed he was dubious about the growing footprint of the company he'd masterminded. As he walked along a bucolic stream where he was vacationing in Germany, an errant McDonald's cup polluted his view.

In order to assert his position, Ray decided that his secretary/treasurer, unofficially known as vice president of equilibrium, had to go, too. June's unlikely rise to success in a chauvinist company couldn't save her now. The fact that she admired and supported Harry equally as she did Ray made her, in Ray's estimation, a liability as he worked to reestablish total authority. June also received the promise of a $100,000 annual pension, even as her share of the stock continued to multiply to $50 million. Her exit didn't mean she was in Ray's doghouse; she was invited to join the board of directors of McDonald's in 1969, and served on the honorary board for the rest of her life. Eventually, she moved to Florida, where she built a spectacular waterfront home in Palm Beach and immersed herself in civic and philanthropic causes.

With the men whose name and toil had invented the business gone, and so, too, the brains and the soul of McDonald's, Ray, with his abundant confidence and courage, now had the control he wanted. At least, professionally speaking.

Time marched on for Joan in Wretched City. Slowly. She joined the board of the local library, where she rubbed elbows with the wealthiest and most civic-minded people in town. Putting food on the table was no longer a concern. Rollie had done so well with his first two stores that he was granted the right to open two more, one on the north side of Rapid and the other up in

Manitoba, as part of the company's expansion into Canada. With his success, he'd been able to join the Arrowhead Country Club, where he played round after round of golf. Up in the clubhouse, Joan sat behind the keyboard for hours, encouraging anyone who could to sing along and give voice to her music. (She knew her limits; she couldn't hold a tune.) From time to time she'd make an appearance at other pianos around town. Admirers dispensed the highest praise: She was so good, she "played like a man."

Her daughter, Linda, finished high school at an Episcopal boarding school back in Minnesota. When she enrolled in college, the Smiths decided to move closer to downtown. Over the years, two floods had swelled Lime Creek in front of their home to overflowing, pushing water and mud into the family home on 38th Street. Flush now with cash, Joan and Rollie traded up for a swank floor-through condo at the newly constructed seven-story Dahl Towers, with views in every direction and parties that quickly became local legend. Most mornings, Joan would rise early, throw a coat over her robe, light up a cigarette, and take her dog for a stroll in the neighborhood, chatting up local teenagers heading to school as she meandered to pick up a pastry at the grocery store.

She befriended the madman sculptor Korczak Ziolkowski, whose obsessive vision was to carve the side of a mountain not far from Rushmore with a face that in his estimation was more important than (or at least as important as) that of the presidents, the Native American warrior Crazy Horse. Joan shared a rebellious streak with the artist's wife, Ruth, who'd defied her father's wishes by moving clear across the country from Connecticut to marry this older, burly man with a seemingly unattainable dream. Joan balanced her interest in the arts with support of commerce, as a frequent customer at Haggerty's department store at the Baken Park Shopping Center, where clerks were familiar with her affection for fancy Vanity Fair sleepwear and lingerie.

In the seven years since her aborted attempt to marry Ray, she'd made peace with Wretched City, or at least had stopped warring with it. But then, an invitation arrived in the mail from corporate to attend the 1968 Western Regional Operators' meeting on Coronado Island, California, just outside San Diego. The lavish meetings were becoming legendary among franchisees. When she saw Ray listed as keynote speaker, Joan didn't hesitate to RSVP yes.

Wherever he went, Ray carried a three-ring binder into which his secretary inserted the daily sales performance numbers at each of the McDonald's outposts. He'd pore over the figures with the attention a biblical scholar would give the Scripture. Only a few years ago, a thousand stores had seemed a preposterous dream. Yet he'd just marked the opening of that milestone store, arriving in a chauffeur-driven limo for the ribbon cutting, outfitted in splendor for the occasion in black tie. (Jane stepped out adorned in a mink stole.) There had been a time when he needed no reminder of the names of his franchisees, or the sequential numbers of their stores, nor of their spouses' or their children's names. Nothing made him feel more like a titan of the business world than on Christmas Day, when he would sit and call three hundred owners, spending a minute on the phone with each of these participants in his hamburger empire. They were happy to have even a word with the man who'd made them rich. Now, with so many stores up and running, the pages provided a necessary cheat sheet.

Life thrummed on with lows and highs. His dear companion Art Trygg, who'd dutifully produced a monthly newsletter and ferried the boss around, passed away. McDonald's stock split again. Ray had a new driver who was preparing the Rolls-Royce to squire him from his home in Beverly Hills down to the convention. He'd been asked to give a speech. When he perused the roster of registered attendants, the names leaped off the page: Rollie and Joan Smith from Rapid City.

The Smiths arrived in California attended by a chaperone: Joan's mother. Mrs. Mansfield felt it was "like throwing gasoline on the fire" for her daughter to be in the same state, much less the same convention hall, as Ray. Warily, she accompanied Joan and Rollie to a small pre-convention dinner hosted by the big boss, hoping to keep her daughter out of trouble. Just as he'd been struck by Joan's loveliness a dozen years before, he now found himself overcome by a wave of emotion at the sight of his blond beauty. It had been six years since they'd last seen each other, they each maintained. The rest of the group was amused by his flirty command to Joan to sit by him, while he admonished Rollie to stay on the other end of the table. After the meal was over, drink in hand, Ray delivered an impromptu speech.

"I've attained everything in life I've ever wanted except one thing," he declared. Only Joan, and her husband and mother, could decipher this cryptic message. The "thing" missing from his life was right there, beside him.

Eager to keep the party going, Ray had a piano brought up to his suite for after-dinner drinks and music, and bellowed select guests to join him, the Smiths among them. They obeyed, and up in the room, Joan beelined for the keyboard. She and Ray were soon lost in song, and an exasperated Rollie excused himself. Fred Turner, who'd witnessed their first meeting, observed with amusement how hard Ray was working now to win her. One log after another burned on the fire, and the night became the wee hours of the morning. Now it was Ray's chauffeur's turn to function as a chaperone, though he fell asleep on the couch. At four a.m., an angry phone call from her husband beckoned Joan home.

A few hours later, with his head spinning "like a top out of control," Ray resorted to a cocktail of eyewash and Alka-Seltzer and aspirin to fortify him to deliver his opening remarks. He made his way to a ballroom full of devotees and scanned the crowd for evidence of his beloved. Neither she, nor Rollie, nor Mrs. Mansfield was there.

The mood aboard the private yacht was festive and celebratory as it glided along the stately, snug Intracoastal Waterway in Fort Lauderdale. Champagne flowed and caviar was served; a band played at an upbeat tempo befitting the occasion. Ray and Jane were soon to set sail on a large ship that would take them on a round-the-world cruise in celebration of their fifth wedding anniversary. Senior executives of McDonald's had flown with their wives to Florida to attend this lavish bon voyage party. Ray loved being around the boys, his boys, the men in the constellation of McDonald's who revered him. Any chance for them to fête the man responsible for their fortunes was one they eagerly seized.

Tonight, though, Ray's mind was anywhere but here. Nor was he focused on the months-long itinerary before him: Acapulco. The Panama Canal. Hong Kong. He'd rationalized with himself that he could make it, at least part of the way, but the more he considered what it would be like to be cooped up on a ship with Jane for weeks on end, he knew he could never last his way out of the harbor.

As the merriment unfolded around them, Ray asked for a private word with his lawyer. Off to the side, he let him in on a secret: He wanted a divorce, and even poor, unsuspecting Jane wasn't aware of her husband's intentions. Ray tasked the man with breaking the news to her on the spot, and laying out the terms of the deal to end the marriage: She could keep the house and the $3 million in cash in their bank account, and, if she didn't contest the terms, her family could continue to operate their McDonald's units without interruption.

It didn't take long for the news to spread and cast a pall over the occasion. Revelers circled Mrs. Kroc to console her as she wept. The trip was off. The marriage was over. Her husband had left her. Literally. Ray had vanished from the party without saying a word. His driver had spirited him away to the next chapter of his life.

That chapter began back in Las Vegas, where Ray and Joan returned in order to establish the required residency of six weeks necessary for them to obtain divorces. They chose as their temporary accommodation the luxurious Riviera Hotel, the city's first high-rise built during the fifties boom years of the town. Each of them loved to play cards, and Ray's wealth subsidized the indulgence. Ever conservative, Ray felt it necessary to explain to his lawyer that his relationship with Joan had been, up to that point, chaste, and that they had taken separate rooms until they could be legally married.

By February 21, 1969, the court had decreed Joan and Rollie's marriage officially over. A week later, Ray and Jane's bonds of matrimony had been dissolved, too. Among executives at McDonald's, in service of illustrating the big boss's fairness and honor, the story circulated that Ray insisted Joan send her wardrobe back to Rollie. It was one thing to take another man's wife, but it was another to allow her to keep belongings that man had worked hard to buy.

Untethered, Ray and Joan headed back to California, stopping in at the Santa Barbara County courthouse to register for a marriage license. On their application, Joan listed her occupation as "unemployed."

Two days later, in front of the great stone fireplace at the J and R Double Arch Ranch, they were united as husband and wife. The groom wore a tux, the bride, her hair elegantly swept in an updo, a pale pink suit — the perfect complement to her new eleven-carat heart-shaped pink diamond. The newlyweds embraced while clutching cocktail glasses.

The "J" now stood for Joan, the bride Ray had actually wanted all along. And Joan was no longer without work. She had a new job now. She was Mrs. Ray Kroc.

7
THE *JONIRAY*

There is no literal gold on the glorious streets of the refined, tree-lined Chicago neighborhood known as the Gold Coast. But it feels as if were you to meander long enough, you might stumble upon a trove. To paint a picture of this exclusive area — one of America's richest — would require a muted palette with shades of reddish brick and stately limestone, punctuated in spring and summer with an abundance of verdant green.

Almost a hundred years before the Ray Krocs landed here to begin, at long last, their married life together, another May-December couple lay the groundwork for this exclusive enclave. In the mid-nineteenth century, Potter Palmer had, starting with modest means, amassed a small fortune as the owner of a dry-goods store. For innovating such revolutionary concepts as free delivery, no-questions-asked returns on merchandise, and the notion that the customer was always right, Palmer would come to be considered the father of modern retail.

The successful bachelor businessman first laid eyes on his future wife, Bertha Honoré, when she was just thirteen years old and shopping with her mother in his store. As the belle from Kentucky grew into womanhood, she attracted a chorus of suitors. Palmer, twenty-three years her senior, finally won her hand, marrying her when she turned twenty-one. He gifted her with a grand eight-story hotel, the tallest structure in the city. The Great Chicago Fire of 1871 destroyed this wedding present, along with much of the rest of the central business district, leaving hundreds of thousands of people without shelter. Yet the disaster fortified the couple's brand-new marriage. Palmer, out of town to attend a family funeral, commanded his wife to harbor as many of their distressed fellow citizens as she could; the compassionate Bertha had already opened the doors to their grand home, despite the fact that it, too, had suffered damage. Overwhelmed on his return with the enormity of rebuilding, Palmer felt compelled to just walk away from the city. Bertha persuaded him that he owed it to Chicago to stay.

Fortified by his beautiful young wife's commitment, the enterprising Palmer filled the swampland north of the Astor Street District with sand and enticed his friends to join him in relocating to this new neighborhood he'd established. He set about building the Mrs. a majestic, turreted palace, soaring eighty feet high. As the initial budget of $90,000 skyrocketed past a million, Palmer told the architects to quit showing him the bills. There was one expenditure that would not be necessary: exterior doorknobs. A staff of two dozen servants was to be available day and night.

With his elaborate nest feathered, Palmer left another indelible imprint on the city by goading officials to build a road outside this home, a winding stretch that hugged the curve of the formidable Lake Michigan. Were it not for this expanse, the water would practically lap up on their doorstep. Eventually this thoroughfare would become known, appropriately, as Lake Shore Drive.

As society would expect of the wife of such a prominent figure, Mrs. Palmer adorned herself with lima-bean-size diamonds and relished her role as the grande dame of the city, hosting royalty in her own personal castle. An invitation to step inside was coveted by tout le monde. But while she reveled in her largesse, she emerged as far more than an indulged, entitled glamour-puss. A lover of art, she was just as likely to buy the works of Impressionists as she was the latest fashion when shopping in Paris. As an intellect and an activist who supported the progressive causes of workers' and women's rights, she was dubbed by the *Chicago Tribune* "the embodiment of the new woman."

A new woman is exactly what Joan hoped to become as she arrived on Lake Shore Drive in 1969. There was no other neighborhood in the city, really, that the chairman of a multimillion-dollar corporation and his beautiful younger bride could possibly consider for their residence. By then, the Palmer mansion had been long lost to the wrecking ball to make way for high-priced condominiums, all the better to maximize the number of residences boasting spectacular lake views. The soaring vistas from the twenty-seventh-floor duplex purchased by the newlyweds matched Joan's expansive dream for her new life. The 5,300-square-foot condo cost ten times the average $14,000 price of a brand-new home.

To help them appoint their marital nest, Ray had enlisted the help of interior designer Raymond Jacques Dayan, an ambitious man of French-Moroccan descent. Dayan got his foot in the door at headquarters when he sold June artificial plants to spruce up the Chicago-area stores. She'd then hired him to decorate her home, which led to work on one owned by Harry, and then a chance to become a franchisee. The designer planned a gala welcome party for his clients at the swank Four Georges Room at the Ambassador West Hotel, which rated a mention in the society column in the *Chicago Tribune*. For her debut, Joan cloaked herself in white jersey, accented with aquamarine and pearls.

The condo retrofit Dayan would oversee required the installation of an "organ that hides in the wall and a piano that does not," necessary accoutrements for this couple who'd met, and bonded, over music. A state-of-the-art air-conditioning-filtration system offset another of their common passions — cigarettes — and would consume a copious chunk of the expected quarter-million-dollar renovation. However, ornate mirrored walls and ceilings, installed by the previous owner, were deemed too over-the-top even for the hardly subdued Ray and Joan.

Then there was the winter retreat. On the very day they'd registered for their marriage license, they'd expanded the scope of the designer's assignment, contracting with him for the task of decorating a top-of-the-line condominium they'd purchased as a second home at the swank Port of Americas building in Fort Lauderdale, replete with private beach and more eye-popping water views, this time of the Atlantic. After that botched foray into swampland real estate sales in Florida decades before, Ray would be returning to the state in style. The world was theirs, indeed.

Joan's new reality was anchored with far more than luxurious real estate. There were extravagant cars, chauffeured. A private plane — a Gulfstream jet now, no longer the single-engine Cessna from the old days, this one paid for by Ray and leased back to the company for a dollar a year so the chairman could travel in style. A fleet of "Big Mac" buses he'd bought and distributed to operators around the country to strategically deploy for community outreach. A more unusual form of alternative transportation would be at her beck and call, should she desire. The year before they married, Ray had indulged, on a whim at auction, in the ultimate extravagance — a private rail car, used only once by its previous owner, purchased for $63,000. He confessed he had no idea what to do with it.

The Woodland Hills escapade eight years earlier, the family's frustration, their long-hidden relationship and the shame of divorce — all that was now a distant memory. But this didn't mean Joan's life would be easy from now on. In exchange for these marital goods, naturally, Joan's new station in life came with expectations. There would be no more morning strolls to walk the dog in her bathrobe and curlers. Ray's exacting standard of grooming and presentation demanded that Joan frequent the finest stores on the fancy shopping stretch, State Street, another legacy of Potter Palmer, and a far cry from Haggerty's in Rapid. Of course, she never need trouble herself with the bills. (Occasionally a merchant would commit an uncomfortable faux pas — this was not Mrs. *Jane,* but Mrs. *Joan.*) She'd visit the hairdresser frequently for upkeep on her meticulous coiffure. To offset the stress, she'd indulge in a massage.

There were civic obligations, of course. Mrs. Ray Kroc was thrust onto the circuit with the likes of other high-society wives whose lives were dedicated to the betterment of the communities where their husbands had become (or been born) rich, boosters of the underclass and afflicted.

Fancy luncheons and demure garden parties filled the days, in the service of planning galas that occupied their nights, all in the name of supporting important and worthy, if predictable, causes: children's hospitals and museums and the committee to save, fix, or cure this and that malady or social ill. Occasionally, spontaneous merriment would erupt, like the time a well-heeled lady jumped into a swimming pool at the luncheon where Ray and Joan were announced as the "angels" of an upcoming benefit dinner. The lives of the carefree well-to-do! These women were servants of their men and their expectations, acting on the script they were expected, as members of the upper class, to follow. They had no identity apart from the names and fortunes of their husbands. Joan found it all so boring she wanted to cry.

Even when he made personal donations in both their names, it was Ray who got the honors. Over the next five years, he received a flurry of awards, many bestowed in the hopes the accolade would beget another, larger gift. One year he was decreed Outstanding Chicagoan, and at the banquet in his honor, after conferring with Joan during opening remarks, he surprised the organizers by announcing a donation of $1 million to multiple sclerosis research. The Lions' Club proclaimed him American of the Year. Twice he was named Distinguished Citizen by the Boy Scouts. The Horatio Alger Award, in honor of the author who wrote about honest, hardworking boys who rise to greatness from humble beginnings: Didn't Ray Kroc personify that story line? Sometimes the institutions he supported invited him to become more involved. Henrotin Hospital was eager to have the newly rich former patient on its board, since they'd cared for him after the chopped-fingertip incident. (When he learned the hospital was a not-for-profit, he quit in a huff.) Other times, Joan would be pressed into service on her husband's behalf, never because of what she might offer, but simply because she was a proxy for Ray.

It had been one thing to be the wife of "Mr. McDonald's" back in South Dakota. There, at least, she'd commanded equal footing. She was Joan, the lady who played piano so well, the lady involved with the library, who happened to be married to Rollie, who happened to own the local McDonald's. She took enormous pride in what they'd built and in the larger corporation. She bragged to total strangers about it, how it wasn't just the arches that were golden.

The company loomed over her life, but it didn't occupy her every breath. Though they loved being involved with the business, ketchup didn't run through Rollie's veins quite as thickly as it did for Ray.

Now that she was the wife of the king, a constellation of people who *were* similarly entrenched orchestrated her and her husband's world. They plotted her vacations, usually out to the ranch with a handful of Ray's closest associates and their wives. They arranged the parties, for either suppliers or franchisees or other folks in the wide circle of the company. They advised Ray on his finances, including where he strategically gave charitable contributions in the community. Joan wasn't Joan anymore. She was merely Ray's watch fob, his parlor ornament. The visible, invisible half of the Mr. Ray Krocs.

Back when she was ordering an adequate stock of potatoes at Rollie's first store on Main Street, learning how to wrangle the Keating French fryer, and counting out her life's savings in change, the luxuriousness in which Joan now basked was an unimaginable dream. And yet somehow the suffocation she felt in the Black Hills was nothing like what was strangling her now that she sported a glowing eleven-carat pink diamond. Her new circumstances weighed heavily on her soul. She availed herself of the private plane she had at her disposal to take her back to see her girlfriends in Rapid City. The characters who'd inhabited her former life now seemed genuine — real. She invited Rapid to her, commissioning the artist Korczak Ziolkowski to sculpt a bronze of Ray — the last one he did before he turned attention full-time to his mountain opus. When he arrived at the penthouse on Lake Shore Drive to mold a plaster cast as a study, the two men visited for hours, and Ray liked the bearded man so much he not only overlooked his distaste for long hair and whiskers, which the artist possessed in abundance, but even forgave his choice of cocktail. The unmanly Manhattan was Korczak's favorite drink.

Apart from Joan's strong will and raging desire to make her own mark, there was something else that intensified her identity crisis. There was a volatility in Ray that seeped over to their relationship. One fierce personality battling another in the name of, what was it, love? To one confidante, she said she felt as if she were going crazy. With her eyes shielded behind shaded sunglasses in the back of a darkened restaurant, she cried to another that she felt she'd married her father, hinting at the unspoken darkness from her childhood years. The more she consulted and pondered and read and studied, she began to believe that perhaps the root of her problem had to do with Ray's affinity for Early Times. She had begun to notice that it ratcheted up his already tempestuous personality into a storm.

Back in his native Chicago as his permanent residence, a dozen miles and a world away from the boyhood home where he learned to play piano, Ray languished in his role as the celebrated multimillionaire chairman of the company that had changed the way America ate. He indulged a bit of nostalgia, asking his chauffeur to ferry him to suburban Arlington Heights so he could stop for a moment in front of the modest house he'd first bought when he was a young milk shake machine salesman. How far he had come. The press loved this celebrity businessman, quoted him in stories, asked him to comment on TV. In his private jet, he toured around the country with his hand-chosen successor, the man he considered as close as a son, Fred Turner, now firmly installed in charge of McDonald's day-to-day. Ray was rich now, but he still drank the same rotgut booze he'd enjoyed on the way up, even though he lived an otherwise top-shelf life in every other way. The chairman and his charge made a grand two-week tour around the south, from Texas to Alabama, rising each morning at six thirty and investigating every last nook and cranny of each McDonald's they visited till retiring at eleven. Charming Ray, Chairman Ray, was the toast of the town — and best of all, he got to come home to his Joni. That they squabbled and fought with great passion and intensity, plates flying, occasionally coming to blows, well, that was just part of it. Her strong will was one of the things he loved about her. She was the love of his life.

It wasn't that Ray was entirely unconscious of his behavior. He was unashamed of it and its consequences. He described his own personality to a reporter: "hot tempered, emotional and, on occasion, an outright son of a bitch." At his core, he confessed, was a soft spot. He believed himself a romantic. Romance was evidenced in the $600,000 seventy-two-foot boat he commissioned for Joan from the Burger Yacht company in Manitowoc, Wisconsin. The fact that the company's name echoed his core product was merely a coincidence. Burger built the best boat around, Ray discovered as he'd been test-riding one down in Florida, where they'd upgraded from condo to house. What was the point of having a place on the Intracoastal Waterway in Fort Lauderdale if you didn't have a vessel in which to glide up and down? A custom boat with white oak paneling. Fabrics in brilliant primary colors, inspired by tile from old-world Portugal. Carpeting, made to order. A gourmet kitchen, and the luxurious modern convenience of a built-in central vacuum. An escape hatch on the forward deck designed to double as a cocktail table, so there was no need to go inside for a drink. As there was on the entryway to the ranch, and his cars, on the lapel of his jacket, and the diamond ring on his un-chopped finger — anything he owned, really — the boat was branded with an insignia of golden arches.

Sipping cocktails serenely on the peaceful waters with his beloved: Life was a dream. The most intimate part of this romantic gesture was not its intention, but the name with which he christened the boat: the *Joni-Ray*. It was evidence that, at least to him, they were so close they had no spaces.

There was, however, another side to his illusion. In November 1971, after a gala Halloween brunch held in honor of the Ray Krocs at the Ambassador West Hotel in Chicago, Ray had flown out of town on business. On his return, an officer from the Cook County sheriff's office greeted him on the tarmac, bearing a summons to appear in court, a filing for divorce, and a restraining order to keep away from their apartment — and to keep his hands off Joan. Ray found, when he arrived on Lake Shore Drive, that it was true: The locks had been changed. The court papers from the divorce division, case 71 D 21992, Circuit Court of Cook County, laid out the charges:

> The defendant has a violent and ungovernable temper and has in the past inflicted upon the person of the plaintiff physical harm, violence and injury . . . the plaintiff has just cause and reason to, and in fact does, fear that, upon being apprised that the plaintiff has instituted the present action, the said defendant will perpetrate or attempt to perpetrate upon her person physical violence, harm, damage and injury . . . by reason of the past conduct of the defendant in inflicting upon the person of the plaintiff physical harm, violence and injury, the physical and mental well-being of the plaintiff would be endangered,

imperiled, and jeopardized by the continued presence of the said defendant in and
upon the premises formerly occupied by
the parties hereto as their marital home . . .

The legalese was distilled into a news
item, picked up by newspapers across the
country, buried on the business pages:

United Press International, November
11, 1971:
Ray A. Kroc, 69, president of the multimillion-dollar McDonald's hamburger franchise chain, was sued for divorce in Chicago by his third wife, Joan, 43, who
alleged physical and mental cruelty. She
was awarded a temporary order restraining her husband from harming her. She
estimated Kroc's fortune at between $350
and $400 million and asked for alimony,
the family apartment in Chicago, its fur-
nishings and paintings.

Bereft, Ray took up residence a half mile
away from home at the local haunt he loved,
the Whitehall Hotel — the same place where
he'd taken refuge on return visits to Chicago
after he'd left Ethel and moved west. It was
one thing to drink in the wood-paneled dining room and, a few times a week, eat Chef
René's signature chicken-crab gumbo and

214

delectable osso bucco with the guys, of his own volition. Now he was sentenced to the place for the foreseeable future.

Ray's lawyers pressed into action. They informed Joan's attorney — the best in town for aggrieved wives of high-net-worth men — that they needed access to the condo to fetch Ray's suits. A pickup was arranged. Trial dates were set and reset. Meantime, the Boy Scouts presented Ray with the Good Scout award for his support of a national beautification program. Ray offered Joan's attorney a franchise to settle the case. His own attorney hinted that incriminating witnesses would be called to the stand to discredit Joan.

Just after the new year, Joan called her lawyer to announce she was calling off the separation, and the couple suddenly and mysteriously reconciled — even more mysteriously than they'd united to begin with. As hard as it was for them to live together, it seemed, Joan had decided they shouldn't be apart. No explanation was ever offered, other than that. With Ray now back home on Lake Shore Drive, Joan tucked this episode on her list of subjects never to be talked about again.

Soon, another personal legal matter would

demand Ray's attention.

His daughter had the capacity to sing in the smooth, buttery style of Doris Day. Her bright smile and mane of light brown curls masked her sadness as she worked her way through the standards under the stage name Lynn Scott. She'd recorded a demo record with a full orchestra that showed her impressive range, from the upbeat "Buttons and Bows" to the moony "How Deep Is the Ocean" and the dramatic "September Song." But despite her pluck and her engaging head shots, like so many with a talent, she hadn't managed to become a star.

Lynn's life had been a strain, with the faltering career and the conflict between her parents. Her mother, Ethel, had succumbed at age sixty-four to heart disease just after Thanksgiving, 1965, the same year Mc-Donald's had gone public and made Ray a multimillionaire. (Ethel's brother-in-law, the franchisee in Florida, shouted angrily at the chairman at an operators' meeting, "You killed my sister.")

In her mid-forties now, Lynn was desperate to negotiate an advance on the inheritance assured her in her mother's divorce agreement. That document made her rightful heir to a third of what Ray possessed, which was, when Ray and Ethel parted ways, nothing. Today, though, his fortune hovered in value around half a billion dollars, depending on the trading price of a share of McDonald's stock.

But Lynn couldn't wait for the promise of vast riches due her one day in the future. A cruel disease was slowly killing her, and it was unlikely she'd outlive her father. She was willing to trade her right to a future slice of Ray's enormous wealth in order to get a smaller, more immediate payout.

Ray agreed to put a million dollars into a trust, which would yield a weekly stipend of a thousand dollars to Lynn and her husband. Once she died, she was assured, what might be left of the principal would be deposited into her father's foundation, to go toward medical research. He also agreed to pay for her condominium, a mile from the home where her parents' marriage had fallen apart.

Lynn, in return, assured her lawyer that she understood that by taking money now, she was giving up her claim to a far greater sum.

Two years into the arrangement, on September 11, 1973, Lynn died at Northwest Community Hospital. Advanced cirrhosis of the liver caused the gastrointestinal bleeding that claimed her life, a month shy of her forty-ninth birthday.

Ray was in Europe at the time. That same week, a cartoon hamburger appeared on the cover of *Time* magazine, along with the headline: "The Burger That Conquered the Country." The company he called his "only child" had become the largest purveyor of meals in the nation, dispensing even more food than the United States Army.

Since the aborted divorce, Ray's advisors had been searching for something to keep Joan busy. Perhaps if she had something compelling, something of her own, to occupy her, she might be more content — and less trouble. Ray appointed her vice chairman of the board of his foundation, and even changed the name, dropping the "Raymond A." to emphasize that "The Kroc Foundation" was a family affair, hoping she'd get more involved with the work his brother, Bob, was undertaking. Then an investment proposal crossed Ray's desk for a new concept, a chain of "pet motels" to appease finicky, overprotective owners who wanted not only a safe place to board their beloved animals, but one where they would be assured all the comforts of home — and then some. The owners of the American Pet Motel, in fact, intended to go above and beyond the typical accommodations of the average Fido. Music would be piped into their private rooms to soothe them; pet-size brass beds covered with clean sheets would be provided; calls from their owners would be held to their ears on phones adorned with that famous dog Snoopy; food would be individually prepared to the client's specifications. This grandeur wasn't just the domain of Fido. Special and equally swank provisions would be made for other pets, like horses, cats, fish, and snakes. The notion was to build a prototype motel and franchise it around the country, mimicking the franchise philosophy: consistent look and service, repeated from site to site.

Ray was so taken with the idea that he decided to invest a million dollars of his fortune in it. This was a perfect pursuit for his Joni, the inveterate animal lover. As a condition of the deal, he stipulated she be given the title of vice president. Entrepreneur Robert X. Leeds was so happy to have the backing of one of America's most celebrated businessmen that he naturally agreed. The deal was sealed with a boozy celebration at Ray and Joan's place on Lake Shore Drive. It took a year to build the prototype, and of course, as with most any construction project, there were cost overruns. Joan met with Leeds to assure him that it was okay, that the business didn't need to turn a profit. She and Ray were rich beyond measure, and their goal was to make Leeds rich, too.

At the gala opening of the facilities outside Chicago, Ray and Joan arrived with their schnauzer, Burgy, in tow, decked out in a white doggie collar and black tie. Ray made a fuss after discovering that his favorite brand of booze wasn't stocked at the bar. Leeds dispatched a staffer to the nearby liquor store to make sure his benefactor had his beverage of choice. Cocktail in hand, Ray posed for a photo, grinning, with Joan at his side and flanked by Leeds and his wife. But the smiling relationship skidded downhill from there. Except for a lunch or two, Joan never exercised her power as vice president. Ultimately, the partnership came to an acrimonious end.

Joan didn't want an occupation or a project foisted on her by Ray or anyone in his circle. She was searching to carve her own path. Even her butler observed her ambition, her desire to do more than minister to hamburger franchisees. A calamity unfolding back in South Dakota gave her a sense of the power within her reach. The rains had poured down in a torrent back in the Black Hills one June day. Fifteen inches, fallen in the span of hours, had swelled the city's namesake Rapid Creek to overflowing. Canyon Lake Dam burst, turning streets into rivers, ripping dozens of houses from their foundations, launching the structures with such force they became dangerous horizontal missiles, sweeping up cars, trucks, and even people in their path. The entire swath of town where Joan used to live was left without power, shutting off communications to frantic family members separated from one another. As she watched the carnage on the nightly news from the cozy comfort of home, Joan couldn't believe the place she'd once lived — the place where the father of her child still lived — was the scene of the second-worst flood in the nation's history. At the Baken Park shopping center where Joan used to buy lingerie, terrified people clustered on the roof for safety, praying to be spared from the passing debris. Before the food at the store on Main Street spoiled, Rollie and his crew stepped up to disperse provisions to rescue workers — a quintessential McDonald's reaction to a crisis. The toll was unimaginable: 238 people dead. Twelve hundred homes destroyed, along with five thousand cars. More than $160 million in damage. It would take a long time before Rapid returned to anything resembling normal.

Joan and Rollie had experienced a mud and water incursion when they lived back on Lime Creek. That was nothing in comparison. She felt compelled to do something. But what? She arranged for a meeting with the recently elected mayor, twenty-eight-year-old Don Barnett, a Vietnam veteran who'd earned a Bronze Star and resigned his post as the chief of the South Dakota Consumers' League to lead city government. He'd heard about the local woman who'd left the city to marry the head of McDonald's. Everyone in Rapid knew the story. To make sure he was appropriately groomed for the society lady, the young mayor made a beeline to the barber for a shave and a haircut. It wasn't every day that a private jet with a bullet-shaped nose adorned with a unique "M" insignia made of arches landed at Rapid City Airport, or that he got to shake hands with a multimillionaire.

Joan arrived bearing good news. She hoped to help her fellow Rapidians by making a donation to the fund for victims. There was one condition, though: There must not be any publicity. She pulled out her purse, fumbled for her checkbook, and wrote out the grand sum of $50,000 — the largest donation the mayor had received. "Holy cow" was the mayor's corn-fed reaction. He vowed to honor her request. If word got out, she repeated, she'd stop payment on the check.

That fall, as the city was settling in to its reconstruction, the library on Quincy Street that had been in the works for years opened its doors. Joan wrote another check to Rapid, this time for $20,000, to pay for books and artwork to be displayed in the new facility. A dozen years earlier, she'd been scrambling for change to pay for lunch, picking up extra money by giving piano lessons, and now here she was, dispensing money around her old haunt like a fairy godmother. It was a grand taste of the power she had at her disposal, and a symbol of how far she'd come.

In the library lobby, Mayor Barnett innocently decided to hang a portrait of this former citizen, paying tribute to his silent benefactor. He didn't realize he was rekindling a town scandal. When people asked why the former Joan Smith was on display, the mayor shrugged. "She was just a wonderful citizen," he'd say coyly, keeping his promise. But some of the locals didn't think

Joan was so wonderful. She'd left Rollie, after all, to run off with a rich man — his boss! The gossip around town lingered, and people still whispered about what Rollie must have been given in "exchange" for giving up his wife — the crass speculation that he received more stores. Employees at the three area McDonald's were under strict orders not to utter Joan's name, or, for that matter, Ray's. Rollie, for his part, had hardly wallowed in his grief. He was able to golf to his heart's content, and built a brand-new house in a new subdivision a mile from the Arrowhead Country Club, where he was an active member. He was even given the opportunity to name the road. He called it Heidiway Lane, in honor of Heide, his new, younger wife.

In the winter of 1973, an eleventh-hour wrench in the planned move of the San Diego Padres, the cellar-dwelling worst team in baseball, dominated sports headlines and changed the course of Ray and Joan's lives. The team's owner, C. Arnholt Smith, grappling with charges of tax fraud and embezzlement, needed a quick cash infusion. He'd sold to a group of investors who'd plunked down a $100,000 deposit on the $12 million purchase price. As a condition of the sale, the Padres were to be relocated from the balmy paradise at the southernmost tip of California, most famous for its world-class zoo and military bases, to the nation's capital, Washington, D.C. New baseball cards had even been printed that displayed a prototype uniform emblazoned with the team's proposed new name, "Stars."

The city fathers of San Diego were apoplectic about this abandonment. Reneging on a long-term lease on the stadium was a serious breach of contract. (Never mind that the team was a crashing dud. The Padres were *their* dud.) A suit was filed to block the sale. The legal dispute was an obstacle Smith couldn't afford to endure. He needed cash, now.

Enter Ray. He listened intently to the drama as it unfolded in the sports news. He happened to possess two things: an ample pot of cash and a lifelong love of baseball. As a salesman, he'd snuck off so many afternoons to cheer at Wrigley Field, he sported a tan from sitting in the stands. For years, back when he could scarcely afford box seats at a game, he was so sure he'd one day own the Chicago Cubs he'd even bragged of his intention to disbelieving friends.

Once he had become a multimillionaire, his PR counsel set about helping his client's dream come true. Al Golin floated the idea of Ray's buying the team and had been flatly dismissed by the Wrigley family in a terse letter: "Some things in life aren't for sale and the Chicago Cubs is one of them." The San Diego Padres would have to suffice, then. Such symmetry: This was the same city where he and Joan had decided, the second time, to marry. But before he went ahead with the purchase, just to be absolutely sure, Ray made one last inquiry about the team he really wanted. The answer was still no. So he signed off on the deal — more symmetry — while sitting in the living room of his old friend Jim Zien, who'd ultimately opened seven McDonald's, later sold them back to corporate for millions of dollars, then relocated his family to San Diego. For Ray, $12 million was a mere rounding error in his fortune. Being able to pay for it all on his own fluffed his peacock feathers, too, as did the fact he'd paid a premium, even if it was for a losing team. The year before, shipping magnate George Steinbrenner had bought the venerable New York Yankees for only $8.8 million, and he'd done it in a group.

San Diegans went wild with the news.

Sports reporters crawled over the story of this new celebrity owner with glee. Team management breathed a sigh of relief at the prospect of the "Sugar Padre" who'd saved their game. Even the players were intrigued by Ray; some hoped it might be a way into ownership of a McDonald's. About the only person who seemed lukewarm about the purchase was Joan. She was so ignorant about baseball that when she heard "Padres" she assumed her husband was buying a monastery.

"I just wanted a hobby," Ray explained to a reporter on the day the deal won final approval, as he sipped a gin and tonic by the pool at his sprawling, 10,000-square-foot home in Fort Lauderdale. An extravagant hobby, he allowed. And certainly nothing that would replace his "one and only child, McDonald's." This baseball team would never be more than a "stepchild" to Ray. Was he in it to make money? another reporter asked. He insisted the desire to make money had never been his motive for anything. His only interest now was to see if he could work the same magic on this crummy team as he had on the hamburger shack in a one-horse town. He wanted to win.

Like any skilled entertainer, the organist

Danny Topaz had a flair for drama. He'd changed his surname, Topuzes, to the more melodic and glittering moniker of a gemstone, which happened to represent November, the month he'd been married. Topaz had first been hired to provide the live music in the stadium when the team got started in 1969. The excitement of the new community "toy" quickly waned when would-be fans discovered the Padres were losers and just stopped showing up for the games. Topaz quit, figuring he could find a more enthusiastic audience at nightclubs and other venues around town.

But the arrival of this new multimillionaire owner renewed San Diego's fallow hope for a winning team, and Topaz's interest in providing their accompaniment. That both Ray and his wife were keyboard aficionados made the skilled player's repeat audition a cinch. His flair and precision on the stadium's great Lowrey organ wowed them, and he was rehired on the spot.

Before he got to play a single chord, the Padres lived up to their reputation, starting the season with a characteristic crashing thud and losing all three games of the opening series to the Los Angeles Dodgers, 8–0, 8–0, 9–2. At least, Ray figured as he boarded one of his Big Mac buses to trek south for the home opener against the Houston Astros, there were 159 games to go.

April 9, 1974, proved to be a frosty night for a southern California spring, but fans were so elated that baseball was still being played on local soil, against all odds, that they bundled up and crammed the San Diego stadium nearly to capacity for the first time since the team's formation. When the mayor introduced the man who saved baseball, the fans erupted in a hero's welcome.

Aside from Topaz's energetic playing, the other animated and reliable showmanship on game night took place off the field, up in the announcer's booth, awkwardly positioned on the first base line. John DeMott was a local morning drive-time broadcaster who moonlighted at the games on the public address system. He'd developed a distinctive style of introducing the players he called "hot-dogging." When the visiting team was at bat, he'd announce their names low-key and straight. When the Padres were up, he'd milk it, drawing out each individual player's name as he made his way onto the field with drama: "Number eleven ENnnnnnnZzzzzz-O." But no matter how they were introduced, the Padres kept getting trounced, and tonight was no exception. By the top of the eighth inning, the score was a pathetic 9–2. Denny, the usher who served in the owner's box, suddenly appeared in the doorway of the booth with a question: Could Mr. Kroc please address the crowd?

"Certainly," DeMott answered without hesitation, "it's his crowd." Just then, the announcer's wife and four-year-old son, Chris, ducked into the booth to warm up from the cool night and say they were heading home. What was the point of staying up to see the Padres flame out again? Having visitors was against the rules, lest an interloper distract the man with the microphone, or try to seize it, but DeMott figured nobody would notice or mind if his family stuck around for a few moments.

Suddenly, Ray appeared in the doorway, cocktail in hand. The public address announcer cautiously introduced the new owner to his family, who squirmed uncomfortably at their infraction. Ray didn't appear to know or care that their presence was against the rules. He asked when he please might speak. DeMott told the new owner he could talk as soon as the Padres struck out — which happened, characteristically, one, two, three.

DeMott pressed down on the foot pedal

to turn on the microphone, so he could introduce Ray. Ray, in turn, stood by his side, waiting to speak to the crowd. The awkward configuration meant Ray's back was now toward home plate. His audience was DeMott's wife and little boy.

"Ladies and gentlemen, this is Ray Kroc," he began. "I suffer with you." Almost as if on cue, a streaker leaped out of the stands and darted across the outfield. The crowd went wild at the sight of a naked man, their shrieks drowning out Ray, who turned around just in time to see that the din had nothing to do with his remarks. "Get that man, arrest him!" Ray yelled, his shrill voice reverberating over the stadium loudspeakers. Security guards were already on the case, whisking the intruder out of sight. Ray resumed his commentary: "There is good news and bad news," he said. "First, the good news. You loyal fans outdid Los Angeles. They had thirty-one thousand for opening night and we have nearly forty thousand. God bless you. Now for the bad news. We are putting on a lousy show for you. I apologize for it. I'm disgusted. This is the most stupid ballplaying I've ever seen."

With that, clutching his cocktail glass, Ray excused himself to return to his owner's box, unaware of the firestorm of support, and ire, his speech was about to unleash. The Kroc era in major league baseball had begun.

8
THE SECRET EVERYONE KNOWS

Perched in an elegant suite at the Pierre
Hotel on Fifth Avenue in New York City,
her blond hair styled in a perfect nest, her
fashionable eyeglass frames sparkling in the
springtime sun, Joan sat, cigarette in hand,
poised for an interview with a reporter from
the venerable *New York Times.* Until now,
she'd done what she could to avoid journalists. She knew better than to think they were
interested in *her.* What they wanted was
insights into Ray. What was it like to be married to one of America's most successful
and venerated businessmen, the man who
changed the way the world ate, the man who
spoke his mind — the man not only rich
enough to *own* a baseball team, but unafraid
to publicly *humiliate* it.

She couldn't and wouldn't admit the truth
about life with her husband, certainly not
with most outsiders, and definitely not with
the press. The publicity surrounding the

divorce filing had vanished into the ether, without a trace of meddling follow-up. That was fine by Joan. It had made life easier for it to just disappear. A lingering wrinkle, although a private one, made matters sticky: Ray's attorneys in the matter were friends with whom they socialized on trips to the ranch and other occasions. One of them, in fact, had been assigned to her as her own personal attorney, to give her a sense she had an advocate all her own. It was hard to know whose interests were being served.

Virtually everyone seemed to be looking for something, and more often than not, it traced back to money, or McDonald's, or both. As if to prove it, while she was with the reporter, the phone rang in her suite with a call from a man offering to trade a $300,000 emerald for a franchise. She curtly explained that she had nothing to do with the company, and referred him to Ray.

Wealth, Joan was finding, came not with strings attached, but with ropes. It attracted sycophants, opportunists, and people who believed having an abundance of cash made life better, solved every problem. The only thing money did, as far as Joan was concerned, was prevent poverty. Having abundant riches simply meant no longer having to look at the right side of the menu in a restaurant. She was, of course, happy not to be poor any longer, but she wished she could disabuse people of the idea that money equaled happiness.

Yet, as burdensome as it could feel, it could also prove liberating. Joan couldn't deny to herself that access to the fast-food fortune unlocked a certain amount of power. She was learning to wield this to her advantage, like a sword. In her husband, she had an excellent tutor. He hadn't denied himself what he wanted before he was rich. Now that cash was as plentiful as air, all the more reason not to let cost stand in the way.

She had begun to assert herself in the marriage more forcefully. Ray wanted to live on a yacht in San Diego during baseball season and dispatched his men to locate an appropriate vessel. The *JoniRay* wasn't big enough. Besides, that was their East Coast yacht. This new "house-yacht" had to be larger than a hundred feet, the size of the boat belonging to Gussie Busch, the owner of the St. Louis Cardinals, so Ray could have bragging rights. A suitable vessel was located, but Joan nixed the plan. It was too fraught with potential for bachelor-pad shenanigans, and not good for Ray's health.

Besides, Joan's daughter had moved to San Diego with her husband and children, which was reason enough to have a real residence there. As a favor to the city, Ray had stepped up and bought the ailing local hockey team, the Mariners, whose owner couldn't make payroll. Ray tapped Joan's son-in-law, Ballard, a lawyer who'd left his post as district attorney in Crawford County, Pennsylvania, to serve as general manager of this venture.

Off the Krocs went to house shop. They fell in love with a place in the fancy enclave of La Jolla, and, without even inquiring about the asking price, Ray offered a million dollars. Hours later, after the owner's maid refused to allow them back in for a second peek, he killed the deal, marched up the street, and bought another house.

Ray's main focus now was on deploying his fortune in the service of his new, expensive hobby. By pouring enough money into the Padres, maybe he'd coddle the team into winning. Little luxuries, like wooden toilet seats and fancy hangers — not plain wire ones — to make the players feel special. Big ones, like a private plane decked out in the team colors, gold and brown. The dawn of free agency was beginning to drive up player salaries from relatively modest to obscene. When the best pitcher in baseball, Catfish Hunter, came on the markct, Ray was intent on getting his mitts on the guy. He dispatched top team brass to close the deal with instructions to pay an incredible four times Hunter's last deal. At the climax of the negotiation, a special ship-to-shore call was placed to the *JoniRay* as it sailed in sparkling waters. The price tag, Ray's employees informed him, was actually close to ten times higher than the $400,000 annual salary they were authorized to spend.

"Four *million?*" Ray shouted, incredulous at the sum. Baseball players didn't command such lavish salaries. In the confines of the boat, Joan, who couldn't help but eavesdrop, started shouting in the background, just as incredulous that Ray would spend so much of their money on one salary for one player in a frivolous game she didn't understand. A mammoth domestic dispute erupted over the proposed expenditure, loud enough that every word of the fight could be heard by the callers back on land. It was his money to spend, goddammit, and Joan just needed to shut up, Ray shouted. Joan was equally vocal in her opposition. In the end, after Ray's lawyers tried to insert a condition in the deal that Hunter as a Padre would do double-duty as a spokesman for McDonald's, the star athlete signed, instead, with the Yankees.

Reconciliation hadn't quelled the volatility in Ray and Joan's relationship. What had changed was Joan's approach to the situation. She was learning to stop reacting and start acting. Money might not equal happiness, but it could buy her what she wanted. And that was why she sat now in the suite in the Pierre with this reporter. She put down her cigarette. She had something vitally important that she wished to convey.

If purchasing the Padres qualified Ray as a believer in the "great hereafter," breakfast with the players during spring training in Yuma, Arizona, was heaven on earth. To sit down at the hotel café with the team — *his* team — before heading out for a hard day's work on the field was the ultimate in inside-baseball. Besides, the travel required to keep up with his "stepchild" gave him a marvelous excuse to field-check outposts of his beloved McDonald's he might not otherwise visit.

As hungry players wolfed down their eggs and coffee, the outfielder Ivan Murrell approached Ray at the booth where he was holding court to tell the new boss how much he loved McDonald's. One day, in fact, he hoped he might own one back home in his native Panama. Here in Yuma during spring training, he bragged, he used much of his meal allowance at the one in town. He'd noticed, though, that the French fries stuck together.

The mere suggestion that there was something wrong with his sacred product launched Ray into action. He demanded to be driven to the nearby store, immediately, frantically consulting his omnipresent leather binder along the way for the name of the franchisee, stewing about what could possibly be wrong. Was it the temperature of the fryer? Was the oil not fresh? That player, he mused aloud, he wants a store in Panama? Those Latin Americans were all too dirty to maintain the high sanitation standards necessary for McDonald's! By the time the car arrived at the store's parking lot, Ray was all but frothing at the mouth. The vision before him agitated him even more.

The front door of the place was propped wide open, a violation of company code. Violation two: a limp, wet towel festering on top of the trash can. The third and most egregious violation of all: a young, female employee, a cigarette dangling from her lips, rushed from her half-finished cleanup duty to stand behind the counter and serve this customer who'd just arrived. It was the cigarette, not her gender, that was the problem. The edict prohibiting female employees had been lifted several years earlier, although franchisees had been cautioned to only hire women who were flat-chested and as unattractive as possible. Good-looking women presented too much of a distraction.

What the hell is that? demanded Ray, gesturing at the errant towel.

Who the hell are you? demanded the employee.

Ray shouted to no one in particular that whoever this girl was, she was fired, now — immediately.

A whirl of activity: tears from the young woman, a manager appearing, and then, on his heels, the franchisee, as Ray demanded to know, "What the fuck is going on? The French fries are sticking together."

"What do you mean," said the chagrined store owner, having no idea what Ray was referring to, "the French fries?"

"I want four batches made — rehire that girl so she can help. I want as many fries as will fit into four of these cardboard boxes."

As Ray stood watch, his order was obediently executed. The goods were loaded into the back of the car, a delicate exhibit A. Back at the hotel, the maids were embarking on their morning rounds. Ray grabbed extra towels and tossed them onto a freshly made bed. Then, as the cleaning crew gazed on in bewilderment, he began tipping sleeve after sleeve of the spuds on the mattress, sifting through in search of sticky offenders.

It wasn't until he got down to the bottom of the bags that any offending fries were revealed. That outfielder, said Ray, he was right. The fryer must have been off by a couple of degrees.

Having seen it for himself, and having put the franchisee on notice with his tirade, Ray was satisfied. Now he could get on with the day, back to the field to watch the boys play ball.

It was one kind of difficult when the histrionics were private. It was another when they were public displays. Like those remarks at the Padres opening game. Joan had been so ashamed. She'd quizzed Ray on the phone in the aftermath. Had he been drunk? He swore he wasn't; if he had been, he said, his remarks would have been far worse and "set baseball back fifty years." Even the sportswriters agreed that no man in his right mind would insult his team in such a way. "Kroc was washing down his hamburgers with something not sold at McDonald's stands," wrote the columnist Dick Young. "Something that made him a bit bold." Ray insisted it was just an impulsive comment, made worse, he said, by the presence of the streaker. He'd been misunderstood.

Joan had learned that Ray's perspective on alcohol and its impact was all wrong.

That her scientist brother-in-law was spending the money her husband had earmarked for charity on such indecipherable matters as mechanisms of intestinal electrolyte transport, total lymphoid irradiation on autoimmune disease, and peptide hormones of the brain and gut was, to Joan, a frivolity. She was eager to put the foundation's resources to use tackling what she considered "human problems," not to invest in science experiments. In Joan's estimation, Bob was overlooking the most important disease that afflicted their family.

The very word "alcoholism," used in polite society, carried criminal connotations. It conjured up images of a no-good scofflaw lying on the curb, a person who was a drain on, not a contributing member of, society. To Ray's inner circle, Joan's suggestion that her husband drank more than he should was an outrage. He was their hero, a superman, their beloved captain — who also happened to be the life of the party, funny and biting and brash. Rarely did he *seem* drunk. Though he might have had a steady drip of Early Times throughout the evening, late into the night, he still rose early the next day without fail, eager to plunge into work. He'd built an empire! He was rich! He'd made so many other people rich along the way. This was not the behavior of someone with a drinking problem. And how dare this emotional blond piano player suggest it — risking his reputation by making the accusations she had and filing for divorce.

From her perch inside the marriage, Joan struggled to understand the unanswerable — what led some people down the path of addictive behavior and "alcohol misuse," while others could imbibe within reason. If Ray loved her, why didn't he just cut back, or stop altogether? Why couldn't she cure him of his desire, his need, to drink? Did she somehow aggravate the problem? She wasn't the only one asking these questions. All across the United States in the 1970s, a growing movement was emerging to publicly recognize excessive drinking as a problem, understand the impact of the problem on society, and shift the popular perception of alcoholism as a moral shortcoming caused by a lack of willpower to the idea that it was a disease that could be treated.

Just how and where treatment was most effectively administered was also under the microscope. "Familization therapy" — involving relatives in patient care, and even going so far as inviting them to live with the patient in a treatment center — was a newly emerging option. So were new variations on the all-volunteer support system, Alcoholics Anonymous. For decades, since Prohibition's end, AA had been widely believed to be the most effective form of treatment for a person who had reached the breaking point and was ready to say, out loud, that drinking was making their life, and the lives of the people around them, hell. Showing up at one meeting, and then another, and ultimately committing to sobriety within the protective nest of AA was a system that had worked for millions of people. The foundation of this system was known as the "twelve steps."

The first of the steps involved admitting dependency on and powerlessness over alcohol. The last was to continue the cycle by helping others just beginning to march down the path of recovery. The crucial centerpiece of the process involved accepting the existence and guidance of a higher power from the faith tradition of the seeker's choice. (For those who were uncomfortable with religion or spirituality, this presented a thorny obstacle to overcome.)

The "anonymous" part of AA was the other critical part of the equation. It put everyone who participated on equal footing, regardless of his or her place in society, from janitor to chief executive to housewife. And it guaranteed participants the privacy that was felt necessary to address the addiction without fear of shame or retribution.

Four days after the world watched astronauts walk on the moon in 1969, Americans witnessed a groundbreaking televised spectacle of a different sort: a three-day congressional hearing on the wide-ranging and growing impact of drinking on the American people. With eight billion dollars a year collected in tax on alcohol, Senator Harold Hughes of Iowa found it curious that only four million was spent by the federal government to address alcoholism, and that doctors were ill-equipped to address the disease. He had a personal interest in the topic: He was an alcoholic in recovery.

Hughes found it a challenge to convince his peers to take the stand. The founder of AA, affectionately known as "Bill W.," was one of a handful who agreed to testify. When

245

his time came to speak, cameras were dramatically trained away from his face, to preserve his anonymity. Today, he said, splashdown day for the Apollo astronauts, was also a turning point in the public dialogue about alcoholism. He described how he'd been told that if he didn't stop drinking, he would die; how he'd reached the depths in detox and experienced, despite his initial resistance to the notion of a higher power, a sudden spiritual awakening. This, he said, freed him from the desire to drink that had consumed his every waking moment for years. Once he'd made a commitment to stay sober, Bill W. had begun to work with another alcoholic in recovery, which gave way to what eventually grew into the international movement.

Senator Hughes had also enlisted the Academy Award–winning actress Mercedes McCambridge to talk about her own struggles to overcome addiction, a public confession some told her would destroy her career. She proudly defied the warnings of her friends. "My body is thoroughly allergic to alcohol," she said on the stand. "Therefore my disease carries no more moral stigma than diabetes." She decried the publicly accepted veil thrown over women of a certain class who suffered from the disease to shield them, and their loved ones, from the shame of it — the euphemisms of deceit.

Not long after these frank revelations, Congress passed the Hughes Act, which provided funds for the government to invest in treatment and research, quintupling the number of rehabilitation facilities over the next decade. But that didn't offset the fact that the medical profession still wasn't addressing addiction head-on. Even if the doctors who monitored Ray's other health problems had inquired about his drinking habits, Ray acknowledged it was possible for a drinker to bamboozle his doctor.

A monumental breakthrough in the public consideration of alcoholism occurred when the former first lady Betty Ford stepped forward with a blockbuster confession: "I'm Betty, and I'm an alcoholic, and I know my drinking has hurt my family." In a well-publicized memoir, she detailed how her children staged an intervention, which she credited with saving her life. She revealed that the former president had stood, proudly and honorably, by her side through her thirty-day inpatient rehabilitation program at Long Beach Naval Hospital, encouraging her to reveal the truth about her condition. She feared that, in doing so, she'd taint or shame him. "There will be no embarrassment to me," said President Gerald Ford. "You go ahead and say what should be said." Her declaration immediately catapulted her into the limelight as the publicly acknowledged champion for the cause of sobriety. If a former resident of the White House had suffered dependence issues and worked to get a grasp on them, surely now others could step forward and seek help, too.

Joan's trouble wasn't just that she couldn't get Ray to accept help. She couldn't even persuade him he had a problem. He was pleased she was immersed in a project that consumed her, and happy to support the pursuit. But to Ray, the therapists and addiction specialists she brought around were quacks, not to be trusted. Experts in the disease whom she invited to the house or the ranch marveled at his case: They'd never met someone who could drink and drink and drink, and yet never suffer a hangover. Desperate to feel some sort of progress, she was convinced by a friend to attend Al-Anon, the support group for people affected by the drinking of a loved one. Her attendance at meetings changed her life. Here, she came face-to-face with others who lived with the roller-coastering rhythm of life with someone who drank to excess. She found solace in the group's "serenity prayer:" accepting the things she couldn't change, mustering courage to change what she could, and having the wisdom to know the difference. She learned to quit blaming herself for her husband's drinking and for her inability to get him to stop. She began to believe that alcoholism was, indeed, a disease — a disease that impacted an entire family.

Her investigations sparked an epiphany. Joan resolved to launch a "social revolution" to make the word "alcoholism" as acceptable and common in society as was the well-worn and acceptable practice of drinking and getting drunk. Having only a high school education and no formal training didn't deter her. She had suffered, and she wanted to direct others to help — even if she couldn't help her own husband. After all, she had something at her disposal that most people didn't: access to hundreds of millions of dollars, or, at the least, the $15 million or so in the coffers of her husband's foundation.

She also had at her disposal a magnificently appointed ranch with a conference facility. To help her plot her social revolution, she told her brother-in-law, Bob, that she was inviting key figures in alcohol education and rehabilitation to a meeting there. With Ray's approval, and that well-stocked self-serve bar at the centerpiece of the facility, this small group frankly discussed breakthroughs and deficiencies in the field of addiction science and treatment, and new ways to appeal to the legions of the affected — including and especially the families.

They left brimming with ideas, an eight-page list of media that could be created to improve the public understanding of alcohol misuse and its impact on the family. This included the development of comic strips, books, television shows, and public service announcements to appeal to a wide audience. If she could make just one film, she'd be happy.

Even before she'd begun in earnest, she'd chosen a name for her efforts: Operation Cork. "In case you didn't get it," she explained to a reporter for the *Chicago Daily News,* "Cork is Kroc spelled backward." It did not, she insisted, mean "putting the cork back in the bottle." The clever inversion of Ray's name hinted at the real reason for her interest in combating the problem, while at the same time masking it. Did her husband come up with "cork"? the reporter asked. "Oh no, I did," she responded, "but he thinks he thought of it, so I let him."

On her husband's seventy-fourth birthday in 1976, Operation Cork was officially incorporated into The Kroc Foundation. As foundation president, Bob Kroc wasn't particularly enthused about this development. Joan was clearly muscling her way onto his turf. Ray casually delivered the news to Bob about his wife's new venture on a car ride up at the ranch. When Joan informed him that she'd hired one of the addiction experts from whom she'd been seeking counsel, Rev. John Keller, as Cork's president, his hackles rose again. This newcomer now had equal rank to him! Finally, Joan and Ray both told reporters, the foundation was addressing human problems. Bob defensively countered that they were minimizing the importance of his work. The type of scientific research he was investing in, after all, *was* crucial to humans.

Whether she was ruffling her brother-in-law's feathers was not Joan's concern. The Kroc Foundation belonged to Ray, and thus to her, and she had every right to claim a piece of it. She jumped into her work with the fervor of an evangelist. Operation Cork gave Joan a focus and purpose and renewed energy, as well as a sense that no matter how difficult Ray might be, she was putting the fortune, and her suffering, to good use.

Now that she had a name, Joan invented a mascot — a smiling, wide-eyed cartoon cork — named, naturally, "Corky." Several people tried to dissuade her from using the character, because they felt it diminished the importance of her message. But Joan was insistent, and proud of her creation; she was, in essence, the ventriloquist behind Corky, who could express feelings and speak the words she herself could not. She even commissioned Corky figurines made of solid gold as gifts for the women in her office. Corky debuted in a series of advertisements run in the San Diego newspapers:

Hi! My name's Corky. I'll be popping up quite a bit here in San Diego so I thought it was a good time to say "Happy new you!" No, it's not a misprint. It just kind of says what OPERATION CORK is all about. Now, more than any time of year, so many of us are celebrating on the outside but suffering on the inside. The drinking puzzle touches almost every family in this country.

The next order of business was distribution of a forty-page glossy pamphlet written by John Keller, *Alcohol. A Family Affair.* The primer explained the warning signs of problem drinking and how to find help. Joan wrote in the foreword that she hoped it would help ease the pain of afflicted families and help them understand they weren't alone. Nationally syndicated advice columnist Abigail Van Buren decided to give it a plug, cautioning that when she did, Cork staff had better be prepared for a deluge of inquiries.

When Abby ran the column, asking readers to send a dollar to defray mailing costs, as she predicted, more than thirty thousand requests streamed into Cork's office. One reader from Saudi Arabia enclosed four dollars. Another apologized: "I only have fifty cents. Please help my daddy."

Helping children who lived in homes plagued by problem drinking was next on Joan's list of action items. To reach that audience, she sought out the animator Bill Melendez, the man who'd brought Charles Schulz's comic strip, *Peanuts,* to life. A series of public service advertisements Melendez created was mailed on videotape to every television station in the country.

In one of the spots, a little boy cries in the family kitchen.

"Mom, you put salt in my cereal!"

The mother throws up her hands in despair.

"Oh, I'm so upset I don't know what I'm doing. I didn't sleep a wink worrying about your dad and his drinking."

The poor little kid hugs his despondent mother.

"Mom, that's okay, I don't care."

Corny little Corky, wearing a baseball hat adorned with an Operation Cork logo, steps authoritatively toward the camera.

"They really do care. I'm Corky, and I care too."

Thousands more requests streamed in. Operation Cork had touched a nerve. Joan's social revolution was in full throttle.

Reaction to this work fueled Joan's desire to accomplish even more. In her suite at the Pierre Hotel, she told a reporter with *The New York Times* about Cork's latest project, a made-for-TV movie. Joan had hired a filmmaker, Gerald Rogers, known for his brutally honest depiction of addiction, to make a movie for Cork. The film *If You*

Loved Me chronicles the decline of a handsome, doting suburban father named Don as he becomes dependent on alcohol to get through the stress of his days. His wife, Nancy, is racked with self-loathing for helping to cover up her husband's absences from work. Then a friend convinces her to find support at Al-Anon. The title echoed the impassioned exchanges in a troubled family: "If you loved me, you wouldn't drink" and "If you loved me, you'd get off my back."

After a gala premiere screening at the Adler Planetarium in Chicago, in the Kroc Universe Theater Ray had underwritten, Joan's team arranged for *If You Loved Me* to air, nationwide, on NBC. She enlisted the assistance of her friends at Hubbard Broadcasting, where she'd long ago worked as an organist. Joan was so much more now than the beautiful young musician juggling three jobs and a family. She was an activist, a publisher, a bona fide film producer, in production on a new film, *Soft Is the Heart of a Child,* which told the story of another alcoholic father and an enabling mother from the perspective of three young children, so distressed by their home life that they bravely run away. The kids are rescued thanks to the intervention of a kindly school

255

guidance counselor who deduces their behavioral issues as a signal of problems at home.

Soft Is the Heart of a Child aired on PBS stations around the nation in 1979, and went on to win a host of awards that made it standard viewing at rehabilitation clinics and other treatment programs. One on-air screening was followed by a live conversation with experts about addiction. The switchboard was overloaded with calls.

Reporters didn't quite know what to make of the crusade being waged by the wife of the founding chairman of McDonald's, a woman sporting a pink diamond so big that it looked like it had fallen out of an ice-cube tray. The skeptics hinted that Cork might be a dilettante hobby for the bored wife of a rich man. Why was she so interested in alcoholism? With each interview, Joan's story morphed a bit. She'd started Cork because half her household staff was impacted by drinking. To another reporter, she credited the struggle of a cherished uncle. To yet another, it was a lecture at the library that prompted her concern. And to another still, she maintained there was no problem in her family, then quickly added, borrowing a cue from the AA pledge, that she couldn't really answer the question.

Alcoholism, she explained, simply wasn't a disease that got a lot of attention. It was up to her to shine a spotlight on it.

Though some reporters were confused by this earnest wife's motivation, at least one journalist was downright dismissive, deeming Corky "a kind of alcoholic's answer to Ronald McDonald." If the marketing of Joan's Operation Cork in any way resembled the company that was indirectly funding her work, it was because she'd been learning all these years from the men who built the chain. She'd had a ringside seat to how advertisements had shaped and distinguished McDonald's, and made her first husband well-off and her second husband rich. She bounced all of her Corky ideas off Ray, she told a reporter: "He is, after all, well — a merchandiser." The input was more than informal. The PR firm that had been hawking the company for twenty years had been hired to help her craft her message — and to keep a watchful eye to make sure she didn't reveal too much personal information. When Ray wanted to accept the invitation to talk about his wife's work on a television show, he was advised that that wasn't a good idea.

To prove she wasn't a prohibitionist, during one interview Joan nonchalantly ordered and sipped a glass of rosé and declared that alcohol was the best social lubricant out there. The liquor itself wasn't the problem; it was the user of it who was. The fact that she drank, she believed, made her more effective as an advocate.

The flowing presence of booze presented problems at the Cork conferences Joan continued to convene at the ranch. That mammoth self-serve bar proved torturous to visitors who'd committed to sobriety. "Cocktail hour" on the printed agenda was renamed more sensitively "You name it hour," but the name change didn't dissuade consumption of copious amounts of alcohol (which Bob meticulously inventoried after each meeting to make sure it was properly accounted for and stocked). For dinner, Joan might dip into the cellar to retrieve a case of Château Lafite Rothschild. Later in the evening, as guests relaxed in the lodge's living room, Ray emerged in his robe to lounge around the fireplace, Hefner-style, the confident man of the house, a long cigar in one hand and his ever-present cocktail in the other, funny and charming as hell, and angry at anyone who seemed to be overindulging. "God is among us," one visitor explained Ray's ineffable presence, "and he happens to be an alcoholic."

As mysterious and contradictory and cryptic as Joan might be — even to some of her staff, many of whom had no idea what inspired their boss's passionate commitment — she developed a reputation in the close-knit addiction field for being enthusiastic about new ideas, with deep pockets to match. The burgeoning network of addiction counselors around the country took curious note of the activities of this Operation Cork. Her wide-ranging advocacy landed her on a syndicated television show about addiction called *It's Great to Be Alive!* and on the cover of *Alcoholism* magazine, smiling slyly and confidently for the camera. A young social worker arrived at the Cork offices to show off a nearly complete book designed to help children of alcoholics — one of the first of its kind — and left with a check in hand from Joan that allowed her to finish the project. When a young journalist in recovery came to ask Joan how she might get involved with Cork, Joan commissioned her to write her own story. The resulting book frankly addressed the writer's shame as a child when she realized her parents had been alcoholics, and how she'd grown up to be one herself:

> I want to tell you a secret. It's something I tried to hide — even from myself — for many years because I thought it was so awful and dirty. I decided no one should ever find out about it. You can stop being so scared and miserable if you do a very simple thing: share your secret. Let me tell you mine.

Joan still wasn't able to disclose her own personal secret, but she delighted in working with this young author to help reveal hers. She pushed her to express her deepest feelings, and told her she shouldn't worry about violating her family's privacy — she could byline the book with a pseudonym. The woman chose the name "Cathleen Brooks." But she was still stuck on a title for the work.

Joan had a ready answer.

"How about," she said knowingly, *"The Secret Everyone Knows."*

Operation Cork detoured in a new direction because of an unrelated invitation extended to Ray by an unlikely suitor: the Ivy League Dartmouth College in Hanover, New Hampshire. Ray had the same disdain for professors as he had for therapists, and sniffed at institutions of higher learning. In his estimation, the world was filled with "too many baccalaureates and too few butchers." What this country needed, he believed, was more practical education like the training academy McDonald's had set up back in 1961, "Hamburger University," where franchisees and employees enrolled for indoctrination in the ways of the company. He vowed never to write a check to a university unless it installed a trade school, and he'd quoted Calvin Coolidge so often that people began to attribute Coolidge's words to Ray:

Nothing in this world can take the place of persistence. Talent will not: nothing is more common than unsuccessful men with talent. Genius will not; unrewarded genius is almost a proverb. Education will not: the world is full of educated derelicts. Persistence and determination alone are omnipotent.

Despite his misgivings about higher education, it would have been difficult for Ray to refuse the invitation extended to him in 1974 to speak to students at Dartmouth College's Tuck School of Business. The request came via an alumnus of the school,

Fred Fedeli, the financial wizard who'd thrown McDonald's the $1.5 million lifeline that saved it from bankruptcy in 1960. The 22.5 percent stake his group had received from McDonald's in return for its cash infusion had, when stock started trading, yielded a mammoth $20 million, catapulting Fedeli into the ranks of visionaries in the world of finance. The banker had run into his former classmate Paul Paganucci, who now taught at their alma mater; Paganucci asked for an introduction to Ray; and soon, in the dead of winter, the hamburger king was en route to Hanover, New Hampshire.

A major snowstorm rerouted Ray's jet to Boston, where, luckily, one of the fleet of Big Mac buses was at the ready to squire him and his entourage an hour away to campus. The frank, off-the-record talk he gave to students was one of the first times he'd walked through his life story, from paper cups, real estate, and Multimixers to his deal with the McDonald brothers — natives of the very state where he was speaking — to their buyout and subsequent initial public offering. There wasn't a proper, patrician, Ivy League bone in Ray's body; and especially since this crop of students was from the first generation to grow up eating at McDonald's, to have the bombastic

262

senior chairman in their midst was no less thrilling than a lecture by a rock star.

Now that Dartmouth had lured this iconic business executive with a grand and growing fortune to their off-the-beaten-path school, administrators were positively giddy at the prospect of expanding the friendship — especially after they did some more homework. Paganucci had the help of an inside source: He'd attended law school with Ray's chief counsel, who shared some facts. In the nine years since Ray had first struck gold, he'd given away an incredible $30 million — more than any Dartmouth alumnus had ever gifted to the school. (Much of it had been tucked away, to his tax advantage, into his own foundation, but this figure also included a gift of $10 million to build a wing at Children's Memorial Hospital in Chicago.) Since Ray himself had no affiliation with a college, there was no alma mater to sentimentally tug at his purse strings. Paganucci was advised that this "awesome total" was just the start. And, since Mr. Kroc was now in his seventies, with myriad health concerns — and no apparent offspring — there was no time like the present to get closer.

The Tuck administrators envisioned a relatively modest gift of a million dollars that would bear Ray's name. As the irascible chairman of McDonald's returned to Dartmouth for two more classroom visits, it seemed certain that this famous businessman had begun to consider Dartmouth "his" school. They were so gleeful at having won his favor that, having learned of Ray's affinity for Early Times, they made a special note to stock the booze for whenever he was on campus. (Hedging their bets, they also recorded that Ray's protégé and now McDonald's chairman, Fred Turner — also without a college degree, and therefore ripe to be swayed to the school's favor — preferred Crown Royal.) Ray had been pleased that he hadn't had to ask for his favorite liquor. Details like this, Paganucci noted, could one day yield "big casino" for the school.

Keeping a potential donor's drink of choice on hand was one way to impress him, but a university's more traditional method of luring money from a wealthy prospect was by awarding him an honorary degree. Advised of his tremendous potential for giving, the awards committee overlooked Ray's absence of a formal education, and he was chosen to be awarded a doctorate of humane letters. On this special visit, he brought along a sizeable entourage of a dozen, including his usual McDonald's cabal of advisors, as well as Joan, Joan's daughter, Linda, and her husband, Ballard, now working for Ray at the Padres, Ray's brother, Bob, and his wife, and the chief of Operation Cork, Rev. John Keller, and his wife, Doris.

At a celebratory pre-graduation dinner the night before commencement, Rev. Keller found himself seated across from the dean of Dartmouth's medical school, Dr. James Strickler, who did his best to mask his disappointment at not scoring a place at the more interesting end of the table with another honoree, Earl Blaik, the retired Dartmouth College football coach. The doctor and the addiction specialist struck up a conversation about whether medical students at Dartmouth received any sort of special training in addiction issues. Just that week, Dr. Strickler was able to report, the head of the school's department of psychiatry, Dr. Peter Whybrow, had submitted a proposal to fund a faculty position that would teach and conduct research on that very topic. Just as the nation was waking up to the impact of addiction, so were college campuses.

Rev. Keller was excited to introduce the doctor to his boss after dinner during cocktail hour.

"Joan, I'd really like you to talk with Dr. Strickler here about what Dartmouth Medical School is doing about alcoholism," Rev. Keller said. He and Joan frequently discussed what the medical profession was *not* doing in that regard, and figuring out how to address that was on Operation Cork's short list of priorities.

"That's very interesting," Joan said, distracted. "You're a medical doctor?"

"Yes," responded Dr. Strickler proudly.

"My daughter had a car door slammed on her upper leg this afternoon and it's hurting her and I really think she ought to see a doctor," Joan said, calling over the beautiful, statuesque Linda, then hoisting up her skirt over her hips to illustrate the injury, in the process, exposing her panties. An embarrassed Dr. Strickler said he doubted the woman had broken anything. He suggested they all visit the campus emergency room after the cocktail hour was through.

The next day, Ray achieved a milestone he'd never imagined or even desired. In his seventy-fifth year on earth, he donned the traditional mortarboard and gown, and marched up onstage to receive a diploma from the president of the school. Just as his name was called, on cue, the bells in the

266

campus clock tower began chiming the catchy McDonald's theme song, "You Deserve a Break Today." The students roared with approval.

Weeks later, Drs. Strickler and Whybrow found themselves flying across the country to the J and R Double Arch Ranch as guests of Joan and Operation Cork. They hadn't intended to upstage the business school by muscling in on Kroc territory. It had just worked out that way. The fact that Joan was contemplating a collaboration with the same school that was courting Ray surprised his attorney, since Joan had become so insistent in carving out her own way.

A private residence for Ray and Joan had been erected on the property, a round building on top of a hill — not a garish facsimile of a hamburger, as neighbors had feared, but an elegant retreat from the rest of the bustle on the property for the namesake owners of the ranch. Clues to their respective personalities could be found in their private bathrooms: In hers hung a Cezanne; in his, a picture of a naked woman on a bed with a smoking gun in her hand, and a hairy arm falling over the foot-railing with the caption, "No credit."

Of all the eye-catching artifacts and

curiosities on the property, the two doctors were struck by the well-stocked self-serve bar with twelve spigots. Cocktails before dinner. Wine with dinner. Cocktails after dinner. Affable Ray in his bathrobe reclining in the living room, holding forth with a cigar in one hand and his cocktail glass in the other. The reason for Joan's intense interest in and concern about drinking, and its consequences, began to seem clear.

Joan and Rev. Keller talked with their visitors about their desire to help change the attitude of doctors and medical students toward alcohol. The standard one-hour training on alcoholism offered in all of medical school wasn't enough, they believed. Could the doctors write a proposal for a program to develop a curriculum to teach young doctors in medical school about the hazards of alcohol misuse? By the end of the summer, Operation Cork had received the document outlining how a team at Dartmouth would do just that.

Meanwhile, Ray's lawyer received a five-page memo from Paul Paganucci detailing possible gifts Ray might make to Dartmouth. Half a million dollars, for instance, would underwrite a lecture series; a million dollars would endow a Ray Kroc professorship; $20 million would attach Ray's name to the medical school. "The Ray A. Kroc Medical School" had a catchy ring.

Joan gave the go-ahead to the proposal for the Dartmouth doctors to start work on the updated medical curriculum. Shortly before Christmas 1977, Dartmouth received notice of a gift of twenty thousand shares of McDonald's stock, worth about a million dollars, to establish the Ray and Joan Kroc Medical School Fund. It wasn't what the school hoped to get, and it also wasn't the gift Ray had hoped to give.

Hamburgers were not on the menu at the book release party for Ray's memoir, *Grinding It Out.* Since the publisher was footing the bill, slightly fancier fare was offered, including egg rolls, meat in pastry puffs, and ham and turkey sandwiches. There was, of course, an open bar, and Ray eagerly made his way back to it after a guest fawned over him about the amazing things he'd "done with hamburgers." The features editor of the *Chicago Tribune* had been hired to spend a year in his company, refining and crafting what Ray had begun to commit to paper on that cruise back in 1966. Ray even declared in the pages of his memoir that books bored him. Yet now he had one to his credit. None other than Paul Paganucci of

Dartmouth contributed the foreword.

As the celebrated chairman made the rounds of the nation's most influential television programs on his book tour, he turned on the salesman's charm and deflected what little criticism was lobbed his way. On the late-night program *Tomorrow,* Ray presented host Tom Snyder with a Big Mac, and Snyder reached across to light his guest's Pall Mall with a pack of McDonald's matches, asking why the company had switched from real ice cream to milk shake mix. Ray smacked his lips; the answer was simple. "We can trust a machine better than the human factor for uniformity," he said. "When it's done by an individual there are all types of variances. Too much of this and that." All McDonald's sold was wholesome: "meat and potatoes and bread and milk. When that's no longer good nutrition, we'll be out of business."

On the *Donahue* show, the family-minded host grilled Ray about his personal life as if he were on the witness stand:

"You fell in love with your present wife before you married your second wife."

"Yeah . . . yup, yup," said Ray, grinning as the mostly female audience fell silent.

"But she was . . . not ready," Phil Donahue countered.

"That's right," said Ray, unashamed.

"So you got married to somebody else. You're married to somebody else and she calls and says, 'I'm ready.' "

"Well, not quite that way." Ray paused and explained. "Sometimes it takes ladies a long time to get ready."

The smooth rhythm of the classic symphonic swing song "April in Paris" filled the ballroom at the Continental Plaza in Chicago. There could be no better band to entertain at Ray's seventy-fifth birthday gala than the great Count Basie Orchestra. Seven hundred of Ray's closest friends and business associates had flown in from all over the world. Even Ray's childhood chum from his Oak Park Elementary School days Eunie Hagen was on hand.

The evening's emcee, veteran PR man Al Golin, promised the guests a show that "Vegas would envy." He'd lined up the dynamic vocal quartet the Mills Brothers, along with the Oscar-winning lyricist Sammy Cahn, who'd been hired for $12,500, plus expenses, to rewrite popular songs with inventive lyrics that lampooned Ray and his constellation of intimates.

"I'd stop at nothing to get an invitation to this party. I even agreed to do this," Golin quipped. Never mind that it was he who'd plotted the whole shebang. Salutary birthday greetings were read aloud, dispatched by the mayor of Chicago, the governor of Illinois, the president of the United States — silence after the words "Jimmy Carter" were uttered, given Ray's famous conservatism — and the prime minister of Canada, all lauding Ray's humanitarian work and his embodiment of free enterprise.

"I think we all have the same thing in common," Golin said to the crowd of birthday well-wishers. "We've all been lucky to have our lives, our paths, crossed with Ray's. Needless to say, I think we've all been a lot richer for it and I mean that in every sense of the word."

Indeed, most of those present had seen their fortunes soar, if not quite so grandly as Ray's, because of their affiliation with the company. The man Ray credited with as much, or even more, of the success of McDonald's had put aside their differences and was in their midst. When Ray asked Harry Sonneborn to rise and take a bow, a long, hearty round of applause ensued among the old-timers, who knew it to be true: If it hadn't been for Harry, none of them would likely be here tonight. Also representing the early roots of the company was June Martino. Dick McDonald, however, was not invited. (Mac had died in 1971.)

The pomp continued as Ray introduced the junior chairman of the board, his protégé, Fred Turner.

"I'm still the senior," said Ray, slurring a bit. "I don't like the terminology. It sounds like a rest home. Anyway, god bless you, Fred."

Fred emphasized that Ray hadn't changed since they'd first met twenty-one years earlier, even if his accoutrements were finer now. The crowd tittered. He certainly didn't mean Ray's choice of beverage; everyone who knew him knew about the Early Times. Perhaps Turner meant Ray's mode of transportation — or, maybe, his wife? On with the proceedings: Fred presented a birthday gift for the man who had everything — $200,000 comprised of donations from colleagues, friends, and other associates, to replicate a charity that McDonald's had adopted on a national scale. Ronald McDonald House was its name.

Ray shouted from the wings. "Fred, tell them what the Ronald House is. Tell them, they may not know."

"Now you know how he got to be senior, and I got to be junior," deadpanned Fred, who explained that the houses, of which

273

there were currently two, were places where parents could stay at low or no cost while their child was in the hospital. The idea had been hatched in Philadelphia, when a player for the Eagles, Fred Hill, was grappling with his three-year-old daughter's treatment for leukemia. A local advertising agency had approached McDonald's for financial support. Donating proceeds from the sale of shakes created especially for St. Patrick's Day developed into a deeper commitment.

Just as Ray had co-opted a sleepy hamburger stand in the desert and took it worldwide, his corporation had taken the wonderful idea of creating a safe haven for families with sick children and turned it into a showpiece charity, branded with its now famous mascot. A facility to help people at a time of dire need was a dream come true for the PR-minded McDonald's, as was the idea for the benevolent birthday gift. (This was a riff on Ray's magnanimous seventieth birthday gesture, which included a donation to establish an exhibit on ecology at Chicago's Field Museum of Natural History and his friends raising additional money to launch the Ray A. Kroc Environmental Fund.) In recent years, wage issues, price-fixing, and underrepresentation of minorities were a few of the new problems that had been added to the persistent criticisms about nutritional quality of the food sold by the company and its aggressive marketing to children. Branding this organization to help families in need was a perfect counterpoint. The fund would allow franchisees to kick-start the opening of Ronald McDonald Houses in their markets, multiplying not just the impact of the charity but its halo effect. Each time a new house was built, to reinforce the tie to McDonald's, a plaque would be placed in honor of Ray.

The program for the evening reminded Joan of one of those boring balls she used to attend when she was first married. This was all about public relations, not about her husband. Who had seven hundred intimate friends? Before the gala, she and Ray had had one of their explosive blowouts. Ray had informed Joan that as a birthday present to himself he was going to buy the naming rights to the Dartmouth Medical School with a $20 million donation. His advisors loved the idea of the gift. They felt attaching Ray's name to such a venerable institution would be an excellent monument to his greatness, and great PR, too. But Joan refused. Not only did she not believe in funding buildings, she had designs on the coffers of The Kroc Foundation. She wanted as much money as possible left in them to ultimately control. If Ray had gone ahead and pledged the gift without telling her, Dartmouth might have been $20 million richer and have a medical school named for a scion of fast food.

By the time it was her turn to speak, Joan was shaking a bit with nerves about addressing the crowd.

"My name is Joan, and I belong to Ray," she said, asking her husband to bring up her drink. "I've got a little toast for you, honey." Okay, shouted Ray. As he rose at her command, the partygoers did, too:

> To you, Ray, a rare unique and wonderful human being, who has known the heartbreak of failure and the enormous fulfillment of success.

He may be tough, continued Joan, and he may have caused some tears. But to those who love him, she said, he's given much greater cause for happiness. Joan said she counted herself among them.

Glasses hoisted and clinked, and applause filled the room. Now it was the vaunted senior chairman's moment to address his well-wishers. Assembled before him were an encyclopedic array of people who'd aided

276

and abetted him throughout his life. Ray fumbled for his glasses to read a poem written by Dr. Carl Dragstedt, chair of the Northwestern University pharmacology department. Ray said it summed up how he was feeling on this momentous occasion.

Life's prize is not a big medal,
That is yours when you get to the top;
When you've outscrambled all of the
    scramblers,
And now are boss of the shop.

Ray recited with emphasis on the couplets.

Life's prize is not a big trophy,
That you can win in a game;
It's something entirely different
From wealth or power or fame.
It's the look of respect and affection,
That one can see in the eyes
Of the folks who know all about you,
That really is Life's great prize.

It was true that most of the people at the party knew all about Ray. Some had incurred his wrath. Others had been fired, and rehired. Others still had stood watch when he was out on the town or scuffling with Joan. All who were present tonight had stuck with him, regardless.

No one could know this was the last time they'd all come together.

While a team at Dartmouth crafted a medical education that addressed addiction, Joan commissioned two more films from Gerald Rogers: *Our Brothers' Keeper,* a dark drama about a successful doctor who loses both his family and his practice as he fails to admit his alcohol dependence, and *Alcohol and the Physician,* a frank, chilling documentary designed to teach the medical community about diagnosis and treatment.

Though Ray groused publicly about how sick and tired he was of subsidizing a losing team, he cheerfully squired reporter Norm Clarke of the Associated Press around the ballpark in his golf cart, giving special attention to the vines being trellised at the rear of the stadium to mimic his beloved Wrigley Field. Afterward, Clarke called with a follow-up question. Ray mentioned several ballplayers about to become free agents whom he hoped to lure to the team.

A few minutes after they'd hung up, Clarke's phone rang. A worried Padres staffer explained that Ray had said some things on the phone that he shouldn't have. The baseball commissioner wouldn't be happy to learn his intent to go after certain

278

players. Saying so, and publicly, constituted tampering — patently against the rules. Clarke responded that his editors wouldn't be happy to hear he let himself get talked out of a story.

Clarke wrote up Ray's remarks, and after a public outcry, the baseball commissioner slapped Ray with a $100,000 fine. Outraged, Ray dashed off a check and declared "baseball can go to hell." Then he handed over complete control of the team to his stepson-in-law, Ballard. He was tired of the frustration. The fun of the game was gone. There was, he said, more of a future in hamburgers.

But the future for Ray, now seventy-seven, was becoming bleak. Two days before Christmas, 1979, he suffered a stroke. Continuing to drink now would be a certain death sentence. Joan made it clear: If he didn't consent to treatment, she would leave him, once and for all.

He was transported north to Orange County, where he was admitted to Care Manor Hospital, a rehabilitation facility. There, he was treated by the same doctor who'd successfully helped Betty Ford battle her addiction. It was team president Ballard, rather than McDonald's corporate officials, who released a carefully crafted statement to the media announcing the senior chairman of the board's hospitalization. The patient was, the statement read, resting comfortably. As if to illustrate that one of America's most famous businessmen was still in command of his faculties, despite this turn of events, he was even quoted: "I am required to take medication which is incompatible with the use of alcohol." Entering addiction care, he added, was a move advised by his doctors and simply part of his continuing treatment.

The veil had been lifted, even if just a bit, on the secret Joan and others had long known.

9
1984: Two Widows

The blood had barely been mopped from the floor of the McDonald's in San Ysidro, California, when the light blue Rolls-Royce barreled into town. From high on a hill above the lush oceanfront village of La Jolla, the car wended its way south twenty miles down Interstate 5 to this poor dusty border community. In a matter of a little over an hour, this community had earned the miserable distinction as the site of the worst massacre in US history to date by a single gunman.

Palm trees lilted softly in the breeze, their leaves glowing in the magic crystal light of the California sunshine. The chauffeur-driven car exited the freeway. Under ordinary circumstances, San Ysidro was sleepy. But in the aftermath of the shooting spree at the McDonald's, all activity in the community had ground to a complete halt. The smell of death hung heavy in the air.

Passing the murder scene, the Rolls made its way to the home where Mrs. Etna Huberty and her daughters were taking refuge. It wasn't safe for them to stay in their own $475-a-month apartment on Averil Road. Everyone knew their address. The place was just several hundred yards from the restaurant on San Ysidro Boulevard — so close that, as the sounds of the gunfire rang out, Etna's younger daughter, Cassandra, playing with friends next door, had cowered. Told it was her father wielding the gun — brutally, gleefully, shooting dozens of people, including an eight-month-old child — the girl had cried in disbelief, "My father could never kill a baby."

When Etna had made the startling connection, she'd called police, remembering her husband's last words. Before he'd left home in his camouflage pants and dark t-shirt that afternoon, he'd kissed her goodbye and declared: "Society has had their chance. I'm going hunting humans." She'd dismissed his bluster as empty chatter.

If only I had stopped him, Etna thought. If only I hadn't pried his fingers from the pistol when he'd tried to kill himself last year. After, he had burst into tears, and admonished her, "You should have let me kill myself." If he'd died then, this disaster would never have happened. In these last forty-eight hours, she'd replayed the scene a million times. He was right. If only . . .

In nineteen years of marriage, it had been impossible for Etna to predict James Huberty's seesaw volatility. Would he erupt into a violent rage? Would he wither into a pool of self-pitying sadness? At times he was the angriest man in the world. Other times, the weakest. It was just like Jim, Etna thought, to leave her holding the bag. He'd been doing that since they'd met at college in the Midwest twenty years ago. Her mother had never been keen on him, this pale-faced, skinny man who trained as an embalmer but had never possessed the social skills to interact with grieving families. His awkward combativeness had been the reason he'd lost his most recent job, as a security guard, just a few weeks before. On more than one occasion, he'd even threatened his own children with one of his treasured weapons. He'd also tortured his elder daughter, Zelia, by forcing her to ride on a motorcycle with a perilously waxed seat.

Etna was always battling Jim, and never following through on her promises to leave him. Yet he had finally made good on his promise to find help. He'd called a mental health facility the day before his rampage, but the call had gone unreturned. Could Etna have imagined this finale? Twenty-one people dead. That baby. A seventy-four-year-old man. Schoolmates of her daughters. Nineteen others hit by his bullets had survived, their lives scarred forever. So many people, engulfed by her husband's madness and pain.

Etna had run down to the McDonald's to try to convince him to stop, but her coaxing, and the police's, had proved fruitless. Inside, James Huberty casually helped himself to a soda, took a sip, and defiantly kept shooting, his sound track provided on a portable cassette deck he'd brought along, on which he played the Cars' album *Heartbeat City*. He tossed French fries onto one of his victims. When his twelve-gauge Winchester pump-action shotgun jammed, he switched to the automatic pistol and semi-automatic Uzi, and fired off 140 rounds in a little over an hour. An eternity elapsed — one hour and seventeen minutes — before the SWAT sharpshooter, perched atop the roof of the post office next door, was given the go-ahead to fire the shot to the heart that felled Huberty and finally silenced the mayhem.

Swarms of media appeared, diverted from the Democratic National Convention up in

San Francisco and the pre-Olympic setup under way in Los Angeles. Macabre camera-wielding tourists immediately arrived to rubberneck. Mostly what they saw, besides the shattered glass windows of a McDonald's, were the bewildered faces of grieving locals, sitting vigil outside the crime scene tape. They wielded a petition, demanding the restaurant turned death chamber be torn down and a shrine erected in its place. No one dared touch the homemade signs hoisted to the surrounding redbrick fence that spelled out in words, in two languages, what was plainly evident on the faces of all who lived here: WE ARE SAD and UNIDOS EN ESTA TRAGEDÍA.

Etna ached for the people of San Ysidro to understand how much she'd suffered, the anguish that consumed her now. To convey her feelings, she'd even written an open letter to the local TV station:

I am truly sorry for the problems my husband caused. I don't believe he came into the community with this type of intention. In a normal state of mind, he loved children. In particular, little girls. He would never harm a child.

How could anyone believe that? The

bereaved people of San Ysidro taunted Etna and her girls, pointing fingers — as if it were she who had pulled the trigger. The head of the local mental health services could talk all he wanted about how she and her kids would need counseling more than anyone, since they were the ones who'd have to shoulder the magnitude of Huberty's actions. But few people could muster any sympathy.

That Thursday afternoon, the day after the murders, no one seemed to notice the Rolls-Royce that arrived to deposit Joan, accompanied by her daughter and a friend, to pay a condolence call to the husky, wild-eyed woman with short, mousy brown hair. Joan felt compelled to comfort this stranger. She considered Etna an innocent victim.

After all, this unspeakable horror occurred not only in Joan's backyard, but on the grounds of the business that made her family's entire existence possible. The unfortunate connection Joan had to the incident was only a small reason she found her heart swelling with compassion. She knew a thing or two herself about volatility and redemption and forgiveness, about the bargains one made with oneself to stay in a marriage.

She also knew about loss. For Joan, too,

was now a widow.

Ray had returned to the hospital in early December 1983. His decline after that first stroke had been steady, with a series of other strokes following, leaving the once feisty salesman feeble and mostly dependent on a motorized cart to get around. Those last years, he defied the odds, holding on, as he had his entire life. Joan presided over his care, miring herself in what business dealings he had left, protecting him, protecting the fortune she knew she would inherit. She'd already staked her claim to The Kroc Foundation, finally wresting it away from her brother-in-law and Ray's advisors in Chicago. Its assets of more than $30 million had been transferred over and tucked into her newly formed Joan B. Kroc Foundation, ready for her to give. Still, she coyly refused to answer a reporter who asked her not long before Ray died who would take charge of his controlling interest in McDonald's. ("It's a matter of family planning," she'd said.)

He'd been so sick and close to dying for so long, Joan, in preparation, had purchased a family plot in 1980, and the McDonald's media relations team had drafted plans for a memorial ad and service. And yet, Ray made it to celebrate his eightieth birthday at the stadium in 1982. He and Joan were squired around the field in the back of a convertible so they could wave to the enthusiastic crowd of 43,000. To one acquaintance, Joan described the last few years of her life with Ray as their marriage's happiest.

In late 1983, it seemed the end was imminent. Fred Turner had flown into San Diego for a final visit with the man who had plucked him from behind the griddle and defined his career. Ray was so distressed by his inability to work that he'd asked Fred to take him off the McDonald's payroll. As senior chairman, he received $175,000 a year. Though he had long ago ceded control of the company to his chosen successor, he had proudly kept a hand in the business. He'd make his way into the office in San Diego, even if for just an hour a day, sometimes conspiring on the phone with his old friend from the club at the Whitehall Hotel, Chef René Arend, who had capitulated to Ray's repeated entreaties to join McDonald's and traded in gourmet cooking for more populist fare like Chicken McNuggets and the McRib. Though Ray's condition now made anything more than superficial involvement impossible, Turner still refused the request. To him, Ray was the reason the company they loved had grown to 7,500 stores in thirty-two countries around the world. What Turner didn't tell his mentor was that he'd commissioned a portrait of that other integral player, the first president of McDonald's, Harry Sonneborn, for the management gallery at headquarters. He wanted to preserve Harry's part in their history as well.

From the hospital, Ray kept a pinkie in baseball, too. When manager Jack McKeon told him he thought relief pitcher "Goose" Gossage would help the team win a pennant, Ray signed off on an $11 million deal to hire him. Baseball salaries had continued to zoom into the stratosphere over the last ten years, a consequence of free agency, the newly founded players' association, and the advent of cable television. Ray lit up when the star player arrived in his room to shake his hand, so hopeful he was that his addition to the lineup would get the Padres out of the cellar, once and for all. So happy, as he'd always been, to be one of the guys.

Two days later, on January 14, 1984, Ray's heart gave in to his afflictions. He was dead at age eighty-one.

Flags were ordered flown at half-staff at McDonald's stores around the world for a week, as devoted franchisees who'd never even met Ray lamented his passing. Twenty-five hundred people arrived at Christ Church in Oak Brook on January 20, 1984, for the service the company had been carefully planning for years.

The widow arrived on this freezing cold day in a stretch limo, clad in sunglasses and fur to insulate against the day's fierce elements, and took her place with her family in the front of the church. The music was fitting for the occasion, but it was exactly the sort that Ray had hated, himself, to play: Prelude: Fugue in E-flat Major by Bach and "A Mighty Fortress" by Pachelbel. The printed program for the service featured, in ornate lettering, the Calvin Coolidge quote so often attributed to Ray: "Press On." Employees watched via closed-circuit television as son-in-law Ballard spoke about his love-hate relationship with the man who put him to work on the San Diego Padres. For his part, Fred eulogized his friend more fondly. By this point, many of them only knew the legend of Ray, the stories of the scrappy, precarious start-up days that were as unimaginable now as the idea that Ray Kroc was anything less than their multimillionaire founder with a finicky penchant for cleanliness.

Ray was the best boss, his best friend — a second father, said Turner.

He gave us an example — to be generous, to be thoughtful to others, to be fairminded, to have balance, to do nothing to excess. We loved his sense of humor. And we accepted his shortcomings.

Those shortcomings, McDonald's hoped, would be laid to rest with the remains of the founding chairman, as would some of his long legacy, like Ray's practice of making casual, handshake deals. (On the very day he died, a verdict was delivered in a long-standing suit against the company. A jury had concluded McDonald's had broken an agreement Ray had made back in the seventies with an ice cream supplier. Turner had told the supplier to forget Ray's "shadow" and abandon the deal.) Only now that Ray was gone would Fred Turner hang the portrait of Harry. The new generation should know about the contributions of both men.

A private funeral was held in southern California, where Ray's body was interred in a modest crypt in the hillside Mausoleum of the Bells, at El Camino Memorial Park in San Diego. Modest — for a man worth half a billion dollars.

And with that, his blond beauty was free.

On a typical day, Joan eagerly bathed in the vast flow of news and information available in the modern world. At home and office, her TV set was perennially tuned to the three-year-old phenomenon known as CNN. Twenty-four-hour cable news, the heartbeat of the world, delivered straight to your living room. She treated the news like an entertainment event; she'd invite friends over to watch with her, devouring Big Macs while sipping Diet Coke or, on occasion, crystal flutes of pink Dom Pérignon, as if they were watching a movie. Reality was far more compelling than anything made up. Long a voracious reader of nonfiction, when Joan liked a book, she'd buy dozens of copies and give them away to friends. Her own life story was proof that truth was stranger and far more interesting than manufactured drama. In the car, she'd station-surf, tuning in to everything from Rush Limbaugh to NPR, not for any ideological kinship but to keep up with the pulse of the news and the variety of voices commenting on world events. To understand, she believed, you had to be informed. To a friend, she floated the idea of buying a radio station, where both liberal and conservative viewpoints would be equally represented. The news kept her honest, transporting her to the larger universe beyond her own, allowing her to stay in touch with world events and informing her about the harsh realities so many other people faced.

Her reality was surreal. The rest of the world didn't fly on a private jet, or own dazzling jewels. The rest of the world didn't employ butlers, fend off art brokers clamoring to sell them great masterpieces to hang on the walls of their luxurious homes, or possess 6,700,000 shares and controlling interest in one of the world's most influential corporations. And even among the world's other multimillionaires, few owned major league sports franchises.

Now, at age fifty-five, Joan Kroc had all of this to herself. To do with as she pleased. Pure, unfathomable abundance.

She'd had a glorious taste of what she was capable of achieving with Operation Cork, and she'd already begun to dabble in other work, this time tinged with glamour. At a restaurant in Beverly Hills, she introduced herself to the actor Jack Lemmon and invited him to throw out the first ball of the Padres' 1983 season. In the owner's box, he'd expressed frustration in getting a pet project off the ground, a film based on a 1980 Broadway play by Bill C. Davis called *Mass Appeal,* about an opinionated, old-school Catholic priest with a drinking problem and a young initiate with decidedly opposing values. Like a fairy godmother, she'd underwritten its production with a $7 million check. Nothing quite like that had happened to Lemmon in the thirty years he'd been in Hollywood. In her capacity as producer, she left three marks: She refused to pay a million-dollar salary required to cast a hot new actor named John Travolta (an actor named Zeljko Ivanek got the part instead). Her daughter appeared in a non-speaking role. And she insisted that the film bear a dedication to Ray, who didn't live to see the final product.

She plunged into her new role as a philanthropist, dipping into the coffers of her newly formed foundation at the start of 1984, days before Ray died, and writing checks to support the Olympic torch relay and to an organization that combated child abuse. Come spring, she placed a call to the dashing intellectual Norman Cousins, the former editor of the influential magazine *Saturday Review.*

Though he wasn't a doctor or medical professional, Cousins had been invited to join the medical school at the University of California, Los Angeles, because of his controversial work in the new field of "psychoneuroimmunology," the biochemistry of attitudes and emotions. Diagnosed with a mysterious illness deemed terminal by his doctors, he'd begun reading about the impact on the physical body of negative emotions like fear and suppressed rage. That led him to ponder the effect of positive emotions on health. He'd given up medicine and painkillers, and claimed that ten minutes of hearty laughter, induced by watching Marx Brothers movies and the television show *Candid Camera,* would give him hours of pain-free sleep. Some heralded him as a genius and called him the father of holistic medicine; others derided the ideas presented in his bestselling book about this discovery, *Anatomy of an Illness: As Perceived by the Patient,* as kooky and New Age.

For Joan, who'd spent the last ten years trying to understand the biochemistry of addiction, there was special resonance in this mind-body connection. She firmly believed in the idea that positive thinking could change one's physical state. Intrigued and concerned about the aging process, she'd convened, around her fiftieth birthday, a conference at the ranch on the subject —

after which she had a face-lift — and had hinted to one of her contacts at Dartmouth that care of the elderly would be the next frontier she addressed. She called the UCLA School of Medicine and told the dean she wanted to meet with Cousins.

Who could refuse her invitation? Cousins trekked the few hours south to meet Joan at one of her favorite lunch spots in La Jolla, La Valencia. She explained that the mission of her new foundation was to address "the human condition," and asked if she could support his work with a $2 million donation. Blown away by her generosity, he invited her to sit in on the discussions of how her gift would be put to use. She flew up on her helicopter, which she called the Luvduv, for the meetings, landing on the UCLA hospital's helipad, and listened intently to the committee members who debated how best to spend the money. The idea was to research these questions: How did hope, the will to live, faith, laughter, festivity, purpose, determination register in the brain? What effect did they have on the body? Was it possible that the brain might play an active part in the healing process? Might the brain be consciously directed for that purpose?

The summer of 1984 had already been

filled with tension and hope, with the historic nomination of the first female vice presidential candidate, Geraldine Ferraro, at the Democratic National Convention and New York governor Mario Cuomo's derision of President Reagan for what he deemed his obliviousness to the poor. Joan had been pondering other questions, too. Could Ronald Reagan be unseated? Could the arms race be scuttled? Was nuclear proliferation inevitable? With her conservative husband gone, Joan could now express her unbridled enthusiasm for a Democrat and fellow Minnesotan, Walter Mondale, whose political views Ray would most definitely not have supported. She'd kept her politics in check all these years, believing it was wrong to express her opinion, since it was so different from Ray's. Mondale was about to earn his party's nomination — and the fact he'd tapped a woman, Geraldine Ferraro, as his running mate, endeared the candidate to Joan even more. How far women had come in Joan's lifetime! Ray thought Joan so bleeding-heart he called her a "patsy." If that was "patsy" behavior, she reckoned, so be it. Her years of keeping silent were through. It was time to get to work.

Television reports allowed Joan to witness

the carnage in San Ysidro. A parade of grisly images filled her screen: A wounded mother clutching her baby, her face twisted in distress. Uniformed workers fleeing McDonald's in terror. Medics on the ground, tending to the injured. Perhaps the most arresting picture was of a little boy lying motionless on top of his bicycle, the golden arches prominent in the background. From his hospital bed, towheaded ten-year-old Joshua Coleman later recounted the story to TV viewers around the world. He'd ridden to McDonald's to meet some friends for ice cream.

"I didn't hear no gunshots until I got there," he said, his voice unwavering. "He shot me first, then my two friends." The two friends died instantly. Only because this little boy had had the presence of mind to play dead had he lived.

It was this grave scene that sparked an idea.

Till now, Joan had been an under-the-radar presence in San Diego. Now, she was standing before an assembled press corps with the city's chief of police by her side, shocking the community by announcing the formation of a victims' fund with a personal donation of $100,000. "I think that anyone who has the means that I have would do the same thing," she explained, asking her fellow San Diegans to do everything in their power to help those impacted by this awful tragedy. Individuals and corporations — McDonald's and the competition, like Burger King and Wendy's — should pitch in. Money was no compensation for the loss of life, she acknowledged, but at least now families of victims who couldn't afford burials or counseling would have access to funds to help.

Included among the victims who'd benefit from this fund, Joan made clear, would be Etna Huberty and her two children. They were suffering, too, and would continue to suffer, psychologically and economically. They'd need all the help they could get in rebuilding their shattered lives. She was sure, she said, that if Ray were alive, he'd have done the same. Most people who'd known him didn't quite think so. His reaction to a crazed gunman shooting up patrons at one of his stores would hardly have been so charitable.

Broadsided by her actions, McDonald's corporate stepped up and added a million dollars to the fund the next day. Turner and other top executives in Oak Brook had been on tenterhooks since Ray's death in January, waiting to see what their largest individual shareholder would do next. What if Joan wanted to exercise some power in the company, the same way she'd asserted herself with Ray's foundation? She made it plain that she did not by asking her son-in-law to take a seat she could have claimed on McDonald's board. She wanted to make a difference, but serving on a corporate board, on any board, wasn't what she had in mind.

The victims' fund continued to grow. More modest donations poured in by various means. A man who described himself as a bum showed up at a bank in San Ysidro, handing over a $300 cash donation. Another man came to the teller window and emptied out a bag containing $65.42 in small change. Envelopes arrived from around the country. A chain of drugstores announced it would auction off the hottest toy of the moment, Cabbage Patch Kids, to raise money. Sports star Jimmy Connors, a paid spokesman for McDonald's, volunteered to stage a tennis exhibition fund-raiser. The nation united in grief.

As did these two widows from parallel worlds. Joan dispatched the Rolls back down to San Ysidro, this time to ferry Etna and her daughters to the Cypress View/

Bonham Brothers Mortuary on Imperial Boulevard, where the body of the gunman was set out for its final viewing before cremation. They were the only visitors. This time, reporters caught sight of the lavish car and researched the license plate to sleuth out its owner. News stories carried the fact of the gunman's wife being ferried by the wife of the deceased founder of McDonald's. What would Joan do next?

Services for Huberty's victims began the next day. Thousands of people crammed the grounds of the hexagonal church on a hillside, Our Lady of Mount Carmel, the grandest building in all of San Ysidro, where the stations of the cross were depicted in modest stained glass, captioned in Spanish. Twenty-two pots of carnations ringed the altar, representing each of the dead — one, even, for the killer. So intense was the grieving that the locals didn't notice the arrival of Etna, clad in purple. She made her way to a pew reserved for dignitaries, escorted by police into and out of the overflow crowd, virtually unrecognized. Joan sat a few rows behind her, wiping back tears and waving off a reporter. Behind her, a team of McDonald's executives had slipped into town unannounced, not wanting to call attention to their presence.

301

The bishop of the San Diego diocese, Leo Maher, commanded the crowd to allow the suffering to unite them in a "great love of one another." The parish priest, Monsignor Frank Aldasor, advised that when death comes, families must continue living. "You must fill the vacuum caused by the death of a loved one," he said. "You must use all of your energy."

Joan hardly needed a reminder.

Five days later, she headed back down to San Ysidro, carrying a message from executives in Oak Brook she knew would be welcome: The company had decided not to reopen the restaurant on the site after all. The locals rejoiced. In the middle of the night, while sleepless San Ysidro residents wrestled with their nightmares, a crew arrived to raze the golden arches and the cheerful Ronald McDonald–themed playground attached to it, with the only slide in town. They spirited off the twisted detritus before it could be immortalized by television crews. The mourners cheered; the physical remnant of the worst day of their lives had been extinguished. The "We are sad" signs vanished, too, replaced by new ones that proclaimed, "Thank you, McDonald's."

Almost immediately, though, the mourners were beset with another concern. Etna Huberty and her girls were en route to Ohio to bury her husband's ashes. Word leaked that she'd received a thousand-dollar payout from the victims' fund to pay for her trip, and that she had been signed by a Hollywood agent to help her sell the rights to her husband's story. Angry talk of a protest march circulated.

Joan called another press conference, this time with her new friend Norman Cousins by her side. He revealed that he'd accompanied her on the condolence call Joan had paid the gunman's widow. The money that subsidized Etna Huberty's travel was taken from a contribution of $2,500 he'd personally made.

"I think it's monstrously unfair that more attention has been given to this $1,000 than the $1 million given by McDonald's for all the survivors and the $100,000 given personally by Mrs. Kroc," he said. It might look like Etna Huberty was receiving preferential treatment, but, he continued, that wasn't the case: "I have no apologies to offer, nor do I think there are any required."

As to the prospect of a television movie about the murders, Cousins announced that he thought such a film would be a constructive way to help the public understand mental instability. He didn't explain that it was he who'd made the Hollywood connections, nor that Joan was staunchly opposed to the idea.

Joan had other concerns. She addressed the cameras angrily, scolding the media for stirring up the already distressed community. "Now some of the victims are feeling more pain. And it's partly your fault, guys, for not getting your facts right." There was nothing more to say. She had done what she felt was responsible, and now she had to get back to her job.

Joan had two jobs now. The first involved giving away money. Several Cork-related gifts were pending, including a grand $7 million sports pavilion at the rehabilitation center in her home state, Hazelden, so that patients undergoing treatment would have a place to work out. Joan had been enrolling key employees for treatment there, whether or not they had addiction issues, so they could better understand the program. Half a million dollars was earmarked to build a pavilion at Betty Ford's new rehabilitation center in Rancho Mirage. A million-dollar grant to start an addiction education program at the Morehouse Medical School in Atlanta. Another million to Dartmouth to continue the work there. All of these projects would bear the Cork name, keeping her program alive — and quietly, indirectly, memorializing her struggles with Ray.

There was also Ray's baseball team to oversee. She'd fused her interest in alcohol education with the sport by hiring the fallen pitcher Bo Belinsky, whose starry career had been destroyed by his addiction. One moment, he'd been celebrated for pitching a no-hitter; the next, he was drinking himself into a stupor under a bridge. Joan offered him up as an Exhibit A to other teams in Major League Baseball, with the hopes of encouraging players to feel safe about stepping forward and seeking help. League brass bristled at her offer: There were no problems with drinking in the game, they maintained. Team owners who weren't cynical about her work were invited to a conference at the ranch with the baseball commissioner. Joan underwrote one more film from Gerald Rogers, called *Dugout,* starring Belinsky as himself, paternalistically sauntering into a Little League clubhouse to counsel young players as they precociously, petulantly down beers and smoke pot after a loss. Little League officials were so upset with the suggestion that some of their own might actually imbibe that they made her erase the logo from the kids' uniforms. Belinsky, after more dramatic recoveries and relapses, wound up selling cars in Las Vegas and becoming a devout Christian.

Her reputation as a crusading do-gooder didn't help endear her to the Padres. Neither did her quips about not knowing "first base from fourth" or her unashamed retelling of how she'd met a nice man named Willie Stargell at a benefit and invited him to be her guest in the owner's box — not realizing that he was a star of the Pittsburgh Pirates, in town to play against the Padres.

She'd long had a bad rap in the clubhouse. Legendary baseball executive Buzzie Bavasi fled his role as Padres president after imperious Joan offered input into the team's affairs. (Ray apologized, but what could he do? It was his wife, after all.) Then, when the frustrated agent for shortstop Ozzie Smith placed a classified ad appealing for a part-time job to supplement his paltry player's income, Joan had said her gardener had offered to help out by hiring him in the off-season, and would even pay a premium wage of $4.50 an hour, a dollar over the usual, because he had a college education. She didn't seem to understand what was wrong with the gesture. As far as the Padres were concerned, women didn't belong in baseball — particularly a woman like Joan Kroc.

Most of the team remained lukewarm, too, about Joan's son-in-law, Ballard. It was one thing when Ray was alive, but now they wondered if Ballard Smith was just a mouthpiece for Joan. Ray might have been a loose cannon who berated them in public, but there had never been any question about his love of and commitment to the sport.

His legacy loomed large. The city council in Yuma voted to rename Desert Sun Stadium, where the Padres held spring training, the Ray Kroc Baseball Facility. (Soon, Einstein Middle School in San Diego would vote to drop the name of the famous scientist for Kroc, too.) The players had dedicated the season to him, and had emblazoned their uniforms with special patches bearing his initials, RAK, a tiny but powerful memorial. The investment Ray had made in the team, and perhaps all his frustration, was finally yielding a dividend. Miraculously, as if he were pulling the strings from the great beyond, the Padres were, for once, winning.

This did not, however, mean the season had been entirely smooth. An ugly series of three testosterone-infused brawls erupted during a game with the Atlanta Braves, humiliating both teams. Then three members of the Padres blanketed the locker room with pamphlets from the far-right-wing John Birch Society, hoping to recruit. Despite these tensions, the team kept winning, and, by fall, they achieved a milestone that had always seemed unattainable. They made it all the way to the National League playoffs.

The game hadn't even begun at Jack Murphy Stadium, but the sellout crowd of 58,000 was already wild with excitement. If the Padres won tonight, the perennially mediocre franchise would salvage their chance at becoming National League champs for the very first time. They'd already lost the first two games in the series. A defeat at this stage, this year in particular, would be especially cruel. Even the opponent was perfectly cast — Ray's childhood favorite, the Cubs, the team he'd really wanted to buy. The fans were wholly invested in the fairy tale.

Joan glided onto the field confidently. Like every other resident of San Diego, she was consumed with Padres fever. Now, here she was at the helm, a member of a tiny sorority of lady ball club owners, one step closer to grasping the crown jewel of baseball. She was the living legacy of the man who'd rescued their team, the team whose lousy ballplaying they'd tolerated for years. Just the sight of her revved up the crowd. Unlike the players, they had no reservations about Joan's ownership, especially this close to a championship.

To prepare to throw out the ceremonial first pitch, Joan removed the coat she'd been wearing as insulation against the cool breeze of an early autumn evening — dramatically revealing her slender frame clad in a form-fitting Padres uniform, replete with cap and stirrups. A batboy's uniform had been enlisted, her name stitched on the back, J KROC. The crowd roared with approval at the vision of one of the richest women dressed in pinstripes. Joan amped up the drama like the performer she was. Smiling and slowly twirling to address the thundering crowd, she pointed to Ray's initials stitched on her left arm — the only visible trace of Ray evident — wordlessly acknowledging the man who had made this evening possible.

Then she made her way to just in front of the pitcher's mound, facing the burly catcher, Terry Kennedy. She blew him a kiss, and he returned in kind. Vamping her best imitation of a major leaguer, Joan wound back her arm and hurled the ball. As it weakly veered off-line, toward third base, Kennedy gently swooped in to retrieve it. Soon, Joan returned to the owner's box. She feasted on her usual, prime rib and diet soda, her family surrounding, watching the team salvage their shot at making it to the World Series with a 7–1 win.

The Padres tied the series up the next night. But soon they were handily losing the deciding game. Chicago scored three runs in the first two innings. Suddenly, in the sixth inning, the Padres rallied and scored, twice, with four more runs in the seventh. And at 4:08 p.m. on October 7, 1984, the team claimed victory, once and for all.

Jubilant crowds swarmed onto the field, drowning out the victorious organ music played by Danny Topaz. The question in his signature tune, "What Are We Waiting For?" had been answered. This was their moment. Grown men bear-hugged each other with abandon, and champagne bottles exploded like rockets in the clubhouse, showering the revelers in a river of bubbly. Even Joan, primly dressed in a lavender silk blouse, got doused. ABC sports reporter Tim McCarver asked her if this was one of the happiest moments in her life, and she shouted, as if she'd loved baseball from the moment she emerged from the womb, "This is *the* happiest moment of my life, and I dedicate this happy moment to Ray, may he rest in peace and be forever and ever happy." Then she called for Ballard to help hoist up the enormous trophy for the cameras. Goose Gossage swore later it was the loudest crowd he'd ever heard.

The players were so thrilled with their victory that they invited Joan to their private celebration the next night. She was surprised and happy to get the call; the guys knew well about her sobriety crusade, and indulgence was sure to occur at this party. As she entered Gossage's backyard, she called for the champagne, and when catcher Kennedy caught a glimpse of the meticulously dressed blonde, he shouted, "She's one of us. She's history." The $500 million widow, briefly redeemed by the team in the moment of victory, got yanked into the pool. Or did she jump? At least for the moment, she was one of the boys.

The team for the Padres to beat was the Detroit Tigers, a team owned by the scion of Domino's. The media gleefully dubbed the competition the "Fast Food Series." The Padres, in the end, couldn't pull off going "all the way for RAK." Ultimately, pizza triumphed over hamburgers, with Detroit winning the series four games to one.

But despite the defeat, Joan herself emerged a winner. She was the toast of San Diego, for the way she handled the massacre, and for presiding over a victorious team. In a full-page newspaper ad, she proclaimed her pride in the city and thanked her fellow citizens. In one of its only unanimous votes, the San Diego Press Club voted her Headliner of the Year. One reporter anointed her with an even better nickname: St. Joan of the Arches.

Before 1984's end, she'd made several visits to talk with the people of San Ysidro, to soothe them and hear what they hoped might be done with the now vacant lot where the McDonald's once sat. She surprised a crowd of five thousand Mondale supporters when she showed up at a rally and spoke so eloquently in support of his presidential campaign that the candidate said he couldn't have said it better himself. She served as grand marshal of the La Jolla Christmas Parade and addressed Christmas cards adorned with a picture of her on the pitcher's mound and a headline, "DREAMS! CAN COME TRUE." And she hosted the first party she'd thrown since Ray had taken ill five years earlier, entertaining guests by playing Christmas carols on the organ.

She bought herself some presents, too, trading Ray's old plane for a new, spiffy $16 million Gulfstream III, and asking a local priest, Father Joe Carroll, to christen it. (He'd never blessed a plane before.) Her name for her new toy was an indication of how she planned to live her days: *Impromptu.*

The gift she bought for herself at an auction more aptly summarized her state of mind. The room thundered with applause when she placed the winning bid of $32,000 for an engraved reproduction of the Declaration of Independence.

10
"DEAR WORLD, I REALLY LOVE YOU"

An hour into the invitation-only National Women's Conference to Prevent Nuclear War, a siren wailed, startling the two hundred A-list attendees, many of whom believed deep in their bones that a nuclear holocaust was imminent. So committed to the cause was the Oscar-winning actress Joanne Woodward that she had spent the last nine months planning the gathering. And despite her dislike of speaking publicly or talking to the press, she'd decided to serve as chairwoman of the proceedings. Though her husband, the actor Paul Newman, was himself so involved in the push for disarmament he'd been invited to serve as a citizen delegate to the United Nations, neither he nor any man was allowed to attend. "We're not anti-men," Woodward explained. "We're pro-survival. We just thought it best for women to hear what women had to say because we certainly aren't being heard in those behind-the-door meetings."

And so a who's who of women arrived to talk, and to listen: Rosalynn Carter; Coretta Scott King; Bella Abzug; Billie Jean King; Sally Field; Eleanor Smeal, who as president of the National Organization for Women had led the unsuccessful drive to ratify the Equal Rights Amendment for women; and Condoleezza Rice, the young assistant director of the Center for International Security and Arms Control at Stanford University. The backdrop for this austere occasion was the grand, two-story Cannon Caucus Room in the United States Capitol, with its three-tiered crystal chandeliers, ornate rosette-accented ceiling, and storied history. Hundreds of members of the Women's Army Corps had pledged their vows here to serve their nation during World War II. In 1948, the room provided the location for one of the key hearings of the House Un-American Activities Committee, where communist turned informant Whittaker Chambers faced off with Alger Hiss and accused him of treason. Now, with looming Cold War tensions and President Ronald Reagan's recently announced Strategic Defense Initiative to amp up the United States arsenal, Cannon offered a place where women concerned about the accelerating arms race could convene to discuss how they might change the world. On this day, hopes were pinned on the sentiment expressed in the title of the conference, "It's Up to the Women," which borrowed its name from proto-feminist first lady Eleanor Roosevelt's first book.

The siren turned out to be routine, a weekly test of Washington's civil defense system. In short order, the discussion on the urgent matter at hand resumed. The presidential election was less than six weeks away. The goals presented to the group included both the immediate — to defeat President Reagan and elect the Mondale-Ferraro ticket — and a bit longer-term: to convince world leaders to enact disarmament, in time for the commemoration of the fortieth anniversary of the bombing of Hiroshima. To that end, participants were encouraged to sign a proclamation:

> We categorically reject the claim that accelerating the arms race increases our national security.
>
> We furthermore hold that the psychological, social and economic consequences of preparing to fight a nuclear war are too heavy a burden on our lives and too great

a threat to our children's future.

We therefore advocate all measures that will move us away from the threat of nuclear war.

Just before a "call to action roundtable," the activist Dr. Helen Caldicott stepped up to deliver remarks around the theme "November 6: Women Must Make the Difference." Trained as a pediatrician, Dr. Caldicott had left her post at Harvard Medical School to dedicate her life to informing the public about the peril of nuclear weapons. Her second book, *Missile Envy: The Arms Race and Nuclear War,* had been released in June, its cheeky title derived from what she deemed the "psychosexual element" in the decidedly masculine language of the military industrial complex: "Missile erector." "Terminal thrust." "Deep penetration." A reviewer for the *Christian Science Monitor* had declared that *Missile Envy* "may well be the most important book of the year." The doctor had just arrived in the nation's capital city suffering fatigue after an exhausting book tour and deflated by the paltry turnout for a talk she'd just given at a YMCA in New York. Buoyed by the kindred spirits in this grand room, she began to preach to the converted: "What do women have to do if they want their babies to survive? Get involved. This country is run by rich white old men." Dr. Caldicott lamented that the budget for nuclear weapons for the year was $300 billion while two-thirds of the world's children were malnourished or starving. She called President Reagan "profoundly ignorant" — the most dangerous president, she decreed, that the United States had ever had. Women, she continued, were smarter than men, particularly the "corporate prostitutes" who roamed the halls of this building. Attendees rose to their feet. "If we don't get off our tails and do something," the doctor said, "we're all going to be dead soon."

With her remarks concluded and the din subsided, Dr. Caldicott made her way off the stage for the next speakers. A woman approached her and said that Joan Kroc wanted to see her. The activist physician had no idea who Joan Kroc was, but given the esprit de corps at the gathering, she agreed, and found herself being whisked into a private room. The well-dressed blonde who arrived to greet her, she soon learned, was the holder of the McDonald's fortune.

Though the Joan B. Kroc Foundation was prominently listed as a major sponsor on the event program, Joan was one of the least well known people present. She was also, with her fortune now hovering around $700 million, the wealthiest. Unless she'd been plunked down in a community of people involved in the alcohol rehabilitation movement, she was hardly known outside San Diego. In pre-conference press, she hadn't even rated a mention. However, flying under the radar was fine by her. She relished being in such good company and was inspired by the zealous energy with which she found herself surrounded. She'd been receiving a crash course in the issues from a particularly deft guide.

Before he became a proponent of the mind-body connection in health, Joan's new friend, the editor Norman Cousins, had dedicated much of his life to the crusade for peace. The devastation caused by the deployment of nuclear bombs at Hiroshima and Nagasaki in 1945 spurred him to action. Twelve days after the devastation, he published an essay in his *Saturday Review,* opining that the deployment of this weaponry signaled that "modern man is obsolete." Then he'd launched a campaign called "moral adoptions," which allowed Americans to send funds to help children who'd been orphaned by the bombs. Later, he arranged for twenty-five women injured in the attack, dubbed the "Hiroshima Maidens," to receive reconstructive surgery in the United States. Even with four grown biological daughters of their own, he and his wife adopted one of the young women into their family. For his efforts, he'd been made an honorary citizen of Hiroshima. He'd been called "the conscience of America."

The horrific destruction had also inspired him to launch a dialogue between the Soviets and the United States. His Dartmouth Conference, first housed at the college in New Hampshire, had brought key Americans and Russians together for fellowship and discussion since 1960. President Eisenhower had given the gatherings his secret blessing. "I can't talk to the Russians," he said. "But somebody better."

While Ray had been a man of fries, Cousins, indeed, was a revered man of letters. There were few people on earth who could be more opposite than these two men who captivated Joan. While Ray was famous for saying that if his competition was drowning, he'd stick a hose in his mouth, her new friend spent a good deal of time talking about how we should be focused not on bolstering individual tribes but on the interconnectedness of the entire species. He was just the sort of "codfish aristocrat" Ray would have detested.

Since she'd called and surprised Cousins with her intention to subsidize his research, a mutual admiration society and a close friendship had emerged between the intellectual esteemed editor and the wealthy widow. Cousins was so enamored of Joan he stood up at a benefit dinner where she was being honored and announced in a meandering speech to a ballroom filled with seven hundred guests — including his wife — that he was in love with her.

Aside from tackling the weighty matters of the day, Cousins had an affinity for two of Joan's interests: baseball — he'd played semipro ball as a young man — and music. During the life-threatening illness that had detoured him into his work as a proponent of holistic medicine, Cousins was worried that his "unrequited love of keyboards" might never be fulfilled. Freudian nightmares haunted his sleep; keys on a grand organ in a magnificent cathedral melting into water, or a strange presence interrupting him just as he sat down to play. This fear made him redouble his commitment to learning. Joan celebrated their shared passion by gifting him an expensive electrical organ. It was white, trimmed in gold, and adorned with a portrait of her. She maintained an apartment on Wilshire Boulevard in the luxurious corridor near his office at UCLA, and later, she stole off with him on vacation, island-hopping their way around the crystal blue waters of Greece and Italy.

Just as she found herself, for the first time in her life, in total control of her own domain — loving the world and its many possibilities — Cousins swayed her center of gravity. Preventing a nuclear holocaust from obliterating the earth had become her number one priority. To some of her friends in the addiction treatment movement, she apologized for shifting gears, but, she explained, with Ray's passing, it was time for her to focus on other concerns. Americans were spending too much time focused on material things, she worried, and not enough on preserving peace. What if actions by leaders like President Reagan, accelerating the nuclear arsenal, led to an end of life as we knew it?

The country, Joan believed, had been on a "nuclear bender" since 1945. She remembered her mother's curious delight after the bombs had been dropped then, how she fervently believed this meant there would never be another war. Though Joan was just seventeen at the time, this logic hadn't made sense. Yes, the war had come to an end; yes, people were celebrating; but a hundred thousand lives had been lost, and a new era of weaponry had clearly begun.

Standing before her now here in these vaunted chambers in the nation's capitol was a powerful instrument of change: a brilliant woman who had dedicated her life to ending the scourge of nuclear weapons. Joan was so impressed with Dr. Caldicott that she planned to spend $11 million to put her on television as part of the campaign to defeat President Reagan. Dr. Caldicott was breathless. She couldn't believe her good fortune in having attracted such a benefactor.

But when Joan discovered that the doctor was, in fact, a citizen of Australia, and not the United States, she backed off on her promise. It would be unwise, she felt, to pit a non-American so publicly against the president. But that wasn't the end of her patronage. Committed to spread the word about the critical need for nuclear disarmament, Joan struck a deal with the publisher of *Missile Envy,* for the dazzling sum of $1 million, to reprint half a million copies. She intended to distribute Caldicott's book for free, to make sure the work was transmitted to the widest possible audience.

The purchase was conditional. Joan insisted on excising a passage at the end of the seventh chapter. In it, Dr. Caldicott described the secretive, invitation-only, all-male bacchanal that unfolded annually at a secluded campground in Sonoma County. Bohemian Grove, it was called. The event kicked off every summer with an elaborate ritual production, the "Cremation of Care," where the normally buttoned-up titans of capitalism donned ballet costumes and danced and sang, symbolically torching whatever concerns they had from the outside world to prepare to relax into up to several weeks of fraternity. The prevailing credo of Bohemian Grove was "weaving spiders come not here," a reminder that the event was for pleasure, not a place for conducting business. Of course, that was a starry fiction. How could a gathering of important men *not* yield alliances and deals? While that rule was largely overlooked, another unspoken credo was followed religiously: to consume alcoholic beverages from morning through night. Day broke at the Grove with gin fizzes for breakfast. A steady drip of other cocktails was mixed up in enormous buckets at each campsite to make for an easy, continuous pour. "The productive drunk is the bane of all moralists," went another Bohemianism. "It tells the productive they can drink, it tells the drunks they're productive."

Helen Caldicott singled out Bohemian Grove not just because of its chauvinism, but because it was widely believed that it was there, in the summer of 1942, amid the boozy proceedings, that the plan had been hatched to build the atom bomb. It would be "suicidal," she wrote, to allow the gathering to continue:

It is obvious that the Bohemian Grove is extremely important for socialization and contact-making to foster international business relationships. The fact that participants ostentatiously lock out women indicates that these powerful men are again operating on masculine principles, excluding and denying their own feminine emotions and values and those of women in general. It is exactly this dynamic that has produced the mess in the world — a world in the grip of egocentric, power-hungry selfish amoral and killing negative animus.

Joan was unhappily familiar with the camp tradition. Ray had eagerly anticipated his yearly trip. Turner had even referenced his mentor's love of the place in his eulogy. A place to play cards and pianos scattered through the woods, while fortified by a constant drip of booze, enveloped by such camaraderie, was nothing short of nirvana for Ray. He'd been thrilled the first time he'd rated an invitation. Being able to buy jets, Rolls-Royces, baseball teams — that was one signal he'd arrived. Being asked to participate in an exclusive men's club like Bohemian Grove was a higher order of acceptance. With each visit, he'd returned so worn down from the festivities that he'd need to be hospitalized for days to recover. Joan insisted that in the edition of the book she was financing, this passage referring to the Grove must be excised. And so it was. Though Dr. Caldicott wasn't clear what benefit there was to omitting mention of the place, she was so taken by Joan, and the promise of her continued patronage, that she agreed to Joan's edits. This seemed a small trade-off in the service of getting her book, and her message, into so many hands. For Joan's part, she hoped that *Missile Envy* would touch a chord with women, and remind them how crucial it was to speak out. She was relieved she was finally able to do so.

As she settled into widowhood, Joan found herself occupied by other, less weighty concerns. On the grounds of her hilltop La Jolla home, she'd discovered an injured hummingbird and sent it via chauffeur-driven Rolls to the famous hundred-acre San Diego Zoo, twenty minutes away, for medical attention. As an animal lover and would-be veterinarian, Joan enjoyed taking her granddaughters there, often dressed in jeans and with rollers in her hair. For a few hours, she could be like any other grandma. To thank the zoo for reviving the little bird, she'd sent a check of appreciation for $100,000. Not long after, she read a newspaper account about the decrepit state of the zoo's two-acre Asian rain forest exhibition. She invited executive director Chuck Bieler over for a chat. After he explained what was needed to get the facility properly renovated, Joan promised to send in the $3.3 million necessary for the upgrades. The next day, she called Bieler, worried that her gift might convey the message that she was more interested in animals than in people. "What can we do for the humans?" she asked. He cooked up a plan for Joan to sponsor free admission days as well.

First, San Ysidro, now this. With so many hundreds of millions of dollars at her disposal, she said, how could she *not* write the check? The zoo was an attraction all the people in her adopted hometown could enjoy. And unlike the Padres, it would never have a losing year.

Two hours before the 1985 Padres home opener, Joan rolled up to the stadium in her blue Mercedes, chauffeured by a police officer she'd hired as a driver/bodyguard. She'd personally paid for a new $6.5 million scoreboard and was eager to see the finished product. Early arriving fans thronged to give her a rock-star welcome, shouting "Joan, Joan." The formality of "Mrs. Kroc" had vanished. Her brand of benevolence made her so much more approachable than your average millionaire. And at least they weren't calling her "hamburger queen," as newspapers sometimes did. She despised the nickname.

In the owner's box, she and her family — including her sister and her ex-husband, Rollie — stopped for a moment to watch Tom Brokaw and the *NBC Nightly News*. A segment on the show marked an important milestone: Thirty years ago on this very day, Ray had launched his first McDonald's in Des Plaines. Without that first restaurant, none of them would be here right now. (This was just the sort of story that riled up Dick McDonald.)

As game time neared, shadows of her early days of motherhood emerged. Back then, a tiny Linda had performed on live television and brought home that lifesaving prize for the family. This night, Joan shooed Linda, now four times a mother herself, out onto the expansive field to sing the national anthem, reminding her to savor every moment of her time in the spotlight. The local musician Steve Vaus had been enlisted to help. After they sang "The Star-Spangled Banner," Linda and Steve belted out a tune that beckoned those in attendance to "reach for the stars." A blaze of fireworks erupted over the stadium while a video montage of the last season loomed large on the new Diamond Vision screen, as if the crowd needed any reminder of the momentous previous year.

On this particular night she hardly watched the game. In her box, she received an emergency phone call from the wife of Ray's former valet and nurse. The man, just forty-five, had had a heart attack, and Joan assured his wife that the McDonald's franchise that had been lined up for them still would be theirs. She vowed to stop by to see them the next day on her way home from an appointment in Washington, D.C. She was scheduled to accompany her friend the entertainer Danny Thomas as he received a National Medal of Honor from the president. Thomas had done her a favor the year before, putting in special prayers for a Padres victory. Joan had promised that if they worked, she'd write a check for a million dollars to the cause he supported, St. Jude's Children's Research Hospital, as thanks. When the team won the playoffs, she did.

This evening in the owner's box, she invited Linda and her four girls along for the trip — one day of missed school wouldn't be a problem, especially since they'd get to spend the day touring the nation's capital while their grandmother was at the White House. A grand slam got the Padres' season off to a great start with an 8–3 win over the San Francisco Giants. Joan would never have bought a baseball team of her own volition. But the thrill of winning had given ownership a glistening luster. She couldn't imagine not having her hand in the game now.

It had been fifteen months since Ray had died, but it seemed like a lifetime ago. Joan was another woman now, her own woman, the embodiment of the woman she'd longed to become as she sat behind the Hammond organ at the Criterion restaurant so many moons ago. The woman she feared she'd never get to be when she'd felt so trapped in the early years with Ray on Lake Shore Drive. Who was that Joan? Who was that person who'd arrived in Rapid City with $1.56 to her name? Those other, earlier versions of herself were indelibly wrapped inside the person she was now: one of the richest women in the world, emerging as a philanthropist guided by her heart and her passions. At her core, she was just Joan, the same Joan. Wasn't she?

Before it had been moved to conveniently fall on a Monday to make way for a tidy three-day weekend, Memorial Day had been traditionally observed on May 30, in the full flush of spring, so that flowers would be in bloom across the country and available to be strewn on the gravesites of those who'd served and died.

On this "real" Memorial Day, readers of twenty-three newspapers across the United States woke to a dramatic, if mysterious, full-page ad. Prominently featured was a photograph of the thirty-fourth president of the United States, Dwight Eisenhower, dressed in the uniform he wore when he served as a five-star general. The portrait was accompanied by a quote from his famous 1953 "Chance for Peace" speech decrying the "military-industrial complex," delivered not long after his election to the presidency and broadcast around the world on television and radio.

Every gun that is made, every warship launched, every rocket fired signifies, in the final sense, a theft from those who are cold and are not clothed. This world in arms is not spending money alone. It is spending the sweat of its laborers, the genius of its scientists, the hopes of its children. This is not a way of life at all in any true sense. Under the cloud of threatening war, it is humanity hanging from a cross of iron.

The advertisements featuring these words had been placed by the Joan B. Kroc Foundation at a cost of nearly half a million dollars. A small credit on the page listed her office address. Almost immediately, the foundation was deluged with calls and, in a few days, more than four thousand letters had arrived. The correspondence ranged from glowing praise attached to marriage proposals to cries she was a "dumb broad" by detractors detailing where she could shove her Chicken McNuggets. One reader in San Diego compared Joan to McDonald's: "To take President Eisenhower's words out of context as Joan Kroc has done and to make it her credo is as phony as the McDonald's slogan, 'We do it all for you.' "

Such criticism was, to Joan, beside the point. McDonald's bought ads to sell hamburgers. If humanity was obliterated, there wouldn't be anyone left to eat them.

Ads weren't enough to illustrate her passion. She commissioned an artist to emblazon doves, the symbols of peace, on the belly of *Impromptu*. She envisioned her own "mountain of peace," an estate she intended to build for herself on a sprawling parcel of land up in north San Diego County. A new home, all her own. For now, she jetted off to Rome, where a friend with connections at the Vatican had arranged for a tour. In her demure pink Givenchy dress with matching straw hat, Joan looked like a prim and proper churchgoer. She wasn't quite that, nor a Catholic, but that didn't diminish the tug of this sacred place. God, she believed, had a plan for everyone, and at the moment, the focus of her work was clearly divined. Pope John Paul II reminded his audience of eight thousand people jammed into St. Peter's Square that they

333

"all shared in the same search for meaning and were all part of the same human race."

After the mass, Joan was, thanks to her connection, included in a small group invited to receive a personal blessing from the Pope. He tapped her on the head and she gave him a gift in return: a special white leather box containing the movie she produced about a wayward priest, *Mass Appeal,* and a cassette of a special peace song she'd commissioned for the upcoming Hiroshima commemoration. She'd dispatched musician Steve Vaus in her helicopter up to the J and R Double Arch Ranch, hardly used these last few years, for a dose of idyllic inspiration. The song he wrote appealed for peace from the perspective of a child, who becomes frightened after receiving a history lesson about the devastation wrought by the atomic bomb. "Dear world, I really love you," he sings, "I wanna hold your hand. I know my arms won't reach you all. But I'm sure my heart can."

The sentiment was as heartfelt, and as corny, as Corky. Joan loved the song and had it duplicated and mailed to every single radio station in the country. Of course, she hoped they'd play it. But even if they didn't, it was worth a try. This was becoming the undercurrent of her philanthropy: Why not

— what was there to lose? There was nothing stodgy or formulaic about her approach to giving. So what if it registered as unorthodox or downright kooky to traditionalists? Joan was relaxing into the ultimate luxury, of being able to indulge her whims — with no concern about cost, outcome, or, better yet, what anyone else thought.

Now she had the chance to deliver her new song into the hands of the leader of the Catholic Church. As she did, she whispered in the Pontiff's ear her most fervent hope of the moment: "I am praying for an end to the arms race."

Joan continued to do more than pray. She enlisted the local ad agency she'd hired to create a second full-page ad. This one ran in nearly a hundred papers. Price tag: $750,000. This time, the ad carried a call-to-action in the form of coupons, which readers were asked to clip and send to the White House and the Kremlin with a simple request: "Please stop all nuclear weapons testing immediately." On the left side of the page, a small symbol of a missile represented the total force of bombs dropped by Allied forces during World War II. On the right side of the page, the symbol was repeated 667 times, representing the mammoth current supply of nuclear weapons.

Consider the facts: One US Trident submarine carries nineteen megatons, the firepower of six World War IIs. 300 megatons can destroy every large and medium size city in the world. Together, the US and the Soviet Union now have enough nuclear weapons to destroy the world 67 times. When is enough enough?

To punctuate the importance of this message, the next day Joan fielded questions from the press at a news conference, accompanied by Rear Admiral Gene LaRocque. The retired military man had become a staunch antinuclear proponent after his service in World War II and Vietnam. His claims that he witnessed a near-miss nuclear weapons launch in 1963 and his ensuing zealousness against nuclear weaponry had made him a poster child for the peace set while earning him the rancor of the military. Joan explained that her campaign wasn't a criticism of the United States government, and that she felt the call for disarmament was an issue that transcended politics. She didn't mean to suggest that she had a greater voice than anyone; the only thing she had that was greater was her bank account, which enabled her to spread the word.

In Joan's owner's box at the stadium, Norman Cousins cheered the team while she clutched a hot dog and chatted with Vaus about a ride the songwriter was about to take on *Impromptu* to Japan. There, he would work with a translator so "Dear World" could be sung and recorded in Japanese by a chorus of local children.

The millions of dollars Joan had been spending on this multimedia campaign caught the attention of NBC's *Nightly News.* On the eve of the fortieth anniversary of the Hiroshima bombing — which happened also to be the night of baseball's annual All-Star Game, as well as the precursor to a possible player strike — Tom Brokaw informed his audience that there was probably only one person in the world whose interests intersected both events.

As the story about her aired, Joan was on her way east for a trip arranged by Cousins. He was so revered in Japan that after arriving in the country on Joan's jet, he managed to talk his way through customs when he discovered he'd forgotten his passport. Joan's whirlwind tour of Hiroshima included a private dinner with bomb survivors, a visit to the Atomic Bomb Research Hospital, and an appearance on TV. Vaus conducted twenty-nine beret-clad Japanese children as they sang "Dear World" in their native tongue, as Joan's eyes filled with tears. Music, she told the TV host, was a universal language.

Later, she stood in silent remembrance of the souls obliterated in the attacks, as hundreds of doves symbolically fluttered off into the skies. The serene and powerful vision strengthened her resolve to work ever harder.

Father Theodore Hesburgh had known since childhood in Syracuse, New York, that he would commit to the priesthood. He saw it as "a kind of bridge between God and humankind." Hesburgh was a charismatic, powerful man. If he hadn't taken the vows, he could have been elected president, or become a movie star. Like Norman Cousins, his handsome looks complemented his strong presence, rendering him an articulate and thoughtful activist and proponent of social justice. He'd been a charter member of the U.S. Commission on Civil Rights and had stood arm in arm with Martin Luther King Jr. in the fight for equality. In recent years he'd gathered esteemed scientists and religious leaders from various faiths to commiserate on what he considered the key issue of the time: the elimination of nuclear weapons.

Now he had come to San Diego to talk about his desire to build a dedicated peace center at the University of Notre Dame, where he'd long served as president. Students would come from around the world to learn about conflict prevention and resolution as well as peace building. Scattered activities were already under way in the school's community, he told the audience, like a new course that had been launched to examine "The Nuclear Dilemma." Each year, a dozen international students arrived on campus, all expenses paid, and a similar effort was conducted by the university in Jerusalem, under the leadership of a Quaker instructor. Father Hesburgh believed every college student should be taught about the perils of nuclear weapons. The trouble was convincing the uninitiated of the importance. "Peace" was a loaded, wishy-washy word that, to some, seemed frivolous, conjuring up images of placard-carrying hippies and pot smoking.

Not for Joan. She sat rapt with attention in the front of the lecture hall, soaking up every word uttered by this spokesman for everything she believed. How was it that the threats posed by nuclear weapons *weren't* a required topic of conversation at every university? And why *was* the topic so polarizing? The more money she herself pledged to the cause, the more criticism she received. Ray, who ordered flags flown full staff at McDonald's after the Kent State massacre, would never have endorsed her crusade.

Public reaction continued to run the gamut from love letters to death threats. "McNut," one conservative columnist called her, adding: "Joan Kroc Should Stay in the Kitchen." (The sexism was entrenched; Joan had come to the conclusion, from her involvement in the corporate world and the macho sport of baseball, that "the whole world is chauvinistic.") There had been accolades, too. Some felt she should be awarded a Nobel; others said her actions were enough to make them get over their disdain for McDonald's. Without disclosing their close friendship or the millions of dollars she'd given for his work at UCLA, Cousins had written a veritable love letter of a story for the *Christian Science Monitor*, praising Joan as the talk of the town for her benevolence. She was, in his estimation, a "great deal more than just a pretty lady with a lot of money."

Linda had become involved in the movement, too, inspired by that day trip she'd taken to Washington, D.C., with her children. Standing before the stark granite memorial to Vietnam, her four daughters beside her, she'd been overcome with emotion about the state of the planet. Bankrolled by Joan, she launched Mothers Embracing Nuclear Disarmament, or MEND. They'd been floated as a mother-daughter ticket for political office, an idea Joan roundly dismissed. There was enough power, she was finding, that came with the fortune. Why give that up for the petty game of politics? At this moment, she found herself swept up in the questions posed by Hesburgh. She had spent close to ten years and millions of dollars advocating on behalf of families impacted by alcohol abuse. Now, this commanding figure was making an equally compelling argument about the shortcomings of education to address the urgent topic she had so wholeheartedly embraced.

Hesburgh noticed an attentive blond woman in the front row as he concluded his remarks.

There may be no future if the nuclear threat is not immobilized. There is no moral concern more threatening to us ever before . . . the present headlong movement towards the ultimate catastrophe that would be an end to all we hold dear, all that is good and true and beautiful, especially an end to all persons.

As soon as he uttered his final words, his ardent listener leaped to her feet to meet him, and asked how much it would cost to build the institute he'd described. He said he didn't know, but that he'd find out. She gave him her card. The name Joan Kroc held no meaning to the priest, although he learned her identity soon enough. That she had no previous connection to the school and was not a Catholic intrigued him. A series of conversations followed. When Joan learned that building a peace center would cost about six or seven million dollars, she said she'd send in the check in the overnight mail.

During the planning and approval for the building, Joan's gift sat in an account accruing $100,000 interest before the principal was even touched to build the center. School officials offered to return the interest to Joan. She told them to just keep it, thanking them for their honesty. Soon enough, she sent along another $6 million. Joan insisted she did not wish the peace center to bear her name. The persuasive Hesburgh insisted. She grew to respect him and his work so intently that she started a new tradition. Each year on his birthday, she'd dash off a cheery greeting card containing a check for a million dollars.

At the annual awards dinner of the San Diego Press Club, Joan collided with another kindred spirit. The tall, wiry political cartoonist Paul Conrad stood before a crowd of fellow journalists on Coronado Island in San Diego. The artist had been invited from Los Angeles to deliver a talk about his poison pen. He flashed up a drawing of a marine in Lebanon, under attack, hollering into a phone for dear life. A befuddled President Reagan was on the receiving end. "Well, tell him to turn up his hearing aid," read the caption.

Conrad's employer, the *Los Angeles Times,* had been inundated with letters in response to this cartoon. "Con," as he'd been called since his service in the army in World War II, said he wasn't as concerned about the president's ears as he was about what was between them.

Reagan's graduation from governor of California to leader of the free world had been good for the artist's career, providing

343

a steady and even richer stream of fodder, what with the Iran-Contra scandal, the accelerating arms race, and his meddling wife Nancy's imperious interference in world affairs, like her use of astrologers to determine the dates of summits and when Air Force One could fly. The politician's tenure, in fact, had motivated the work that had recently won Conrad his third Pulitzer Prize. For years, the actor turned politician had so often been rattled by Conrad's scathing political commentary that the first lady regularly called publisher Otis Chandler to tell him to knock it off. Paul Conrad was ruining their breakfast.

To Con, who prided himself on his pull-no-punches frankness, this was a proud accomplishment. But it paled in comparison to his crowning achievement: rating a listing on President Nixon's fabled "enemies list." Con reviled both men with such passion that he'd gone to extreme measures, having caricatures of each of them etched onto his rear molars. (The Nixon tooth was so rotten, quipped Conrad, that it had fallen out.)

Con's wartime experience, as well as his deep Catholic faith, rendered him a passionate pacifist. He was committed to using his platform to promote justice and peace. "Editorial cartoonists have a function and a purpose for the millions who have no voice," he told the crowd. "I can't imagine reading the news each day and not being able to respond in the medium of an editorial cartoon." Without this kind of opposition, he said, democracy did not exist.

Joan, the news junkie, sat in the audience in the Hotel Coronado ballroom, lapping up the veteran commentator's stories. This was the same place where, back in 1968, she and Ray had decided, once and for all, to marry. But tonight, there wasn't a McDonald's operator anywhere in sight. She was surrounded by news media as the guest of a reporter at *The San Diego Tribune.*

It had caused some consternation in local press circles that the writer Robert Blair Kaiser had become one of Joan's "consorts." In the aftermath of the massacre in San Ysidro, Kaiser had been dispatched by his editors to profile Joan, and a friendship had blossomed — curiously, given her long-standing aversion to the press. But the journalist possessed a nontraditional pedigree. He was an ordained Jesuit priest who had left the order to marry. He'd covered the landmark second Vatican council for *Time* magazine. Now divorced, Kaiser not only had arranged the trip Joan had taken to see the Pope, but had accompanied her there on the *Impromptu.* The fact that the paper had permitted him to write about the trip, particularly without explaining their personal connection, gave some of the purists in the press corps pause. He'd filed another inside story after accompanying Joan to Texas, where they visited the wildlife preservation ranch of animal rights activist Cleveland Amory, yet another of Joan's beneficiaries. And he'd been right there in the owner's box with Joan earlier in the year at the Padres home opener, chronicling the start of the new season for local readers.

Virtually anyone with whom she kept company, man or woman, inevitably became the object of tantalizing rumor and speculation, even before Ray had died. Once he was gone, Joan had told a reporter that she wasn't looking for love. "Do you know what a romance would do to my life?" Joan had said. "When you're in love, your brains go right out of your head, and I've had that, twice now. It just isn't a part of my life that's missing." Love affairs and marriage were the furthest things from Joan's mind. There was too much else she wanted to accomplish, and she was far too independent. As for Kaiser, he said using the word "dating" to describe his relationship with Joan would be "going too far."

That night, she was just content to have the company of allies in her unfolding political consciousness. Joan shared the artist's disdain for the politicians in his crosshairs. That long-ago Nixon episode, after Ray had made a donation in both their names, had not sat well. Recently, President Reagan had extended an invitation for her to serve on a special business commission, and she'd refused. She believed she'd only been asked as a token female, and she most certainly had no intention of doing anything to support the man behind the nuclear arms buildup.

At the conclusion of Conrad's speech, Kaiser rushed up to him so he could introduce Joan. The artist had no idea who Joan was, but that didn't stop a friendship from unfolding over their shared midwestern railroad roots, politics, and concerns. They found they agreed they were more interested in social justice than in strict party politics.

That summer, Joan rented a yacht to cruise Alaska's Inside Passage, and invited the artist and his wife, Kay, to join her and Kaiser, along with two other couples. A crew of twelve serviced the eight passengers. Conrad drew caricatures of everyone in the group. Talk turned to music. In addition to his talent in the visual arts, Conrad was also an accomplished and passionate self-taught musician who, after the war, had delayed his college education in order to tour with an eleven-piece band. Joan was so excited to be in the company of a fellow musician that she stopped at the nearest port of call to buy a piano to bring on board.

Over duets, Conrad talked with Joan about his work. For years, in his spare time, he'd been experimenting with metal, crafting sculpture; some of it was political, giving his print work added dimension; some of it was religious, reflecting his devout faith. For his magnum opus, he told Joan, he wished to forge a giant nuclear mushroom cloud. He grabbed paper and a pen and sketched out a stubby snarl of chain link, to show what he envisioned. In reality, it would rise twenty-six feet tall, he said. "This is a statement of peace" would read the accompanying plaque. "May it never be an epitaph." Joan agreed to subsidize the necessary $200,000 so the artist could create the sculpture. But, she insisted that her patronage remain anonymous.

By the time the artwork called *Chain Reaction* was finally installed in the Santa Monica civic center four years later, its funding cloaked under the requisite veil of secrecy, Joan had made another political statement, as well as a major purchase. In 1987, Joan — a registered independent — wrote a check to the Democratic Party for a million dollars to train candidates and finance computerized voter lists. It was the largest donation the party had ever received, a gift Joan never could have made while her husband was alive.

The yacht vacation had been so much fun, Joan decided to commission Dutch shipbuilder Feadship to craft her very own $40 million boat — twice the length of the *Joni-Ray* — outfitted, of course, with keyboards. She christened this vessel *Impromptu,* like her plane. To celebrate the unveiling of *Chain Reaction,* Joan had the crew navigate the extravagant boat to Terminal Island in San Pedro. Con, his wife, Kay, and a handful of Santa Monica city officials who were in on the secret of her gift were invited to join the elegant dinner. As waiters swirled in service, *Impromptu* sailed up and down the harbor in the nighttime breeze, and Joan sat happily perched at the organ, serenading no one in particular.

11
IMPROMPTU

When she first ran for public office in 1971, and won a landslide victory the likes of which San Diego hadn't seen in years, Maureen O'Connor was a twenty-five-year-old gym teacher at Rosary High School, her alma mater. She'd paid her way through college working as a chambermaid in a fancy downtown hotel. Now, earning $450 a month, she still lived with her parents, as did four of her dozen siblings. For clues on how to run a campaign, her identical twin (who beat her out of the womb by eight minutes) checked out how-to books from the library. One of their brothers donated a tiny office space as headquarters.

Athletics had been an indelible part of Maureen's childhood. Under the direction of their father, a onetime boxer who owned a liquor store and ran the numbers, she and her six sisters swam together professionally. They were so skilled they had toured the country as part of a televised show called *The Wonderful World of Sports.* During San Diego's bicentennial celebration in 1969, O'Connor discovered that old friends of hers from those TV sporting days, who performed under the name Los Voladores Indians, were being paid a paltry twelve dollars a day, despite the city's lavish budget. O'Connor ventured to City Hall to lodge a complaint, and had, she felt, been rudely dismissed. The slight inspired her decision to run for office.

What she lacked in campaign financing and political clout she made up for with her 750-strong volunteer "Maureen Corps," some not quite voting age themselves. They excitedly fanned out around the city and knocked on every door on behalf of their petite, freckled teacher. With her long dark hair parted down the middle, Maureen hardly looked old enough to drive. The dazzling display of youthful might was tinged with Cinderella: the daughter of a liquor store owner and a nurse, raised in a home where, one particularly lean Thanksgiving, hamburger had to be fashioned into a facsimile turkey, trouncing the established, conservative fifty-three-year-old incumbent businessman.

To reinforce the fairy-tale nature of her

victory, Maureen passed out tiny glass shoes to her supporters, telling the press that in order to prove herself a serious legislator, she couldn't "be a slipper."

At school in the weeks after her victory, she received a fistful of telephone messages from a persistent caller, eager to find out just who was this young woman who'd unseated his old friend. She relented and finally spoke with Robert O. Peterson, thirty years her senior. The young city council-woman wound up marrying him in the French Riviera.

The son of a milk and ice cream sales-man, the enterprising Peterson had started a dance pavilion to pay for his college education, and later peddled milk shake machines. In 1941, he jumped into the drive-in restaurant craze, launching a ham-burger stand he dubbed Topsy's. Later, he rechristened the place with his middle name, Oscar, opening several more around town. When he mounted a giant, starry-eyed clown on the roof of the original store, he renamed it again: Jack in the Box.

An expeditious drive-up intercom sepa-rated the restaurant stand from competitors like McDonald's. The gizmo allowed work-ers to serve one customer while taking the order of the next. When a corporation came calling with an eye toward acquisition, Jack in the Box bit: Ralston-Purina absorbed the chain in 1968, catapulting Peterson into the millionaire ranks. He immediately plowed some of his newfound fortune into more stable repositories — a bank and real estate — and back into the community, by supporting education, oceanography, and the arts. For his breadth of interests, he was considered in some circles in San Diego to be a Renaissance man.

Having married well, and having experienced the power of public service, Maureen declined to run for a third term in office, but she couldn't shake the political bug that had burrowed beneath her skin. Yes, she was in the position to enjoy life and travel, but growing up in a large Catholic family gave her a sense of responsibility concerning the greater good.

The call to serve almost undid her marriage. So unhappy was husband Peterson when she filed to run for mayor that he filed for divorce. A financial settlement had been drawn up by lawyers before the pair suddenly reconciled. She lost the race, anyway, but when a campaign finance scandal forced the winner to resign, Maureen jumped into the race again, and won. It was a dizzying time of growth for the once sleepy port town. On the one hand, technology and medical businesses were welcome additions to the city; but the consequence of the expansion was "Los Angelizing" sprawl, leaving the streets bursting with newcomers, and introducing urban challenges like pollution and homelessness.

Frustrated with the platitudes of bureaucrats in addressing social ills, Mayor Mo, as she became known, decided to conduct field research. Dressed in jeans, backpack on her shoulders, she hit the streets to pose as a homeless woman. Rolling out her sleeping bag in the city's Balboa Park for a night's rest, she couldn't sleep for the serenade of drug dealers peddling their wares and male prostitutes scampering to their trysts. The facelessness and despair of a street person were evidenced by the fact that the lady mayor's distinctive cherubic face went mostly unrecognized. But not entirely. At a shelter where she checked in to rest her weary, blistered feet, she gave her mother's maiden name, but that didn't fool several of the other astute patrons, much less an attending nun, who deduced her identity from her choice of reading material. "You should know," she advised, "homeless women don't read the financial section."

Given Maureen's perch at City Hall and Joan's ownership of the local ball team, not to mention her growing and looming benevolence in and around the city, it was inevitable that the lives of the two women would intersect. Given their similar trajectories from hardscrabble to elite, and the fact that they'd both married (and almost divorced) hamburger barons, it was only natural that Mayor Mo and Joan would become close friends. Those intersecting biographical tidbits were punctuated by their similarly unorthodox approaches to life.

There were plenty of other stars in San Diego's philanthropic galaxy: Dr. Jonas Salk, the inventor of the polio vaccine, who'd migrated to La Jolla in 1960 to launch a research institute. Sol Price, who'd founded the warehouse chain Price Club, where Ray insisted his chauffeur ferry him to buy cigarettes at a discount. The writer Theodore Geisel, better known as Dr. Seuss. Genevieve "Jenny" Craig, who, with her husband, had relocated her weight-loss empire here from Australia. Don Shiley, inventor of an artificial heart valve. Cecil Green, a cofounder of electronics giant

Texas Instruments. The local fabric had been built on the backs of these moguls' largesse: Theirs and other names familiar to locals — Preuss, Scripps, Ratner — were so commonplace among area nonprofit institutions, their contributions were practically seen as inevitable. For these entrepreneurial types who'd either grown up in or relocated to the city's toniest neighborhoods, "giving back" to the community was a happy obligation. But no one around here had ever experienced anything like Joan's radical, unconventional giving.

Joan still possessed the same disdain for banquet dinners and lunches and committees-for-the-betterment that she'd developed after arriving in Chicago, even though — and especially because — it was often she who was being honored. Besides being bored by the proceedings, she had another reason not to go. The more she gave, the more impossible it was for her to appear in public. At a party at the home of Dr. Salk, she was so deluged with requests for sponsorship, underwriting, and donations, she fled early. Friends and employees were routinely approached for hints on how to get their worthy cause on her radar. Yet staying home didn't insulate her entirely. Each time one of her gifts was announced, an avalanche of appeals followed. Over time, it proved so burdensome, she unceremoniously shuttered the Joan B. Kroc Foundation. It was just easier to write checks from her personal account, without the formality or bureaucracy. Not that most civilians understood the difference. The money was all hers; rich was rich. Tax write-offs one way or another were beside the point for a woman whose fortune now approached a billion. Besides, that never had been what prompted her to give.

And so, when she decided to finance the city's first freestanding hospice with a ten-million-dollar gift, she insisted her bequest remain anonymous. The staff of the San Diego Hospice, which provided end-of-life care to the dying but did not have a fixed location, received the call during the Christmas season. Years before, when she occasionally flew commercially, Joan had been seated on a flight next to Dr. Doris Howell, an early proponent of the hospice movement. Dr. Howell was about Joan's age and had bucked expectations of women from their generation by attending medical school, and never bothering to get married. In fact, she dropped suitors when they demanded she give up medicine. After both Joan's father and Ray had been assisted by hospice caregivers, Joan resolved to help Dr. Howell fulfill her dream.

A stunning ten-acre parcel of land on a hilltop mesa, fit for a four-star resort, offered a choice location, and was, fortuitously, about to be put up for sale by the county. It had, in the past, been home to hospitals specializing in tuberculosis and mental health, and now served AIDS patients. Joan's deal was firm: She would buy the land, and pay to build an inpatient facility where the terminally ill could peacefully spend their last days. But her identity must not be revealed.

Just as addiction care was becoming a benefit covered by health insurance during Operation Cork's emergence in the seventies, now end-of-life hospice care was becoming an approved Medicare benefit. This new hospice would be only the sixth of its kind in the country, and the first freestanding one in all of California. As staff set about the approval process in order to purchase the land, they bumped up against resistance from some community members, who had other hopes for the property. Also, several city officials resented what they called the secretive "Howard Hughes" nature of the offer. The deal was moments from being spiked.

An earnest city council member committed to getting to the bottom of the mystery sleuthed out, by process of elimination, that it was Joan Kroc behind the donation. He appealed to her lawyer for permission to reveal her identity in the service of saving the project. By then Joan's friend Maureen had been elected mayor. Norman Cousins cinched the deal with an impassioned speech to lawmakers: "What we are talking about essentially is how people leave this stage of life. Will they go out with style? Or will the final scene be filled with pain . . . indignity and squalor?"

Joan's demand for anonymity in her gifts was hardly ironclad. The priest who had blessed her plane, Father Joe Carroll, needed to build a new wing at the St. Vincent de Paul Homeless Shelter in downtown San Diego. Joan publicly announced her $3 million gift, since she knew homelessness could be a tough "sell" to donors. She hoped, by throwing her support behind the issue, others might be inspired to give. The resulting 313-bed facility was so beautiful it was given an award as "best shelter in the free world." Joan hopped onto *Impromptu* with the priest to pick up the prize from the Building and Social Housing Foundation in London. As they rode in separate limos around the city, Joan called the priest on the car phone and asked, "Pardon me, Father. Do you have any Grey Poupon?"

When her attentions turned to a frightening new epidemic, Father Joe got to help his friend. A young doctor named Carol Harris on the front lines of the newly discovered disease, AIDS, appeared on television in 1986 to talk about her work treating patients at Einstein Hospital in New York with few resources. So little was known about AIDS and how it was transmitted that in some settings, even medical professionals wouldn't interact with the afflicted without the armor of protective gear. Watching at home, Joan was moved by Dr. Harris's selfless bravery, and called to tell the doctor she wanted to give her the $4 million she needed to build a stand-alone clinic. Neighbors of the hospital in the Bronx equated a gift from Joan with one that came direct from McDonald's corporate bank account. Distressed at the impending presence in their community of a clinic filled with people suffering from this menacing, mysterious disease, opponents began lobbying the corporation to keep the place out of their backyard. Father Joe happened to be from the neighborhood. Joan sent him in on the

Impromptu to assuage the critics. She wanted the facility built, but she also didn't want an episode of fearmongering to trouble Mc-Donald's. She knew there was a fine line between asserting her own wishes and insulting the source of her fortune.

Later, she hand-delivered a check for $1 million to the actress Liz Taylor, who'd thrown her support behind AMFAR, the foundation for AIDS research. When Joan sold her home in the desert, she gave the bulk of the $2.8 million proceeds to under-write an AIDS clinic in Palm Springs.

The sad saga of DeWayne Mowery, a twelve-year-old boy with hemophilia in Clinton, Tennessee, who'd contracted the AIDS virus from the tainted blood supply, personified the fearmongering surrounding the disease. A dedicated school bus segregated Mowery from other children, ferrying him solo to his own classroom each day, where he received instruction from a tutor. Blockades of protestors demonstrated to keep the boy from attending school at all, fearing his mere presence might infect other kids. Some of his schoolmates cried with compassion about the plight of their friend, holding up handmade signs that declared, "He's a human, not a rabid dog." When the school district faced financial troubles, layoffs — including Mowery's teacher, Angela Gee — seemed inevitable. Joan swooped in with her checkbook, offering up the $232,000 needed to balance the district's books. She tucked in a thousand dollars as a gift to the boy's parents. Then she dispatched *Impromptu* to Tennessee to pick up the family for a night at the Padres game. The shy boy did the honors of throwing out the first pitch.

Even Gee was invited for the ride, and got her own special present from Joan — a check for $10,000 and a Steuben glass "star" award for her "beautiful attitude." Joan tidily summed up her philosophy toward service in a letter to go along with the gift. She recounted the story of a woman who walked along the seaside each morning, tossing beached starfish back into the water. A fellow stroller sniffed that she was just wasting her time; more would inevitably float back to shore. To which the starfish rescuer replied: "I know that, in the big scheme of things, it doesn't make much difference. But it sure makes a big difference to this one little starfish."

Playing guardian angel was, Joan began to feel, a far more compelling use of her time than wrangling the egos and messes in the pesky "little boy's world" of baseball. The Padres were back to their losing selves, and the hassles of ownership were proving to outweigh the benefits. She would put the team up for sale. Other than for the fun of hosting friends in her private box and occasionally dazzling a boy from a small town, Joan was tired of the rising cost of salaries and the personnel hassles. She much preferred to toss money at a cause or concern that piqued her interest. Almost always, the cause or concern was attached to a person she'd met whom she admired. What kind of impact the gift would have generally seemed less important than the investment itself — her trust in the act of giving.

The organist Danny Topaz had, by now, retired, and about the only person involved with the organization who seemed to like having her around anyway, was the maitre d' in the owner's box, Denny Walsh. (She did, from time to time, enjoy visits from a fellow lady ball club owner, Marge Schott of the Cincinnati Reds.) The troubles never seemed to end, and now she was even at odds, too, with her own son-in-law. Ballard had unceremoniously dumped the winning manager, Dick Williams — the same man for whom he'd fetched Big Macs at Ray's behest when he'd been signed to the team.

To patch things up, Joan asked her chauffeur to drop her at Williams's doorstep so she could plead with him to return. A swarm of press gathered outside, and, to avoid a confrontation, his wife spirited Joan away through the garage. Just months later, she fired Williams anyway, on the opening day of spring training. She'd heard he'd been taking nips of whiskey on the job.

Her disdain for the game rapidly accelerated after the response to her edict banning beer from the clubhouse. She swore it had less to do with her long-standing campaign to combat alcoholism than it was an issue of liability. Star pitcher Goose Gossage blew a gasket over the new rule, peppering his tirade with choice salvos: "Gutless," he called the owner and her son-in-law the team president. "Spineless." They could sell beer and make money from the fans, but they were worried about beer in the clubhouse? What about Joan, he hissed, poisoning the world with her hamburgers?

When Joan suspended the garrulous Gossage for insubordination, his teammates rumbled about free speech. There was even talk they might not show up for a game. The matter was fixed after he agreed to apologize and pony up a $25,000 donation to Ronald McDonald House. Her firm finesse under pressure led one sports reporter to dub her "Iron Butterfly and Tinkerbell."

Offloading a baseball team proved harder than she expected. A deal to sell the Padres in 1987 for $50 million — more than four times what Ray had paid for it — fell apart when Joan learned of the shady reputation of the buyer. She decided to just *give* the team away. At an official meeting with her friend Mayor Mo and the city manager, she said she wished to donate the Padres to their rightful owner: the people of San Diego. A $100 million trust for associated operating costs was a key component of her gift, making it a sweet and unprecedented deal with little risk for the city. The Major League Baseball brass wouldn't have it. Public ownership would expose the inner financial workings of the major leagues. Stuck with the club, in the meantime, her daughter divorced Ballard and married a player's agent, Jerry Kapstein. Joan put *him* in charge. The marriage lasted eighteen months, and so did his tenure.

In a group headed by television producer Tom Werner, Joan finally found a buyer. They paid her $75 million for the team — quintupling Ray's original purchase price. Werner debuted as owner with a flourish of cross-promotion in the spirit of McDonald's. He appointed the star of one of his television shows, Roseanne Barr, to sing the national anthem. The actress grabbed her crotch and shrieked her way through the song. The crowd erupted in a collective boo. Like Ray's screeching debut years earlier, Barr's explanation for her rakish performance was, simply, that she'd been misunderstood.

Helen Copley could relate to the perils of inheriting a husband's lofty empire and being tossed into the shark-infested waters that surrounded power. When her husband, Jim, succumbed to brain cancer at the age of fifty-seven in 1973, Helen slid into the corner office of his family newspaper business. Then fifty-one herself, her only prior experience in the news business was as her husband's secretary. The daunting responsibility of lording over twelve daily papers and twenty-nine weeklies struck fear in Helen's heart. But instead of offloading the task to executives, she chose to plunge in.

Shame had been part of Helen's life as long as she could remember. A devout Catholic, she'd fled her hometown of Cedar Rapids, Iowa, pregnant, having married and divorced the father of her child in the span of a few weeks. A month and a half after giving birth, she picked up a much-needed job as a ticket girl at the Santa Fe railroad depot — fitting for the daughter of a railroad signal man. That the depot was right across the street from the Copley newspaper headquarters proved fortuitous. A reporter she met at a nearby coffee spot helped Helen land a job at the media empire. The esteemed publisher plucked the tall brunette for his own secretarial pool. Was it her looks or her name? He already had two other women named Helen assisting him.

A dozen years later, Copley's marriage had collapsed, and he surprised his close friends by proposing to the leggy, soft-spoken single mother. After years on her own, she finally had a father for her son. Copley adopted David, age thirteen, and David, in turn, adopted his surname.

While Joan, as a new bride, had despised the role of servile corporate wife, the self-effacing Helen Copley, who described herself as "pathetically shy," rather enjoyed it. She loved following her husband's lead so much, she even adopted his drink of choice: Scotch. Now, with no Jim to follow, she hired a speech tutor to prime her for her role in the public eye. Other matters required her urgent attention. Her husband's death saddled her with a $16 million estate tax bill, unbalanced corporate books, and a lawsuit from Copley's first wife and children. Courts ruled she owed them $10 million, and she began paying down the debt month by month, $100,000 at a time.

To tidy things up, she offloaded the corporate jet, various real estate holdings, and several of the revenue-draining papers. In a marathon fifteen-hour session with staff, she appealed for assistance in assessing the state of the two marquee titles, *The San Diego Union* and *Tribune.* When a reporter asked about the long-standing policy of not running local stories on the front page, she changed the policy at once. As for claims of bias and favoritism stemming from her husband's fiercely conservative politics, she explained, "I don't know about any sacred cows, and if there are any, they're ex-sacred cows."

Apart from accusations of favoritism, there were those who expected kid-glove treatment, including Helen's beloved Catholic Church. A newspaper report that disclosed pedophilia and financial improprieties in the local diocese created friction with the local Catholic university, University of San Diego, on whose board she sat. Wanting to appear neutral, she resigned. There were even calls for her excommunication. An editor at the *Union* leaped to her defense, and so did the local monsignor, who doubted that the multimillionaire lady publisher "would sit with a green visor on her forehead and a red pencil in her hand every night checking every line of copy and classified ad."

Indeed, Helen claimed to subscribe to the same philosophy as her friend Katharine Graham, the East Coast publisher of *The Washington Post:* "Hire good editors," she said, "and let them do their job."

As if the typical day-to-day thorniness of journalism wasn't enough, Helen found herself taking charge during a time of immense change and contraction in the industry. The ascent of television news was forcing a decline in afternoon newspaper readership all over the country. That led to a troubling dip in advertising. Publishers faced the tough decision to close or merge their papers. Helen herself decided to fuse her flagship holdings in 1991, ending an era with the creation of *The San Diego Union-Tribune.*

A complicated journalistic legacy wasn't all Jim Copley had left behind. He'd started to sow philanthropic seeds his widow knew he'd wish her to continue nourishing. The

Copley name was plastered all over town, on hospitals, libraries — even on a street. For a donation to the San Diego Zoo, the couple had won the right to name a gorilla — a reward Ray and Joan had also been given for their support of Chicago's Lincoln Park Zoo. For their beast's name, Jim and Helen chose "Trib." The Krocs picked "Jo-RayK."

That was the silliest by-product of their Cinderella lives that Helen and Joan shared, but there was so much more. Starting with their humble midwestern railroad beginnings, their intersections were many: the shame of their life decisions, their ascent into leadership roles, their shared love of cigarettes and the city they'd adopted as their home; they both harbored a sense of obligation to put the enormous wealth they'd inherited from their formidable husbands to good use.

The publisher, the team owner/philanthropist, and the woman who ran City Hall. *Time* magazine declared the triumvirate "Lady Power in the Sunbelt." When NBC's breezy morning program, *Today,* arrived in 1989 to spotlight the tremendous growth of this sunny southern California city, this trio of powerful women rated a segment. No other city could claim such a troika. During the afternoon taping, feigned to mimic the early morning hour when the program would air, not a word was mentioned of Joan's affiliation with McDonald's, particularly not by the spurned creator of Ronald McDonald, Willard Scott, who'd failed up from clown to become the show's famous television weatherman. The women could hardly get a word in edgewise as host Jane Pauley fawned and posed the hard-hitting question: How did they get together without any of their fellow San Diegans noticing? (Joan's retort: They meet up in the bathroom.)

Members of the live outdoor studio audience got a special behind-the-scenes treat. They got to meet the fourth of the "power brokers," the Oscar-winning actress Mercedes McCambridge, who rallied the crowd fearlessly like the skilled performer she was. "When they come down," she said of her three friends, "let's give them a round of applause. They were scared to death, and they did a really good job."

The women might have a stranglehold on San Diego, but they were, at their core, just like any other girlfriends. Their accoutrements were just a bit more grand. Other ladies might run off on shopping trips and spa days, but these four embarked on theirs on a private plane. Other ladies would surely band together to support a friend's artistic pursuit, but most such pursuits didn't involve jetting to see your Academy Award–winning friend appear on Broadway. These girlfriends cheered the home team from the owner's box, and, when they chose to spend the day at the casino, they rolled into Joan's very own private wing. Lots of women loved their pets, but most couldn't imagine tossing in $2 million apiece to rebuild the local animal shelter, as Joan and Helen had.

Like any constellation of bosom buddies, these women anointed themselves with a nickname. Borrowing from the fabled group of Hollywood stars who palled around together in the sixties, they called themselves "the rat pack." A rat pack of Cinderellas.

What she lacked in stratospheric wealth and power, Mercedes McCambridge — Mercy to her friends — made up with glamour and fame. She was an integral rat pack presence, a court jester attending the queens. When Mayor Mo's husband, Bob Peterson, passed away, it was the mellifluous Mercedes who delivered the eulogy. Once approval had been granted for the hospice facility Joan underwrote, it was Mercy who emceed the groundbreaking ceremonies. When Joan had ventured to Amsterdam to pick up that new yacht, Mercy tagged along for the maiden voyage, flattered when they sailed through the Panama Canal and a fan waved in recognition. When *Impromptu,* the plane, returned from a mission to fetch a leopard in Ohio for the zoo, Mercy stood beside Joan at the airport to greet the cat.

Mercy's vocal cords had launched her into fame as a young woman. As a scholarship student at Mundelein College in Chicago, she'd been plucked from her role in a student production in 1937 by scouts from NBC and signed to a five-year contract. The director Orson Welles came to regard her as the "the greatest living radio actress."

Because of her square jaw and severe looks, Hollywood said Mercy had zero chance of crossing over into the emerging domain of talking pictures. "There was no point in trying to improve my appearance," she lamented, "in a world where there was Elizabeth Taylor." But accepting her shortcomings didn't mean squelching her ambition. At her very first Hollywood audition, for a screen adaptation of Robert Penn Warren's *All the King's Men,* she made a fuss about the treatment of actors. She landed the part as the young campaign assistant,

Sadie, and walked away with an Oscar for Best Supporting Actress.

It might have been beginner's luck, but the accolades launched her on a series of roles alongside the great actors of her day — James Dean, Rock Hudson, Joan Crawford. Mercy never became a major star, but she rarely went without work. She found herself perennially cast as the "nasty sister, the nasty mother, the nasty spinster who's running the ranch."

Her masterful vocal skills won her her most haunting and memorable role. Director William Friedkin cast her to provide the invisible, demonic voice of a possessed girl in *The Exorcist*. To achieve the appropriately menacing wheezing sounds of torment, the actress chain-smoked, drank raw eggs, and insisted on being tied to a chair. Her congenital bronchitis aided and abetted the effect. At the end of the film's gala preview, she burst into tears. The on-screen credit she expected didn't appear. Mercy sued and got her credit.

She'd experienced far more piercing personal disappointments. When she gave birth to her second stillborn child, the actress Marlene Dietrich flew across the country to hold her hand. Not long after she delivered a healthy baby, John Lawrence, on Christmas Eve, 1941, her marriage fell apart. Twice, she attempted suicide and was discovered by her son. Before she became sober through her dedication to Alcoholics Anonymous, she earned the sad distinction of being hospitalized for drinking binges around the world.

While Joan was in the throes of launching Operation Cork, quietly suppressing her personal hell, Mercedes was unabashedly broadcasting her own struggles to promote awareness of the disease. After her testimony at the Senate subcommittee, she served as spokeswoman for the National Council on Alcoholism. For several years she gave up her career as a performer to serve as president of a rehab center in Pennsylvania. To show she wasn't a figurehead, she even moved to the facility's grounds.

Mercy's brainy son deftly avoided the family business. After earning a PhD in economics, his work as a high-stakes trader took him to Little Rock, Arkansas. The actress briefly tagged along, appearing on-stage there in a production of 'night, Mother, a Pulitzer Prize–winning play about a woman and her grown daughter plotting to take her own life.

Not long after, life imitated art in the most unimaginably wrenching way. An elaborate financial scheme John Lawrence had been perpetuating for years, using an account he'd created for his mother as a front, was discovered. Mercedes had refused to cover for him, and he'd been fired. Despondent over his family's future, one dark night, he set about the house, murdering his two daughters and his wife before shooting himself.

Next to his body, police discovered a rubber Halloween mask — and a venomous thirteen-page letter addressed to his mother, explaining his crime, exonerating her from any wrongdoing in the financial scam, and outlining, in excruciating detail, his long-festering animosity.

I was essentially raised by live-in maids . . . I was conceptualized to save a bad marriage . . . I watched you try to kill yourself twice. You have never been there for me when the chips were down . . . When I cried on the phone you called me a "sniveling wimp." I wished you'd never done a lot of things you did. 'Night mother.

Crushed by the tragedy, Joan pressed into action, dispatching *Impromptu* to ferry her devastated friend to the funeral services.

To those who'd offered condolences, Mercedes sent a terse acknowledgment: "About what happened, that's all there is to say . . . it happened. A Greek tragedy . . . a cast of four beautiful people. The play closed." She never spoke of the incident again, except to give it a cryptic nod.

"Life is a bitch," she'd say — the words could have served as the rat pack credo — "but you have to survive."

In North Dakota, one state over from where Joan's life began and one state north of where it took shape, an entire community was facing the worst natural disaster in its history. The Red River was cresting in Grand Forks, reaching over fifty-four feet, and the dikes were about to burst.

Though her new $12,000-a-year job was technically part-time, Mayor Pat Owens had been working round the clock. After thirty years as the assistant in the mayor's office, she'd won the seat for herself in a landslide victory. She almost hadn't bothered to run — without a college education, she felt unqualified — when her ninety-two-year-old father weighed in with a convincing argument. "Look in Webster's," he said. "To be educated is to be informed. Who is more informed about city government than you?"

Now, City Hall was underwater, and so

was her own home. The situation was dire for tens of thousands of people. The tiny rookie commanded, then oversaw, the largest evacuation of an American city since the Civil War.

The drama advanced nightly on live national television, as the news broadcast more terrible images of destruction and despair into the nation's living rooms. At home in sunny southern California, Joan was glued to the coverage, shadows of the havoc wrought by floods in Rapid City on her mind. President Clinton flew in and visited an airplane hangar where one family after another lived now on cots, coming to grips with having lost their home and every possession.

Desperate for a change of clothing, Mayor Pat ran into a Sam's Club warehouse store at the edge of the city — one of the few stores still open — to buy herself a fresh pair of jeans. They turned out to be a size too small. For the next week, she wore them anyway during her daily televised press conference, a tiny, fierce leader clad in denim, stepping up to protect her fellow citizens. One afternoon, she was sifting through the hundreds of telephone messages assistants had collected on blue slips of paper, stuffed into a plastic bag for her review. One stood out: "Mayor Maureen O'Connor from San Diego. Urgent. Someone wants to give you $15 million."

It seemed a practical joke, but Mayor Pat felt compelled to respond. Maybe a miracle had been conjured from the disaster. The call turned out to be real. Asking an aide to cover for her at the daily press briefing, she made her way to the airport to greet her now retired counterpart from San Diego, who'd arrived in town on a private jet with her twin sister. The two women explained that their friend Joan Kroc wanted to offer the people of Grand Forks some relief. The mayor's plucky assertiveness in this trying circumstance had struck Joan, who decided after watching her in action on television that she wanted to help "this little fox."

Though Mayor Pat had no idea who this Joan Kroc was, she didn't dismiss the incredible offer. These women wouldn't have come so far to play a prank. Maureen emphasized two conditions: Joan did not want the interference of any official agencies, so the money could get quickly into the hands of those who needed it. And her identity must be concealed.

To start the wheels in motion, the grand, mysterious gift was announced. The news media went wild: Who was this angel who descended to relieve the pain of so many beleaguered people? Journalists speculated about who in the United States could possibly be rich enough to make such an enormous donation. How could anyone be so kind, so good? Tears of joy flowed among locals as they stood in line to apply to receive the allotted $2,000, a sum calculated so it didn't disqualify those who needed it from any federal emergency monies. The specific amount was almost beside the point; that a total stranger would swoop in at a time of dire need was a dash of fairy tale locals desperately needed.

Three weeks later, Joan accepted Mayor Pat's invitation to tour the blighted area. It gave her an excuse to stop off in South Dakota. Her friend Ruth Ziolkowski wanted to show her the progress that had been made on the gigantic mountain sculpture since her husband died in 1982. The 563-foot-tall face of the Lakota warrior Crazy Horse was emerging, slowly but surely, on the mammoth granite canvas. Joan had a vested interest in the site, apart from her fondness for the couple and the fact that the sculpture of Ray that Korczak had crafted was, curiously, on display at the visitor center. She'd gifted Ruth with thirty-eight pieces of western art worth over a million dollars after a thwarted attempt to donate it to a new museum in Rapid City.

While the arrival of a fancy private jet belonging to Joan was, by now, no surprise in South Dakota, up north, where journalists were desperate for clues to solve the angel mystery, it was a spectacle. Though, on arrival, Joan was spirited out of her plane in an airplane hangar and whisked off in a van, an intrepid reporter searched for the tail number N-811-JK and double verified the identity by sleuthing out the credit card slip used to pay for fuel. The cloak of secrecy guarding the identity of the "Angel of Grand Forks" had been lifted. A new round of stories extolling this McDonald's heiress's compassion followed. So did ones excoriating the media for defying her wish for anonymity.

Her compassion seemed limitless, applied at seemingly random moments to a wide range of recipients, typically inspired by the news. She'd been as horrified as any decent person after the gruesome murder of a poor African-American man, James Byrd Jr., who'd been dragged to death by racist thugs in Jasper, Texas. Joan mobilized *Impromptu*'s crew, stopped off at the local sheriff, asked directions to the victim's home, wept with the bereaved, and asked how she could help. They could think of nothing she could offer. Joan arranged to buy the family a new truck, then paid expenses for family members to take time off work so they could attend the funeral. She even offered up the services of her attorney to help bring the killers to justice, but was refused.

There were the more calculated gifts. When Rosalynn and Jimmy Carter came to town to build dozens of houses for the poor through their Habitat for Humanity project, Joan invited them to lunch and gifted them with a hundred thousand shares of McDonald's stock to launch the Carter Center. After the meal, the president picked up a newspaper and found, to his surprise, that McDonald's was trading at around $36 a share; the gift was even more generous than he'd realized.

To outsiders, she was the embodiment of her persona — "St. Joan," surprising staff and patients at the hospice when she dropped by with flowers; squiring local kids around to art exhibits on her custom Greyhound bus; calling in to a talk radio program and surprising her friend Father Carroll with a gift of $825,000 (he'd been talking on the air about how he needed to expand the homeless shelter). She and the rest of the rat pack knew well the irony of the nickname. Joan was neither saint nor angel. She had a bawdy sense of humor, and she smoked like a fiend. She'd invite people along for a ride on the plane, and then capriciously cut them out of the trip when she'd filled it up with more interesting companions. She was demanding of her friends and especially her employees, expecting people in her orbit to be available day or night. There seemed to be a revolving door of employees in her service, except those to whom she was loyal, who stayed with her for years. The phone could ring at any hour. Shades of Ray: When she felt she'd been wronged, the offender was exiled immediately and forever. Explained one baseball employee, "If I said, 'Oh, she was great to work for and it was a piece of cake,' I wouldn't be telling the truth."

As grand as she was, she could be equally parsimonious. Keeping her plane at the ready cost a million dollars a year, but she was stingy with benefits for the crew and secretaries. Yet she'd gift staffers or friends cars and houses and pianos the way anyone else might pick up lunch, and, on a whim, dash off a million dollars to a charitable cause she knew or cared little about.

She gambled like, well, like a woman once

ranked forty-ninth richest in the world. She might win or lose a million dollars in a night, and if she won, the money would trickle down to both her entourage and the dealer. After a Ronald McDonald House event in Philadelphia, she made her way via hired limo to Atlantic City and stayed up all night at the blackjack table, winning a quarter of a million dollars before she had to appear bright and early to talk about the charity in the New York studios of the *Today* show.

She'd progressed beyond the need to suffer through social obligations. Like a bad girl cutting class, she ducked out of the opera to puff away in the ladies' room and said she'd give the company a million dollars if she could just skip the show and go to dinner. (She did both.)

Though she stuck to her proclamation that marriage was of no interest, she did manage to carry on a decade-long, on-again, off-again romance with Phil Bifulk, a businessman from back in her native Minnesota. They'd first met as teenagers in St. Paul, when Joan played piano at the Golden Rule Department Store in the service of selling sheet music, and Phil was a salesclerk in the men's department. After they'd reconnected in 1991, he became Joan's steady escort. The pair even tooled around the country in Joan's new motor home for a while. Yet she'd kept him at arm's length. A full-time man underfoot was too much of a distraction.

She was playful as a cat, though she preferred dogs. Once, she found a lost dog outside a restaurant, took it home, offered a reward to find its rightful owner, then, to help her deduce any clues to its provenance, enlisted the services of a therapist who believed she could converse with animals. Something about the new Gulfstream IV she bought herself in 1990 didn't feel quite right, so she sold it after a week — and bought another. *Impromptu* functioned like a pickup truck, cruising the skies in the service of joyful errands, frivolous ones, missions of sorrow. When Norman Cousins died of a heart attack at a hotel near UCLA in 1990, where he'd gone to meet a young concert pianist, Joan made *Impromptu* available to transport his remains to the family plot in New Jersey. When a friend from whom she sought spiritual guidance, the mystical priest Father Henri Nouwen, expired on a visit to his native Holland, Joan sent the plane to return his body to Canada, where he'd lived in a community of disabled adults.

She had been introduced to Father Nouwen through another such friend, Fred Rogers, the cardigan-wearing star of children's public television. Mr. Rogers had earned his ordination as a Presbyterian minister in the early years of his on-air career. His life's work had been a response to his dismay with the gross commercialization of the medium; he'd long crusaded against advertisements targeted to kids. Still, he'd accepted an offer to write an essay for McDonald's 1988 annual report, and later won a $100,000 award from Ronald McDonald House Children's Charities. It was there that he'd met with Joan, who began to send his production company handsome checks of support. Joan even consented to do something she typically didn't: serve on the board of his nonprofit production company. Phil joined her.

Mr. Rogers. Father Henri. Jimmy Carter. Father Ted. Men of rock-solid faith, earthly manifestations of her higher power, from whom she sought solace, wisdom, and counsel. Was allying with these sages a protective shield? Did these friendships fortify her from her own transgressions? Help her make peace with the tremendous wealth she'd been handed? Assist her in reconciling the pain of her youth, the complications of her adulthood? Associating with these holy souls imbued a sense of equilibrium, of equanimity to her free-ranging life. Though she was deeply spiritual, and said she believed in God, she didn't identify with any one faith in particular — a true maverick. (One of the books she enthusiastically gifted to friends was titled *When Religion Becomes Evil.*) She was as ecumenical in her devotion as she was in the way she doled out the fast-food fortune.

But she never forgot her modest roots. When the recipient of a multimillion-dollar gift from Joan got the seven-dollar wire-transfer fee waived, she was delighted. When Father Ted turned eighty-five, she sat at her kitchen table and made out a check for $5 million, instead of the usual million-dollar birthday gift. She wanted to knock his socks off. She sent a maid scrambling through the house to find a stamp with the new postage rate on it, so she didn't have to overpay by using two of the old ones.

No matter how much she gave, or how grandly, Joan still had this nagging sense she wasn't doing enough. One day in 1997, she asked Maureen to go for a ride to check out the rougher parts of town. Maureen hadn't been mayor for five years, but she still put stock, as she had when she posed as a homeless woman, in field experience. To serve as their squire, they enlisted a veteran beat cop, Police Sgt. Mike O'Neill. He took them out in his Ford Aerostar.

The two heiresses halted the car frequently so they could get out and chat up their fellow San Diegans. They learned about their daily tribulations: The yard sales that brought them much-needed extra cash. Parents who worried where their kids could safely spend time after school while they toiled at second jobs. How unexpected expenses, like illness or repairs, upended the family's monthly budget. These struggles hadn't been Joan's or Maureen's realities for years, but they were realities baked into them from their youth. Coming face-to-face with them gave them pause.

For months afterward, Joan thought long and hard about what she could do to help. In search of a coconspirator, and for reasons that were never entirely clear, she contacted the local chapter of the Salvation Army. To the average person, this was a charity whose members rang bells at Christmas to raise money for the poor; maintained thrift stores where bargain clothing and housewares could be found; and swooped in to help a community at the time of a disaster. Some might know the Army for its work in addiction treatment, or in sheltering the poor. At its essence, though, the Army was an evangelical Christian church — as well as one of the most skillful fund-raisers in the nation. Members adhered to a rigid hierarchical structure. They did not smoke, drink alcohol, or gamble. They lived modestly, and wore uniforms to show their commitment to saving the world, believing they'd been called as God's people. Their reasons for being were simple: saving souls, growing saints, and serving suffering humanity.

At least on that last count, Joan's interests intersected with the Army's. She admired their resolve, and their lifestyle choices, and their dedication, even if formal religion wasn't her cup of tea. Over the years, Joan had sent in modest (for her) donations to the group to subsidize holiday meals. The Army had a reputation for fiscal prudence. She needed a coconspirator she could trust.

Everyone in town lived in hope of getting a call from St. Joan. By now, most knew not to bother asking. If they did, they'd be denied. The Army prepared to answer this mysterious call.

Her intentions became clear over lunch with local leaders of the group, as she recalled her childhood, the impact of a skating competition she'd worked hard to win in the frozen Midwest. Then, she revealed her assignment: Draw up plans for a recreation center where kids who need it can go. "Think big," she told them. "Bigger than you've thought before." The Salvation Army wasn't exactly in the business of dreaming about building a community center, but they didn't say no.

Options were prepared, and presented at the next series of meetings. The most expensive one featured an ice rink. That was the one she chose. Her pledge of $80 million to build and maintain it was the largest gift the Army had ever received.

Just as Ray's minions had scouted out locations for the early McDonald's based on proximity to families they'd hope to convert to customers, the church's team charged with executing Joan's vision now scouted for an appropriate parcel for her center. The criteria were similar: Go where the families are. Army brass zeroed in on a run-down lot in an old San Diego neighborhood eight miles east of the water. The area's undulating topography had long ago inspired the name, with a pinch of Spanish lilt as a nod to the nearby Mexican border: Ro-lan-do. Forces seemed to be conspiring in their favor. The purchase price was half what had been budgeted. More good news: This plot of land — about the size of her own home — had no houses on it, and therefore, no one would need to be displaced. "That's the working of the Holy Spirit," said Joan, swept up in the magic of how her wishes were falling into place.

At the groundbreaking, she jumped into the tractor and gleefully scooped up the first dirt. The long process of excavation and building tried her patience. "For god's sake, put up a shack or something," her staff advised Army brass in charge of the project. The project organizers complied by getting area kids to paint murals on plywood that were tacked up around the site to mask the gigantic hole in the ground. Even before it was complete, Joan was so sure it would serve as a beacon for the community that she whispered to the man in charge of the project her plans to give a billion dollars so that ten more could be built just like it around the country.

Several years, and over $50 million, later — including $40 million she tucked away to sustain the cost of operations — Joan's world-class recreation center had risen where run-down old stores used to be. One hundred seventy-five thousand feet of fun: The regulation ice rink. An Olympic pool.

A skateboard park. A wellness center. Fitness equipment. Meeting rooms. A library and performing arts venue. Fees would be low or no cost, depending on the means of the members. This wasn't just a place where neighbors could come together. It was, in Joan's estimation, a mini–peace center.

The "Corps" in the Ray and Joan Kroc Corps Community Center was shorthand in Salvation Army–speak for "church." The rest of the name spoke for itself. It was the first time since he'd died that Joan attached Ray's name to a gift. This was something, Joan said, she was sure Ray would have wanted her to do.

To lend a celebrity touch to the gala grand opening, Joan flew in Fred Rogers. Residents of Rolando were as dazzled by the presence of a television star as they were with the gleaming new center. As he made his way to the podium, he swapped out his jacket for a cardigan emblazoned with the Salvation Army logo, then addressed the crowd in his trademark soft, deliberate tone:

"Many people in our time look at a neighborhood which could easily breed dope dealing, robbery, and murder," he said. "Their reaction is to build bigger prisons. Not Joan Kroc. Her reaction is to build bigger swimming pools."

■ ■ ■

And buy pianos. A fancy six-figure Bösendorfer, one of the best instruments money could buy, similar to the one Joan had at home, was an essential part of the six-hundred-seat theater on the grounds. The Joan B. Kroc Performing Arts Center would host dance troupes, theatrical groups, and other performing artists when the Salvation Army itself wasn't using it as a church — a tidy unintended consequence of Joan's grand gift.

Nine months after the opening, the pall surrounding the once rundown plot had already begun to lift. Six thousand people had signed up for memberships. Fitness classes and swimming lessons and community meetings and preschool filled the campus with life. Housing prices in the neighboring area were beginning to rise; other businesses snapped up nearby real estate; proximity to the center was touted with pride. Before you knew it, there'd be a Starbucks in the neighborhood.

The night a famous singer came to play would give extra luster to this jewel. Stardom for singer Tony Bennett had grown ever larger since Joan entertained the diners at the Criterion with his music over forty years earlier. She and Ray had found themselves in the dazzling position of, over the years, being able to commission him for the occasional party. This time, she enlisted him to play at a special benefit concert.

The house was packed. The superstar Bennett thrilled the crowd with his standards, "Smile" and "I Left My Heart in San Francisco." With just a guitar as accompaniment, he gave a rousing performance of "Fly Me to the Moon." When he shooed the band off the stage for a break, a surprise guest emerged from the wings to thunderous applause: the benefactress, Joan. She took a seat on the piano bench, and the storied singer began to croon her favorite song, "Our Love Is Here to Stay" — as she played along.

The impromptu performance lifted the crowd out of their seats.

12
ST. JOAN

On the occasion of her seventy-fifth birthday in the summer of 2003, Joan decided to throw herself a party. It would be a small, early afternoon affair, just a handful of guests, gathering for lunch and champagne at her grand 16,000-square-foot estate, which she'd built for herself after Ray's death, in the exclusive Fairbanks Ranch community, the place she called Montagna de la Paloma.

Typically, when she hosted a group, Joan preferred to entertain at Rancho Valencia, the luxury resort down the hill. "The RV," she jokingly called the five-star establishment, where she liked to entertain in the private dining room. Since her custom-designed Lalique crystal dining room table seated just fourteen people, it never worked to have a larger group for a sit-down at home. Besides, too much traffic on the grounds of her property aggravated her collection of dogs.

At this stage, though, home was easier. Everything needed to be as simple as possible.

Now that other, grander decisions had been made, the guest list fell into place. Only Maureen O'Connor, the youngest of the rat pack at age fifty-seven, was in good enough health to attend. Mercedes, now eighty-seven, and Helen, eighty, had both been suffering the consequences of age. Joan had confided to Helen on her peachy insignia letterhead a few weeks before that she herself had been diagnosed with a serious medical condition:

. . . since I don't write the script I do not know how it will turn out.

I've had a walk-on part with a few positive words such as faith, hope, peace, love and justice.

She asked Helen to keep the this information confidential, which she knew she'd understand. Imagine the vultures swirling after hearing her news.

Another on Joan's guest list was a new but cherished friend: The dashing chief of National Public Radio, Kevin Klose, would fly in from headquarters in Washington.

He'd accompany the woman who'd introduced him to Joan, Stephanie Bergsma, a
fund-raiser for KPBS, the San Diego affili-
ate of both PBS and NPR. Despite Joan's
deep affection for public television star Fred
Rogers, she was not otherwise an overly
devoted fan of public media. Like so many,
she conflated PBS (TV) and NPR (radio)
as one entity, and the confusion was aggravated by the station's name. She'd given
a tiny donation to KPBS years before, to
support production of a film on child abuse.
More recently, she'd contributed $3 million
for equipment to furnish the station's new
building, but that was as much to support
Helen and her son, who spearheaded the
campaign. When Joan had finally consented
to a tour of their new facility, administrators observed that she seemed more concerned about where in the building she
could light up a cigarette without setting off
an alarm than seeing the fruits of her donation.

Bergsma and Joan had connected for
reasons that had nothing to do with radio
or television. Bergsma's husband had spent
his last days in the magnificent hospice Joan
had underwritten, and had sent a letter
thanking her for providing such a beautiful,
serene place to die. By the time Joan called

to talk with him, he had passed away. The women had lunch, and, skilled fund-raiser that she was, Bergsma reached out to her counterparts on the network level to see if she might set up informational meetings with Joan. The PBS contacts never returned the calls, nor did they return separate inquiries from Joan's advisors. NPR's Klose, on the other hand, leaped at the chance to meet her. Over a breakfast meeting, he explained how the public radio network gathered news and charmed her with his eloquent discourse about the power and importance of journalism and a free press to democracy, how public radio played a critical role in keeping society informed. Dazzled, Joan stuck a check in a Christmas card to Klose for half a million dollars, a token for her, but only the third time the network had ever received a gift of that size from an individual.

The executive director of the Kroc Institute for International Peace Studies at Notre Dame, Scott Appleby, would attend the party to represent the university. So would his counterpart, Joyce Neu, the head of the second such center Joan had underwritten, housed at the University of San Diego. The 90,000-square-foot Joan B. Kroc Institute of Peace and Justice looked like a cousin of the Taj Mahal, perched high on a hillside. She had actually intended for it to be named after the Indian leader Mohandas K. Gandhi. (This was sure to ensure good "McKarma," wags joked, noting the source of the donation and the fact that cows were sacred in Gandhi's native land.) But Joan had had to settle for having her name attached to the institute as a substitution for the storied man. Certain higher-ups at the Catholic school squirmed over the name of a Hindu adorning one of their buildings.

With her name prominently attached to two major Catholic universities, people just assumed she was one herself. The Catholic bishop of San Diego was on her birthday guest list, after all. Others believed she must be a Salvationist. To represent her coconspirator in the recreation center, Joan invited Commissioner Linda Bond, the church's recently installed territorial commander for the West. The two women had met earlier in the year, and there had been an immediate click. Joan had been impressed by this powerful woman, the thirteenth child of a Canadian miner, who'd risen through the ranks within the church hierarchy. Commissioner Bond, in turn, had been taken by how informed, how well read, how *alive* was this woman who had funded the incredible center in Rolando. In fact, the religious leader found herself wishing Joan weren't so rich so they could have a normal friendship. Joan had suggested to her, when she admired her collection of dogs, that she get a pet for herself. Bond, who was single, explained she traveled too much to care for one. A package from Joan arrived a few days later containing a stuffed bear — covered in mink — to keep her company. It was a lavish possession for Bond, a woman who'd committed her life to God and community service.

Though the Kroc Center was flourishing in the year since it had opened, Joan had had some sticking points with its operation. Staff had rebuffed the San Diego Gay Men's Chorus, whose organizers had hoped to rent the luxurious theater for a concert. Word of the discrimination got out to the local gay press, which ran with the story. Chorus administration didn't want Joan to think they were dismayed with her personally; she was a hero in the gay community for her long-standing support of AIDS patients and research. The group's president wrote a personal note of apology to Joan, ashamed that her good name had been dragged into negative news. She invited him to lunch; then she upbraided Army higher-ups for their intolerance; and *then* she gifted the chorus with a $105,000 Bösendorfer half-grand concert piano, a twin of the one she'd had installed at the center. The present was the grandest the chorus had ever received.

Of course, family was on the guest list: her daughter, Linda, and Linda's daughters, Allison, Amy, Amanda, and Holly, all grown now and living nearby. She had hoped, after their lives had twisted and turned, that they might want to "step into Grandma's boots" as philanthropists. Though she had refused to start up a foundation of her own again, she'd set aside hundreds of millions of dollars in one she called the Four Flowers, in honor of her nickname for them. But she'd been disappointed. The girls never took up the cause, and the foundation had been dissolved, without a penny being spent.

Joan would dispatch the *Impromptu* to fetch her only sister, Gloria, and her husband, Jay, from back home in Minnesota. From the time Joan's brother-in-law left his job in the stockyards to work alongside Rollie in St. Louis Park, McDonald's had come to dominate their lives, too. Jay became a franchisee and at one point owned nearly two dozen stores. He was proud to have followed an advertising agency's recommendation that he install collection boxes at his store's drive-throughs, allowing spare change to be gathered from customers for his area Ronald McDonald House.

On the way west, *Impromptu* would stop to pick up a good friend from her South Dakota days, Thelma. Joan's butler and her maid and her trusted advisors, the coexecutors of her will, would be in attendance. So would her doctor.

One person who would not be present was her companion, Phil. Shortly after Joan had received the news from her doctor, she'd sent him home for good to Minnesota, perhaps to spare him watching her demise.

As soon as the list was complete, the swirl of pre-party busyness began. The bright desert light streamed through the floor-to-ceiling windows, reflecting onto the crystal dining table. Joan remembered the joy she had experienced while building out the place, her own personal oasis. That day the semi arrived on the grounds, piled up with endless trees to add to the mature ones already on the land, the capstone to this grand creation she'd had constructed for herself. The warmth and flicker in the cold desert nights of the fireplace specially designed for the center of the enormous living space. Her beloved piano, which she now didn't have the energy to play.

For a dozen years, this lavish home — the first place she ever lived in on her own — had provided a joyous sanctuary. Nights of silly fun with the rat pack, where they'd have dinner and dial up those pricey call-in astrology numbers — when they weren't off on her plane or her yacht, headed to or from some gambling or shopping adventure. A team of full-time gardeners clipping and pruning the landscaping to keep it pristine, just the way she liked it. Maintenance men tending the Olympic-size pool, always turned up to a toasty ninety-five degrees. The dogs chasing after her as she tooled around the property in her golf cart, a cigarette dangling from her manicured hands.

She could feel the warm rush of nicotine from her lungs to her head.

Since her diagnosis with brain cancer just a few months ago, there had been more bustle and activity than usual on the compound, with so much to organize and to consider. Everyone falling all over themselves to please her, to make their presence known. All wondering, secretly, about her plans for the fortune.

The whirring and buzzing about excited

Joan, even though it was painful to move right now. She was starting to lose her words and her wits in a veil of confusion. One of the staff had caught her feeding cash into a paper shredder.

On the morning of the party, Joan asked her guests to be alerted — those who didn't know the secret — so they weren't blind-sided about her condition on their arrival.

"You are going to see something at Mrs. Kroc's house today that will disturb you," they were told by telephone. "Don't be worried, though. Everything is going to be all right."

Family members were cautioned to please not discuss the details with the other guests, so as not to darken the collective mood. The same cone of silence Joan's circle had abided for years now: to leave what was better left unsaid, unsaid. Everyone who came into contact with Joan knew well this edict: Wall out the inevitable curious outsiders. Especially the press. She hated the idea that someone might write a book about her. Her death wouldn't mean the end of the edict for silence.

The elegant millionaire greeted her well-wishers from the comfort of her new indispensible accessory, her wheelchair. Her hair and makeup were perfectly done, her nails, as always, meticulously manicured. Cosmetics, though, could not mask the drooping of her mouth and eye, nor could they correct her slurring speech. The deeper meaning of the warning call began to click into focus. And yet, the words rang false: Looking at Joan, nothing at all seemed as if it would be all right.

Over the course of the next few hours, cake was sliced and champagne glasses were kept filled to the brim by the attentive waitstaff. Not a single word was uttered about cause or illness or outcome — exactly the way Joan wished.

Toasts were made to the generosity, kindness, and happiness that St. Joan — St. Joan of the Arches — had brought to those gathered here today, and to San Diego, and the world beyond.

With her butler's help to navigate her around the room, Mrs. Kroc managed a private moment with each of her guests to assure them, brightly, that "we are going to do great things together." The guests smiled, sweetly, politely, sadly in affirmation, not quite understanding her mysterious words, uttered as if this were a game of Clue. Before everyone left, Joan joked with Commissioner Bond in front of the others. What would she do, she asked, if she left her house — this sprawling, magnificent acreage — to the Salvation Army? Awkward laughter followed. Didn't everyone here hope Joan would leave them something so grand? They were all already part of an exclusive club of recipients of her generosity.

A crane arrived at Joan's property to hoist the massive Henry Moore sculpture to its new home. The ten-ton bronze *Figure in a Shelter,* a celebration of maternal warmth and comfort, was to reside in the garden behind the Kroc Center library, the latest starry addition to the Rolando neighborhood. Kids instantly treated this museum piece like a very pricey jungle gym. Joan wished to see the monumental work in its new home, and so she was whisked over, pushed in her wheelchair for the view. No one at the center had known, till then, that she was ill. Her hair covered in a kerchief, she gazed from the sidelines at children gliding happily on the skating rink, swimmers splashing in the pool, the words of Fred Rogers at the center's opening echoing:

Our world hangs like a magnificent jewel in the vastness of space. Every one of us is a facet of that jewel. And in the perspective of infinity, our differences are infinitesimal. We are all intimately related. May we never even pretend that we are not.

It was time to go home.

Joan died in her own bed, surrounded by her daughter and granddaughters in her 660-square-foot bedroom, on Sunday, October 12, 2003, at eight thirty in the morning. Her remains were interred directly beneath Ray's, in a crypt that overlooks a thicket of trees in the Vista of Sunset at the Mausoleum of the Bells, just around the corner from the Sanctuary of Love. Her office issued a statement which gave a brief overview of some of her major gifts. In its own press release, McDonald's called her a great woman: "The world has lost a true humanitarian, and McDonald's has lost a true friend."

The memorial service she'd orchestrated was held on the Sunday before Thanksgiving. Guests, hand-selected by Joan, arrived at the glorious "garden of the sea," behind her peace institute at the University of San Diego, with its soaring views of the bay and the Pacific Ocean.

At her request, San Diego's bishop, Robert Brom, led the service. The four speakers Joan had asked to deliver remarks took their turns: Linda Bond, who held inside a tremendous secret; Father Ted Hesburgh; former president Jimmy Carter; and Joan's granddaughter Amanda.

Billowy clouds imprinted on the garden's large reflecting pool. The guests sat flanked by the two sculptures installed amid the shrubbery, facing each other: one a gift from Joan, a bronze by Giacomo Manzu of a seated cardinal; the other of St. Francis of Assisi, the holy man who'd devoted his life to serving the poor. On one side of a card given to guests was printed a prayer so frequently attributed to the saint that it had incorrectly become identified as his own:

> Lord, make me an instrument of your
>   peace.
> Where there is hatred, let me sow love.
> Where there is injury, pardon.
> Where there is doubt, faith.
> Where there is darkness, light.
> Where there is sadness, joy.
>
> O DIVINE MASTER,
> grant that I may not so much seek to be
>   consoled as to console;
> to be understood as to understand;
> to be loved as to love.
> For it is in giving that we receive;

it is in pardoning that we are pardoned;
and it is in dying that we are born to eternal
life.

A photograph of Joan at her most elegant
graced the card's reverse: The blond beauty
perched on the bench in front of her beloved
white Bösendorfer piano, smiling, trim and
radiant in a white pantsuit, long nails
painted red; simple, elegant gold jewelry ac-
centing her neck and wrist. This was the
Joan Ray had fallen for, years ago, only
older, and fiercer, with finer accoutrements,
and the means to exercise her big heart.

No organ, or piano, was played at the
service. The only music was provided by a
harp.

POSTSCRIPT

It was up to Joan's coexecutors, Dick Starmann, the former McDonald's executive who had long served as her advisor, and Nancy Trestick, her longtime assistant, to enact her final wishes. This involved fending off crass, curious callers who wondered if they'd been "remembered" in her will; closing up her home to protect it and its contents; asking the court to seal the names of those listed in her trust, to protect beneficiaries from predators; informing the charities that had been recipients of her final gifts; and routing the money where she intended it to go.

A major part of their work included summoning Commissioner Linda Bond, who left behind Salvation Army business in Oregon to go to California to attend the urgent meeting. When she arrived in San Diego, she was driven to Joan's office building in La Jolla. Lunch was brought in. As they dispensed with pleasantries and ate out of Styrofoam containers, a copy of the trust was slid across the table for her review.

Joan not only had willed Montagna de la Paloma to the Salvation Army, as she'd hinted, but had left instructions that Bond was to convey the enormous news to the rest of her flock: The church was to receive the bulk of her fortune and use it to replicate the center that had been built in San Diego. The sum was $1.5 billion, give or take several hundred million dollars, depending on the economic condition of the markets at the time the money was delivered. It was the largest philanthropic gift ever made by an individual in the United States.

Top Army brass called it a "gift from God," but the major windfall presented a bewitching challenge. Senior church leaders prayed about whether they could accept the gift, which tasked them specifically with building more centers like the one in Rolando — a major undertaking outside of the Army's usual area of expertise. There was fear that the enormous donation would discourage others from giving — "donor creep," it was called in fund-raising. The church only formally agreed to accept the sum just before it was revealed to the public, in January 2004, after the Christmas bell-ringing season. (Wiring the money into the account proved a banking challenge: too many zeroes.)

The plan was firm, but loose: The Army would have to figure out how to enact her wishes. Half of her gift, Joan had stipulated, was to go toward building Kroc Centers, from scratch; retrofitting old buildings was not permitted. The other half would be deposited in an endowment to keep the centers running. The money was to be divided across the four quadrants that split the United States.

Despite the enormity of the gift, it would not be enough to sustain the centers. That left local chapters of the group with the challenge of raising money for this specific purpose. Bids were called for from cities across the country, and locals had to prove they could build and sustain and fund-raise to support their own Kroc Center. In several communities, like Detroit and Long Beach, California, goals went unmet and centers were never built.

Today, twenty-six Ray and Joan Kroc Community Corps Centers have been opened, from Hawaii to Puerto Rico, where kids skate and swim and play after school; where adults lift weights, sweat in exercise classes, and hold meetings — and anyone who wants to participate can worship in "Kroc Churches," even though recruiting converts to the religion wasn't the intention of Joan's gift.

The year after the gift was announced, Bond suddenly resigned her position in the church. She returned to service a year later. In 2011, she was elected to its highest office, General — only the third time a woman had been named its international leader. Two years later, she retired abruptly and vanished from public life.

Kevin Klose received his news via telephone in his office at NPR's headquarters in Washington, D.C. "Are you sitting down?" asked coexecutor Starmann. Then he commanded the executive to pick up a pen and start writing down zeroes. Six of them. Klose had once said he hoped Joan might make a donation to NPR at the elite $25,000 level. In fact, Starmann told him, Joan had left the network approximately $220 million. It was the money that had been earmarked for the Four Flowers. (The sum reached $236 million by the time the gift was delivered.) "Is that the silver club or the gold club?" Starmann quipped.

This was more than twice the network's annual budget and the largest gift NPR had

414

ever received. The quinoa- and kale-eating public radio employees brought in Big Macs at lunch the day the gift was announced in November 2003. One vice president, Jay Kernis, remarked that it was like Christmas and the lottery, all rolled into one. The emerita network host Susan Stamberg joked she was changing her name to "McStamberg."

The bulk of the gift, about $190 million, was earmarked for the network's endowment, which, until Joan's beneficence, only contained $35 million. Interest alone now would amount to $10 million a year. The remaining $20 million plus went directly to NPR's operational costs.

As the Salvation Army leaders had been, top NPR brass was befuddled by the windfall. Would it dissuade devoted listeners from opening their pocketbooks to give to member stations? How would station personnel feel? They were perennially in fundraising mode, paying the network handsome fees for programming. It was they who were on the front lines of the muddled identity between network and affiliates; they would have to explain to listeners that this Kroc windfall didn't trickle down directly into their coffers. And what about the cranks who routinely criticized the network for receiving government funding? (In truth, NPR got a tiny portion of its funds from the government, but this myth was pervasive among the network's detractors.)

By the next year, NPR administrators had hatched a plan: To flesh out news coverage worldwide, seventy new staff positions would be added, along with an internship program named for Joan. Fees paid to the network by member stations were temporarily lowered. Joan's landmark contribution was acknowledged in the lobby of NPR's grand new $200 million headquarters that opened in 2013, and she's thanked on the air each day.

One by one, other gifts were revealed and announced with pride and fanfare. Sixty million dollars to be spread among the 120 Ronald McDonald Houses that had been formed in the United States since that seed fund created back in 1977 in honor of Ray. Fifty million dollars apiece to each of the two peace centers Joan had built. Twenty million dollars to San Diego Hospice. Ten million each to the Zoo and the opera she'd once walked out on. Five million to KPBS. A million to Crazy Horse. Half a million dollars each to two groups in San Diego that helped AIDS patients: Mama's

Kitchen, a meal delivery service for those with the disease, and Auntie Helen's Fluff n Fold, a laundry service for the afflicted.

In all, about $2.7 billion — the lion's share of the fortune.

Joan's first husband, Rollie, preceded her in death by just three weeks. He was killed in a car accident on September 23, 2003. A recreation center, Smith Youth Sports Complex, stands in Whitefish, Montana, a gift made by his daughter before his passing.

As for the rat pack: Mercedes McCambridge died five months after Joan, on March 2, 2004. Helen died six months later, on August 25, 2004.

Newspaper reports pointed to these losses as a reason for the troubling decline of Mayor Mo. In 2013, Maureen O'Connor pleaded not guilty to a charge of money laundering and admitted to taking $2.1 million out of her late husband's charitable foundation to support her gambling addiction, making more than a billion dollars in bets and losing around $13 million. She blamed the problem on a brain tumor. That her good friend Joan was herself a high roller was never mentioned. In exchange for having the charges dropped, Maureen promised to pay back the money.

■ ■ ■

Mac McDonald died on December 11, 1971, in Palm Springs. In 1964, Dick Mc-Donald married his high school sweetheart, Dorothy, and returned to their native New Hampshire. After Ray's death launched a flurry of tributes to the "founder" of Mc-Donald's, Dick waged a campaign to ensure his and his brother's contributions as the true founders were acknowledged. In August 1991, *The Wall Street Journal* ran a story headlined: "McDonald's Pickle: He Began Fast Food but Gets No Credit. History according to Kroc Irks Dick Mc-Donald, Who Rid the World of Carhops." It spawned, as high-profile news articles often do, a flurry of interest and other interviews. It also inspired longtime PR man Al Golin to write an impassioned response in support of Ray's legacy: "When a baby is left on a doorstep of a home — the true father is the one who raised and educated that baby to maturity. The McDonald's Restaurant's father is Ray Kroc." Were that true, wags noted, the famous sandwich would be called not a "Big Mac" but a "Big Kroc."

In 1993, Dick was awarded an honorary doctor of commerce degree from Bellevue

University in Nebraska. He died in 1998.

Harry Sonneborn died in Alabama on September 21, 1992; June Martino, in Florida, on January 29, 2005. Her family asked that in lieu of flowers, gifts be given instead to Ronald McDonald House. Fred Turner died on January 7, 2013. Max Cooper passed away in August 2015 at the age of ninety-nine. At one point he owned more than forty McDonald's outposts in Alabama. Harry had convinced him to get into the business there. Cooper also fulfilled his dream of producing plays on Broadway, for which he won two Tony Awards.

Songwriter Steve Vaus continued to use his musical talents to promote political and social messages, although in a different direction from Joan's. A supporter of the Tea Party and a gun rights advocate, his hit "Wrong's Not Right" was an indictment of Bill Clinton. Under the name Buck Howdy, he won a Grammy in 2010 for his children's recordings. Vaus was elected mayor of Poway, California, in 2014.

As for the fate of several of Joan's beneficiaries: San Diego Hospice declared bankruptcy in February 2013 and was acquired by a local hospital, Scripps. The San Diego Opera announced in 2014 that it was closing due to budget shortfalls, but was subsequently rescued.

Hazelden and Betty Ford merged their treatment centers in 2013. Operation Cork's offshoot at Dartmouth, Project Cork, is in the process of donating its vast database of materials about addiction to Hazelden.

In South Dakota, the Ziolkowski family used its final bequest from Joan to commission a musical laser light show that, on summer nights, explodes onto the side of the mountain where Crazy Horse's likeness continues to emerge. A credit to Joan is given at the end of the show. Joan's gift of western art was not on display when I visited in November 2015. The sculpture of Ray still stands in the visitor center, a random diversion from the Native American art and artifacts that surround it.

What was left of Joan's personal art collection was auctioned by Christie's, along with her jewels.

The *Chain Reaction* sculpture by Paul Conrad funded anonymously by Joan and erected in 1991 was found to be in disrepair in late 2011. Given what they said would be the prohibitive cost of fixing it, the Santa Monica City Council considered the possibility of "deaccessioning" the work. Supporters, including the late artist's son, Dave, and local activist Jerry Rubin, rallied a dedicated group that called itself the "Chain Gang" to raise $100,000 from a host of people, from schoolchildren to well-known figures like Norman Lear, Ed Asner, Martin Sheen, Tim Robbins, Ed Ruscha, and Dr. Helen Caldicott. They also got permission from Joan's daughter, Linda, to remove the cloak of secrecy over the gift from Joan that made it possible for the sculpture to be built. The City Council voted six to one on February 25, 2014, to preserve the monument. It is currently being restored, and there are plans to surround it with a "peace park." There's also talk of a plaque to honor Joan's gift, for making the work possible.

The nuclear mushroom cloud that the McDonald's fortune built stands as one of the more unusual legacies of Joan's inventive giving. It's also one of the enduring reminders of the power of a chance encounter to change the course of a kaleidoscope of lives. Two brothers who migrated west; a salesman in search of a lucky break; a beautiful young woman who dreamed of a world beyond her own. Joan could never have imagined that night she met Ray in St. Paul just how big her life would become, or how many lives she'd touch — all because of the race to sell fast food.

ACKNOWLEDGMENTS

Do what's in front of you.
　　　　　　　— MOTHER TERESA

Like the story of Ray and Joan, this book has itself been a curious collision of seemingly random incidents that could not have been completed without the help, big and small, of dozens of people.

Had Gary Scott and Jennifer Ferro not lured me to work at public radio station KCRW, and then allowed me to make up the dream job of "arts reporter," I would never have gone to the Santa Monica civic center to investigate the fate of the Paul Conrad sculpture *Chain Reaction* on February 1, 2012.

Had inveterate peace activist Jerry Rubin not met me there that day and whispered the secret he figured a public radio reporter would want to know — that it was NPR philanthropist Joan Kroc who had underwritten the artwork anonymously more than twenty years earlier — I would not have gone in search of a biography of her. (There wasn't one, so I appointed myself the woman for the job.)

Had the person I call "Coach" not taken my call, I might have been dissuaded from the pursuit. Coach encouraged me "not to write a coffee table book" but, rather, an honest appraisal of Joan's life.

I thank these three people, for while these last four years have not been easy, reconstructing the lives of Ray and Joan has greatly enriched my own. It's also intensified my belief that something perceived as a negative force often contains positive elements.

While the families of Ray and Joan were reluctant to speak with me, I am grateful for the interactions we did have, and hope they see why I felt this story was an important one to tell. I particularly appreciate Linda Ardell Wendfeldt, Amy Ragen, and Amanda Latimer for their graciousness; Charles Nerger, Skipi L. Smoot, and Shelley Wood-Goldstein for their generous insights; and Ballard Smith for running interference.

My wise agent, Dan Conaway, pushed me to explore the Ray part of the Joan equation from the beginning. I am grateful for his forbearance, as well as that of his assistant, Taylor Templeton. The expert elegance of "proposal whisperer" Genevieve Gagne-Hawes allowed this project to find a home with the amazing Jill Schwartzman at Dutton, a dream editor with whom I'd hoped to work for years. (This is where I once again publicly thank Bob Sullivan for the fortuitous introduction many moons ago.) Thanks to attorney Yuki Hirose, publicist Liza Cassity, and all the team at Dutton for their enthusiasm for this project and diligence in getting it into the world.

Jane Cavolina said, "Don't worry," just when I needed to hear those words.

Chief among my many wise and loving friends, family, and supportive colleagues, I thank my father, Vince, who instilled in me a love of and fascination with history. My brother, James, who is too far away. My aunt Mary McTague gave me quiet harbor in her beautiful home in Delray Beach, Florida; thanks to my other cheering squad of aunties, biological and adopted, chief among them: Kay Napoli, Alice Martin and Marian Moos, Lynn Barnett and Judi Lang Robaina. Dr. Eyassu and Mrs. Lucy Habte-Gabr, and their extended family, have embraced me in their lives in a loving way.

In particular, those who have endured my

musings and angst and offered support through the twists and turns and uncertainties of this kind of undertaking include Brian Averna, Alison Berger, Kate Bergh, Merrill Brown, Matthew Coltrin, Liz Dubelman and Paul Slansky, David Friedland and Diego Vega, Hope Hamashige, Elizabeth Kaplan, Doug Krizner, Judi Laing, Tracy Layton, Fiona Ng, Matthew Mirapaul, Borany Pheng, Alesia Powell, Barbara Rybka, Andy Schwartzman, Katherine Stern Weaver, James Suskin, Michael Tirrell, Carolyn Wagner, Preston Wiles (the world's most patient photographer), and Bernie Woodall. Always and especially, I'm grateful for our household's sage and dear guiding light, Code One, Dr. George Moore.

Despite her busy schedule, Lisa Baertlein volunteered to take charge of our monthly cooking club at the Downtown Women's Center so I could give this project full-time attention.

Lucinda Bartley, Bruno Giussani, Seth Godin, Rick Meyer, and Dr. Peter Whybrow offered their ears, eyes, and early encouragement. Marty Harding and Barbara Weiner warmly welcomed me during my visit to Hazelden.

My colleagues KCRW producer Avishay

Artsy, who was with me on that fateful day in the Santa Monica civic center, and art critic Hunter Drohojowska-Philp were patient and flexible as my many research trips interrupted our normal recording days. For a radio story I did about *Chain Reaction,* Steve Chiotakis did a dramatic read of the Joan Kroc funding credit, which he ably reads many times each day. Marissa Gluck originally covered the story for *LA Weekly* that piqued my interest and was also present the first time I stood under the mushroom cloud.

The largely unexplored period of Joan's Rapid City phase took me to that gem of a city several times, perhaps my favorite part of this research. Despite Joan's nickname for the place, I fell in love with it, in no small part because of the very fine people who helped me there — specifically and especially the very dear kindred spirit, historian and preservationist Jean Kessloff. She, her wonderful husband, Bill, and Kim Morey kindly put their lives on hold to squire me around. Lois Facer and Eric Abrahmson fed me and gave me warm harbor. Thanks to Stanford Adelstein, Katherine Le Clair, Reid Riner, and Mike Quasney.

Art critic Edward Goldman and his "art

gypsies," Michael Krass at Insight LA, Leslie Sherwood James of the Upland Shakespeare Club, and Janet Parr of the Rapid City Public Library all kindly invited me to talk to their respective communities about this story before it had taken shape as a book. The enthusiasm and questions of their audiences convinced me the story of Ray and Joan needed to be told.

Figures in the lives of the Krocs warmly welcomed me into their homes and jogged their memories, including Dr. Peter Amacher, Kay Conrad (whose son Dave graciously facilitated the meeting, while at the same time interrupting his life to work to preserve his father's sculpture), Glenn and Phyllis Jorgenson, Rev. John and Doris Keller, Dr. Alice Hayes, Wendy Gross De-Woskin, Vyonne Glaze, Sylvia Conrad, Mary Lou Lowry, Gila Saks, and Tom Gruber.

James McGrath Morris offered wise counsel. The indispensible resource he created, Biographers International, has been a source of fellowship, inspiration, and solace during the challenges of discovery. I eagerly await their monthly newsletter, *The Biographer's Craft,* edited by Michael Burgan, and their annual conference. Biographer Justin Martin offered welcome mentorship.

A particular thanks to the many skilled

and patient archivists who assisted me — in particular Glenn Griffin, who has been a delightful advisor and coconspirator since I first discovered him at Hubbard Broadcasting. The Minnesota Historical Society is fortunate to share his time and his talents.

So many others contributed time, insights, memories, or connections. I've kept this list for years and apologize for any omissions:

Richard Adams, Dee Aker, Jeanne Anderson, Don Barnett, Robert Berman, Chuck Bieler, Ed Borgman, Claudia Black, Barry Bloom, Cathleen Brooks, George Burtness, Sue Bielenberg, Phil Bifulk, Michael Bigger, Ellen Bishop, John Boop, Elizabeth Braham Spencer, Beth Bruton, Maria Burton, Dr. Helen Caldicott, Kate Callen, Robert Cass, Tim Clancy, Norm Clarke, Ron Cleveringa, Burger Boat Company, Max Cooper, Candis Cousins, Jim Crouch, Marguerite Cullum, Alison Da Rosa, David J. Dahl, Bill C. Davis, Bill Deane, John DeMott, Sen. Byron Dorgan, Paul F. Doscher, Dr. Carl Dragstedt, James Ferguson, Jeremy Farmer, Donnali Fifeld, Peter Fimrite, Shirley Forbing, Chris Fowler, Lynn Fox, Walter Fredenhagen, Barbara Fredricks, James T. Friedman, Judith Freeman, David Garfield Roland, Roger Genser, Andrew Goldstein, Al Golin, Martin Gostanian,

Mike Granberry, Thomas Gruber, Kenneth Gubitz, Scott Harris, David Hasenmeyer, Alice Hattemer, Alan Hess, Stanley Hubbard Jr., Scott P. Janik, Glenn Jordan, Robert Blair Kaiser, Tom Karlo, Mark A. Kellner, CarolLee Kidd at CLK Transcription, Dr. Bruce King, Jean Kinney, Jane Klain, Therese Klosterman, Lois Kroc, Ted Leitner, Chris Lemmon, Dan Lilejedahl, Lawrence Luckinbill, Ellen MacDonald, Joseph Maguire, Sandy McCullough, Jennifer McElroy, Ed McLaughlin, Alan Miller, Marcia Mitchell, Susan Morrow, Melinda Frohling Moser, Doug Myrland, Susan Myrland, Mark Nerger, Steve Oney, Pat Owens, Erasmo Paolo, Ashley Parker, Judd Patton, Judy Perlstein, Dr. Trevor Price, Earl Prince Jr., Don Porter, Michael Quinn, Kay Rippencrop, Officer Rosario, Susan Rosser, Linda Rudell-Betts, Trevor Schaefer, Roy Sea, Ann Seaman, Bob Schweich, Sunny Sherman, Ed Sikov, Andrea Skorepa, Kathryn Slater-Carter, Charlie Smith, Dr. David Smith, Jolene Smith, Dr. James Snoddy, Steven Joel Speirs, Larry Spivey, Andy Strasberg, Josh Stein, Ken Stern, Art Stilwell, Dr. James Strickler, Dr. Louis Sullivan, Mike Sund, Gay Swenson, Richard Taite, Rev. Bruce Thalacker, Fred Tully, Larry Turman, Scott Turow, Rick Waechter, Emily-

Rose Wagner, Melissa Wagoner, Alice Walker, Sis Wenger, Terry C. Williams, Donn R. Wilson, Emily Uhrin, Steve Vaus, Melanie Vogel, Monica Zech, Kerstin Zilm, Jadwiga Ziolkowski, Seyburn Zorthian. My neighbors Nicole Gordon, Mary Anne Hillier, and Jill Hoskins provided sustenance in the way of kindness during the marathon of writing that produced this book.

Thanks, too, to those who spoke with me who preferred not to be listed.

Many times as I have pored through old newspaper archives during my research, I have lamented the demise of newspapers, a time when San Diego was covered by skilled journalists at two daily papers as well as a crew charged with putting out a local version of the *Los Angeles Times.* While I've worked as much as possible to reconstruct these stories myself with original reporting, the work of those skilled reporters who came before me has been invaluable. Many generously filled in blanks.

Learning to love reading at a branch of the Brooklyn Public Library system as a child instilled in me an early passion for libraries, but nothing could have made me appreciate and revere librarians and archivists more than dipping into mid-century

American history. Particular thanks are due to the magnificent repository of information up the street from my home, the Los Angeles Public Library, whose resources, human and tangible, I counted on almost every single day of this project. It also happens to be the location of a life-changing experience I had seven years ago.

This book was predominantly written in my home on Bunker Hill in downtown Los Angeles. I could never have embarked on, much less finished, such a mammoth mental exercise without the physical recreation I allowed myself at the wondrous Ketchum YMCA swimming pool. (The nourishing Jupiter gong performance of Kundalini teacher HariSant helped, too.)

Most of all, though, I've depended on and been nourished by the incomparable love, support, and boundless enthusiasm of my life partner, Ted Habte-Gabr. His joyful patience and curiosity sustain me each day, as do our shared passion, values, and commitment to the world beyond our own cozy existence. That I could complete this work is a testament to that, and to our love.

APPENDIX:
WHERE DID THE FAST-FOOD
FORTUNE GO?

> There are so many gifts you don't know about. When you hear she did one gift, there were probably thirty others.
> — FATHER JOE CARROLL

Before the likes of Warren Buffett, Bill Gates, and Mark Zuckerberg received deserved acclaim for pledging their fortunes to charity, Joan Kroc did just that, with no fanfare. This list is provided to show the breadth and depth of her giving as it evolved over her lifetime.

Data on this list is very specific from 1984 through 1991 because that is when the Joan B. Kroc Foundation was operational. Foundations must report their donations on tax returns known as 990s. (The Joseph and Matthew Payton Philanthropic Studies Archives at Indiana University–Purdue University Indianapolis Library does the important work of archiving these returns, as well as foundation annual reports; otherwise, in this case at least, they'd have been lost to history.)

Many of Joan's gifts, however, were not written out of foundation coffers but rather from her personal funds. Some of the entries here I've deduced from newspaper reports; others, from personal interviews or archives. Compiling a comprehensive list would be impossible, since Joan dissolved her foundation and left no papers, and since she gave so many gifts anonymously. Due to space limitations, we offer an abridged list here; the complete list will be available on my website, www.rayandjoan.com.

A word of caution, and semantics: Each day, twenty million listeners of public radio across the United States hear a funding credit that mentions the "estate of Joan Kroc." Many incorrectly assume the estate is still actively dispersing funds. It is not. After her executors implemented the final wishes of the benefactress, the estate was dissolved. Countless other people who visit the Ray and Joan Kroc Corps Community Centers believe the gift made to establish those centers came from the Joan Kroc Foundation. It did not. By the time they were built, the foundation had long ago ceased to exist.

For a better understanding of philanthropic structure and giving, I recommend Ken Stern's *With Charity for All* and Tracy Gary's *Inspired Giving: Your Step-by-Step Guide to Creating a Giving Plan and Leaving a Legacy*. I also recommend the resources of Guidestar and CitizenAudit.org when investigating any nonprofit you choose to support. These resources will allow you to look under the hood of the charity's finances.

My intention in writing this book, in general, and with this list specifically, is not only to bring attention to Joan's inventive philanthropy, but to inspire others to give, in whatever ways they can. Naturally, most of us cannot give on the scale of the Krocs. But that shouldn't stop us from giving in other ways — of our money, our time, and our compassion.

1965

Ray A. Kroc Foundation established with $84,000 after the initial public offering of McDonald's stock. Over the next four years, a total of $70,875 in gifts are given to Henrotin Hospital, Northwest Community Hospital, Centinela Valley Hospital, the Girl Scouts, the Boy Scouts, and the Salvation Army.

435

1969

Renamed The Kroc Foundation.

1972

Rapid City flood relief	$50,000
Ray's seventieth birthday gifts	$7,500,000

Includes gifts to: The Ray A. Kroc Foundation, PACE Program/Cook County Jail, Recording for the Blind; Northwestern Memorial Hospital; Adler Planetarium; St. Jude's Children's Research Hospital; Lincoln Park Zoo; Field Museum of Natural History; Children's Memorial Hospital; Rapid City, South Dakota, public library; Harvard Congregational Church, Oak Park, Illinois.

1975

National Multiple Sclerosis Society	$1,000,000
Children's Memorial Hospital	$10,000,000

1976

Operation Cork launches through The Kroc Foundation.

1977

Ray and Joan Kroc Fund at $1,000,000
   Dartmouth Medical
   School

1983

After convening more than one hundred conferences in the medical sciences, and granting an unspecified sum in the millions to fund medical research, $33 million in assets are transferred from The Kroc Foundation to establish the Joan B. Kroc Foundation. This occurs after final gifts are made funding medical research at fifty institutions, and after the establishment of three endowed professorships named for Robert L. Kroc at Harvard University, University of California, San Francisco, and Washington University in St. Louis. Among the gifts Joan's foundation made that year:

Old Globe Theatre, San Diego	$25,000
Big Sister League	$50,000
San Diego Zoo	$100,000

1984

Olympic Torch Relay	$150,000
San Ysidro Victims' Fund	$100,000
Winning Wheels, Inc., Prophetstown, Illinois	$17,994

Courage Center, Golden Valley, Minnesota	$25,000
San Diego Hospice Corp.	$5,000
Pepperdine University, Malibu, California	$7,500
UCLA Writers Conference in China	$1,000
Scripps/Chest Medicine Research Fund	$100,000
National Foundation for Ileitis and Colitis	$100,000
County of San Diego adoption training	$1,400
KPBS-TV child abuse community outreach program	$3,000
UCSD Medical Center Ultracentrifuge for Neonatology	$45,000
Center for Defense Information to videotape Women's Conference to Prevent Nuclear War	$1,000
Betty Ford Center Construction of Cork Family Pavilion	$500,000
Mid-City Senior Enterprises	$10,000
American Red Cross Ethiopian famine relief	$1,000,000
American Diabetes Association	$25,000

SHARE San Diego/Food for needy	$5,000
San Diego Department of Mental Health Program for mentally ill adults	$500
Child Abuse Prevention Foundation	$150,000
Rachel's Women's Center (homeless women)	$25,000
UCLA Medical School Program in bio-behavioral sciences	$318,355
Hazelden Cork Sports Pavilion	$2,455,306
Project Cork Institute/Dartmouth	$1,000,000

Other grants in 1984 were made to: organizations involved with addiction-related issues, including education and training programs in chemical dependency for San Diego agencies concerned with child abuse; National Council on Alcoholism; Mothers Against Drunk Drivers, and Deaf Community Services in San Diego for services for chemically dependent deaf persons.

1985

The Beyond War Foundation	$100,000
Center for Defense Information	$500,000

439

Courage Center	$500,000
Grants in support of psychoneuroimmunology research directed by Norman Cousins	$702,400
Hazelden/Cork Sports Education	$6,184,947
Home of Guiding Hands	$25,000
Morehouse School of Medicine	$1,400,000
Salvation Army	$31,500
St. Vincent de Paul Center for Homeless	$500,000
UCLA Medical School purchase of cytometer	$302,460
Union of Concerned Scientists	$50,000
Women's Action for New Directions Educational Fund	$140,000
San Diego Zoo	$3,300,000
Advertisements for peace	$1,250,000
Rights to reprint *Missile Envy*	$1,000,000
Mothers Embracing Nuclear Disarmament	$1,000,000

Additional substance-abuse-related gifts in 1985 included grants to UCSD Medical School in alcoholism research; scholarships for a substance abuse workshop at San Diego State University; a drug-alcohol education program for the elderly at Villa View Community Hospital in San Diego; distribution of films and printed materials; and additional funds for chemical dependence training at agencies concerned with child abuse prevention.

1986

Drug Services Bureau, San Diego County, Adolescent Treatment Services	$250,000
Hazelden Foundation	$4,316,459
House of Hope, Fort Lauderdale	$5,000
Gifts to San Diego community programs	$201,700
Educational programs conducted by Operation Cork	$355,013
The Beyond War Foundation	$10,000
The Catticus Corporation	$100,000
Center for Defense Information	$500,000
Grandmothers for Peace	$500
Natural Resources Defense Council	$500,000
Bronx Municipal Hospital Center Services of AIDS Patients	$5,673

441

Medical Associates Research and Education Foundation Research *for* Children Cured of Cancer	$117,053
National Multiple Sclerosis Society	$50,000
Sickle Cell Anemia Education and Information Center	$1,000
UCSD Medical Center Pediatrics Dept.	$124,942
UCSD School of Medicine alcoholism research	$30,000
The University of Illinois Dept. of Surgery	$25,000
Grants in support of psychoneuroimmunology research directed by Norman Cousins	$601,956
Child Abuse Prevention Foundation	$10,000
The Elizabeth Hospice	$5,000
Home of Guiding Hands	$125,000
Mid-City Senior Enterprises	$25,000
North Coast (San Diego) Family YMCA	$100,000
The Salvation Army Holiday Meals	$15,000
San Diego Hospice Corporation	$274,241
Winning Wheels, Inc.	$32,000

YMCA of San Diego County	$50,000
Citizens Participation Project	$400,000
League of Women Voters of California Educational Fund	$10,000
San Diegans for an Independent Judiciary	$10,000
St. Vincent de Paul Homeless Shelter, San Diego	$3,000,000

1987

Albert Einstein College of Medicine AIDS education	$1,000,000
Cystic Fibrosis Foundation	$25,000
Institute for Child Behavior Research	$6,400
Medical Associates Research & Education Foundation	$119,868
New York City Health & Hospitals AIDS Day Hospital	$3,000,000
KPBS Television	$1,000
Grants in support of psychoneuroimmunology research directed by Norman Cousins	$377,289
The Martin Luther King, Jr., Center for Nonviolent Social Change	$25,000

New Entra Casa, San Diego, California	$63,000
Project I Believe Fund Scholarships for Inner-city Students	$10,000
Rockford Memorial Foundation	$10,000
The Salvation Army holiday meals	$500
San Diego Hospice Corporation	$3,458,810
Tender Loving Zoo, Inc., therapy program	$5,000
COACH, Inc.	$245,000
National Council on Alcoholism	$1,000,000
Better World Society, Inc.	$15,000
Beyond War	$50,000
Bread and Roses Community Fund	$75,000
Catticus Corporation	$170,000
Center for Defense Information	$200,000
Eschaton Foundation	$6,000
Federation of American Scientists Fund	$250,000
Greenpeace USA Incorporated	$62,500
Peace Links	$100,000
Spacewatch	$125,000
Forum Institute voter registration and education	$1,000,000

Democratic Party	$1,000,000
Ronald McDonald Children's Charities	(Donation of J and R Double Arch Ranch; ultimately yielding $6 million)

(Local authorities denied permission for the ranch to be used as a camp for young cancer patients. "I hope," Joan said in response, "it's sold to some crazy rock 'n' roll stars who keep the neighbors up all night." It was, in fact, sold for $6 million in 1990 to the dietary supplement impresario Gerald Kessler, who, for a time, raised ostriches on the property and held seminars for his Human Potential Foundation.)

1988

American Foundation for AIDS Research	$1,000,000
Kettering Foundation Research in Psychoneuroimmunology	$2,000,000
San Diego Soviet Festival	$1,000,000
Medical Associates Research and Education Foundation/research for children cured of cancer	$128,002

Ronald McDonald Children's Charities	$100,000
Scripps Clinic and Research Cancer Research	$70,000
Grants in support of psychoneuroimmunology research directed by Norman Cousins	$1,000,000
Boys Clubs of San Diego	$5,000
Casa Familiar, San Ysidro, California	$67,500
Child Abuse Prevention Foundation	$25,000
Childhelp, USA	$1,000
National Public Radio	$2,500
The Salvation Army	$1,450
San Diego Hospice Corporation	$833,429
San Diego Service Center for the Blind	$5,000
Westside Center for Independent Living	$50,000
YWCA of San Diego County Battered Women Services	$5,000
Carl Rogers Institute for Peace	$10,000
Center for Defense Information	$100,000
Federation of American Scientists Fund	$220,000
Peace Links	$100,000

University of Notre Dame	$6,000,000
Center for Participation in Democracy	$150,000
League of Women Voters, Rancho Palos Verdes, CA	$1,000

1989

Charles R. Drew University	$25,000
Epilepsy Society of San Diego County	$10,000
Regents of the University of California Pediatric Oncology Fellowship	$200,000
Scripps Clinic and Research Foundation/Lung Cancer Research	$25,000
The Jonas Salk Foundation/AIDS Research	$901,028
The University of Illinois Institute for Surgical Studies	$25,000
Casa Familiar/Amanecer, San Ysidro, California	$10,000
Children's Hospital Foundation/Center for Child Protection	$50,000
Children's Hospital of Philadelphia/Hospice Program	$200,000
Clair Burgener Foundation	$1,000
Copley Family YMCA	$500

Family Service & Mental Health Center	$50,000
San Diego Hospice Corporation	$1,429,266
Winning Wheels, Inc.	$25,575
YWCA of San Diego County	$10,000
Horatio Alger Association	$5,000
International Institute for Women's Political Leadership	$25,000
San Diego Youth Symphony	$125,000
United Negro College Fund	$1,000
Peace Links	$25,000
San Diego Theatre Foundation (La Jolla Playhouse)	$400,000
San Diego City County Scholarship Fund	$1,000,000
DePaul University Theater	$500,000

1990

Carter Center	$3,600,000
Desert Living Preserve	$200,000
Design Alliance to Combat AIDS/Desert AIDS Project	$2,600,000

1991

Joan B. Kroc Foundation Dissolved January 14, 1991

St. Vincent de Paul Center	$343,700
Fund for Animals	$103,110

1993

Ronald McDonald Houses $60,000,000

1994

Family Communications $400,000
    (Mr. Rogers)

1995

Ronald McDonald House $50,000,000
    Charities
Betty Ford Center $1,000,000
Special Olympics $1,000,000

1996

University of San Diego/ $3,000,000
    no-interest student loans
St. Vincent de Paul $500,000

1997

Grand Forks/East Grand $15,000,000
    Forks Flood Assistance
San Diego Opera $1,000,000
San Diego Council on $10,000
    Literacy
Money to family of James   unspecified
    Byrd
Four Flowers Foundation   *established*

1998

Four Flowers Foundation   *dissolved*

| The Salvation Army Ray and Joan Kroc Corps Community Center | (pledge) (total $87,000,000) |
| University of San Diego Peace Center | $25,000,000 |

2000

| Kroc-Copley Animal Shelter | $2,000,000 |

2002

| Notre Dame on the occasion of Father Ted Hesburgh's eighty-fifth birthday | $5,000,000 |
| National Public Radio | $500,000 |

2003

Gifts announced posthumously

The Salvation Army	$1,500,000,000
NPR	$225,000,000
Ronald McDonald House Charities	$60,000,000
Joan B. Kroc Institute for Peace and Justice, University of San Diego	$50,000,000
Joan B. Kroc Institute for International Peace Studies, University of Notre Dame	$50,000,000
San Diego Hospice	$20,000,000
San Diego Zoo	$10,000,000

San Diego Opera	$10,000,000
KPBS	$5,000,000
Catholic Diocese of San Diego for construction of Mater Dei High School	$5,000,000
Special Olympics	$5,000,000
Betty Ford Center	$5,000,000
Crazy Horse Foundation	$1,000,000
San Diego Children's Hospital	$1,000,000
Mama's Kitchen, San Diego	$500,000
Auntie Helen's Fluff N' Fold, San Diego	$500,000

NOTES

Epigraph

From everyone who has: Luke 12:48 quote in reference to Joan. Lt. Colonel Donald Bell, "Bell Recalls Joan Kroc's 'Stealth Philanthropy,' " *New Frontier Chronicle,* January 20, 2004, accessed online January 23, 2016, http://www .newfrontierchronicle.org/bell-recalls-joan -krocs-stealth-philanthropy.

Chapter 1: Jewels

When she agreed to Ray's proposal: Skipi L. Smoot (niece of Ray's second wife, Jane Kroc), telephone conversation with author, August 8, 2015.

Ray was notorious: John F. Love, *McDonald's: Behind the Arches* (New York: Bantam Books, 1986), 89.

"chauvinistic corporation": Dave Distel,

453

"Joan Kroc: Madre Who Owns the Padres," *Los Angeles Times,* October 4, 1984, H1.

she sent her Gulfstream jet: Confidante of Joan Kroc, telephone conversation with author, January 13, 2015.

Joan requested her personal physician: Amanda Latimer (granddaughter of Joan Kroc), conversation with author, March 31, 2015.

ready source of cut flowers: Timothy Clancy (head gardener at Joan Kroc's property), telephone conversation with author, January 19, 2015.

"This is the saddest day . . .": Amanda Latimer, March 31, 2015.

unpredictable study in extremes: Confidante of Joan Kroc, telephone conversation with author, January 10, 2015.

spicy hint of Yves Saint Laurent's: Andy Strasberg (former San Diego Padres executive), telephone conversation with author, February 18, 2014. He loved her perfume so much, he'd ask to smell her each time he entered her office.

she might whisk down the hill: Timothy Clancy, January 19, 2015.

dognapping some mangy critter: Confidante of Joan Kroc, telephone conversation with author, February 13, 2013.

purebred Cavalier King Charles spaniels: Hartwell Pelson (owner of dogs from same breeder), telephone conversation with author, January 14, 2016; and confidante of Joan Kroc, telephone conversation with author, January 10, 2015.

Halloween would never be the same: Amanda Latimer, telephone conversation with author, October 8, 2015; and Hala Ali Aryan, "Luxurious Living: Fairbanks Ranch Embodies Wealth with Its Huge Houses, Gated Communities, and Parklike Grounds," *San Diego Union-Tribune,* August 11, 2002, N1.

"I don't want any tears": Amanda Latimer, March 31, 2015.

"I've had a great life": Mike Granberry, "Action: Helping People Is Part of Joan Kroc's Life: 'She Works Very Hard and Earns the Results She Gets,' " *Los Angeles Times,* March 10, 1983.

wide-ranging art collection: *19th Century European Art,* Christie's, Wednesday, April 19, 2006 (New York); and *Important American Paintings, Drawings and Sculpture,* Christie's, Thursday, November 30, 2006 (New York).

whose father struggled: Jeff Savage, "Remembering Dad with Tales and Tears," *San Diego Tribune,* June 20, 1987, B3.

at odds with her mother: Linda A. Wendfeldt (daughter of Joan Kroc), e-mail to author, August 19, 2015.

claimed the fifty-dollar first prize: Linda A. Wendfeldt, letter to author, April 2, 2015.

The unfathomable sum: Linda A. Wendfeldt, e-mail to author, June 11, 2015.

giving had been her greatest gift: Ed Jahn, "Philanthropists Say Giving Is the Reward," *San Diego Union,* May 12, 1985, B1.

helping faceless strangers: Linda A. Wendfeldt, e-mail to author, August 19, 2015.

fix the world's problems: Tom Cushman, "For Joan, the Decision to Sell Was a Natural," *San Diego Tribune,* November 21, 1986, E1.

life was hard: Mike Granberry, "Helping People Is Part of Joan Kroc's Life," *Los Angeles Times,* March 10, 1983, SD_C1.

No one was exempt: Suzanne Choney, "Joan Kroc: A Year of Wins, and Losses," *San Diego Union,* October 19, 1984, A1.

It had complicated her life: Granberry, "Helping People . . ."

rotgut whiskey Early Times: Confidante of Joan Kroc, conversation with author, June 16, 2012.

Members of his inner circle: Confidante of Joan Kroc, telephone conversation with author, January 10, 2014, and conversation with author, December 3, 2012; Donn Wilson (early McDonald's executive), telephone conversation with author, August 19, 2015; and former employee of Ray Kroc, telephone conversation with author, April 29, 2014.

a less Hollywood version: Scott Harris, "Dismayed by Nuclear Arms Race: McDonald's Fortune Fuels Joan Kroc's Peace Effort," *Los Angeles Times,* October 13, 1985, 1.

"Ray loved my mother . . .": Ibid., quoting Joan's daughter, Linda.

She believed he loved her: Murray Dubin, "She's More than the Padres' Madre," *Philadelphia Inquirer,* October 13, 1984, D1.

What was love: Wendy Gross (former PR person for Golin/Operation Cork), conversation with author, April 25, 2014.

started to open up: Ray Kroc Memorial, *Crews Views,* McDonald's internal newsletter, February 1984.

After he'd died: Harris, "Dismayed by Nuclear Arms . . ."

"I liked the dog": Person involved with the building of the Kroc Center, conversations with author, July 23, 2012, and January 16, 2016.

It was *Ray's* money: Max Cooper (PR man/McDonald's executive/franchisee affiliated with McDonald's for more than fifty years), telephone conversation with author, February 5, 2015. He said, "People say she's a great philanthropist. She didn't make the money. She inherited the money."

the old guard cringed: Letter from McDonald's PR man Al Golin to lyricist Sammy Cahn, September 7, 1977, Series 7 Biography, Folder Ray Kroc f1044, Sammy Cahn papers, Margaret Herrick Library, Academy of Motion Picture Arts and Sciences, Beverly Hills, CA.

changed her last will and testament: Confidante of Joan Kroc, telephone conversation with author, January 10, 2015.

an accident of birth: Choney, "Joan Kroc: A Year of Wins, and Losses."

harbored tremendous ambition: Tony Perry, "Philanthropy That Was Deeply Personal: Joan Kroc Chose Her Projects Carefully and Strove for Top Quality, Regardless of Cost," *Los Angeles Times,* January 31, 2004, A1.

Allison, the eldest: Robert Blair Kaiser,

"Linda Smith: Coming of Age, Ballard's Wife Has Dreams of Her Own," *San Diego Tribune*, February 25, 1985, C1.

Love, instead of hate: Amanda Latimer, "My Grandma's Love: Joan Kroc's Granddaughter Shares a Personal Message from Her Grandma," *Caring Magazine* 19, no. 2 (Summer 2012): 16–17.

"never seen a Brink's truck . . .": "McDonald's Heir Gives $80 Million to Salvation Army," *New York Times,* September 24, 1998.

the company had been advised: Love, *McDonald's,* 212.

donations of $7.5 million: Ralph Novak, "The McDonald's Man: What Ray Kroc Hath Wrought around the World," *People,* May 19, 1975.

more than $250,000 to President Nixon's: Celia Torres-Spelliscy, "Justices Should Think of Quarter Pounders in Latest Money in Politics Case," *Brennan Center for Justice Blog,* September 24, 2013, accessed online December 13, 2015, https://www.brennancenter.org/blog/ justices-should-think-quarter-pounders -latest-money-politics-case.

Ray had ordered the flags: Adam Bernstein, "Fred Turner, Savvy Operations Chief Who Built McDonald's Empire,

Dies at 80," *Washington Post,* January 8, 2013.

"ladylike or proper": Choney, "Joan Kroc: A Year of Wins, and Losses"; and Robert Blair Kaiser, "A New Force: Joan Kroc's Out of Shadow and Forging Her Own Image," *San Diego Tribune,* October 10, 1984, C-1.

doing things his way: Joan Kroc, "The Ray Kroc 75th Birthday Tribute," private press, 33 1/3 rpm LP, recorded at Continental Plaza, Chicago, October 8, 1977.

remembered for hamburgers: Paula Story, "Salvation McArmy: Kroc Donates $80m," *Philadelphia Daily News,* September 24, 1998, 6.

the leather-bound Bible: Linda A. Wendfeldt, e-mail to author, October 25, 2015.

The "McEgg," . . . for which she paid: Gordon Smith, "Kroc Introduces 'McEgg'; $3 Million Faberge Jewel Will Garnish City's Arts Fest," *San Diego Tribune,* May 19, 1989, D1. The prolific collector of Fabergé eggs Malcolm Forbes expressed pleasure at the sale price, well over the highest price he'd paid for an egg, though he took issue with its lineage. Rita Reif, "Antiques; Not Imperial, Still Fabergé," *New York Times,* May 28, 1989, accessed online January 16, 2016, http://

www.nytimes.com/1989/05/28/arts/
antiques-not-imperial-but-still-faberge
.html.

"It's a little Republican.": Helen Copley,
Joan Kroc, Maureen O'Connor, interviewed by Jane Pauley, *Today,* NBC, May
25, 1989; Robert Laurence, " 'Today'
show in San Diego," *San Diego Union,*
May 25, 1989, C-1.

too much for breakfast-time TV: Confidante of Joan Kroc, telephone conversation with author, January 10, 2015.

Bulgari, Cartier, Van Cleef & Arpels:
Jeff Miller, "Christie's Magnificent Jewels
April 11 in NYC," *Diamonds.net,* March
13, 2006, http://www.diamonds.net/News/
NewsItem.aspx?ArticleID=14544, ac-
cessed online December 13, 2015; and
Christie's Rahul Kadakia, interviewed by
Matt Lauer, Katie Couric, Natalie Mo-
rales, *Today,* NBC, April 7, 2006.

**"Our world hangs like a magnificent
jewel . . .":** Fred Rogers, keynote address,
Ray and Joan Kroc Corps Community
Center — Grand Opening Ceremony,
June 19, 2002, video posted online No-
vember 12, 2013, by The Salvation Army
Ray and Joan Kroc Corps Community
Center, https://www.youtube.com/
watch?v=dupfehtm5Po.

Each day of her final weeks: Confidante of Joan Kroc, telephone conversation with author, January 10, 2015.

Chapter 2: Land of Crazed Speculation

Millions of oranges: Tom Spellman, "California's Second Great Gold Rush," *Garden Compass Magazine,* November/December 2002.

under the rubric "Giant Orange,": Gary Kinst (editor), "The Giant Oranges," Lincoln Highway Association — California Chapter, *The Traveler* 15, no. 1 (2014), www.lincolnhwy.org/ca/traveler.

They'd watched as their father: Thomas C. Dolly, "Pure Americana: The Founding of McDonald's, the True Story" (unpublished thesis, Bellevue University, 2009), 16.

"The Beacon is one of the . . .": "Big Attractions at Beacon Theater," *Covina Argus* (Covina, CA), August 8, 1932.

root beer stand named Wiley's: *Pure Americana: The Founding of McDonald's,* directed by Thomas C. Dolly (Bellevue, WA: Bellevue College Entrepreneurial Leadership Center, 1992), videocassette.

cut a deal with Sunkist: Dolly, "Pure Americana" (print version), 18.

Foothill Flying Field: Paul Freeman, "Abandoned and Little Known Airfields: California East Los Angeles Area," July 18, 2015, http://www.airfields-freeman .com/CA/Airfields_CA_LA_E.htm.

for film shoots: Jim Wigston, "Remembering the Monrovia Airport," *Monrovia Patch,* August 27, 2011, accessed online December 14, 2015, http://patch.com/ california/monrovia/remembering-the -monrovia-airport.

This venture was so successful: Dolly, "Pure Americana" (print version), 18.

establishment they'd call the "Dimer": Daniel Okrent, "The Man Who Invented Fast Food," *Chicago Tribune,* April 11, 1985; and Philip Langdon, *Orange Roofs, Golden Arches: The Architecture of American Chain Restaurants* (New York: Alfred A. Knopf, 1986), 89.

the workweek would shrink: Dick McDonald to Ray Kroc, Ray Kroc/McDonald Brothers Dictaphone Tapes, June 1957, A.

talk their way into a five-thousand-dollar loan: Dolly, "Pure Americana" (print version), 19.

employee named Ralph Evans: Ibid., 20.

ladies in usherette uniforms: Ibid., 20.

By 1950, forty million cars: Ibid., 67.

hamburger was de rigueur: Ibid., 29.

"winos and floaters . . .": "Over Seven Million Hamburgers Sold," *Drive-In Restaurant and Highway Café Magazine,* July 1952, 4, reprinted in McDonald's Offering Plan, 1958.

a cast of twenty carhops hopping: Letter from Richard J. McDonald to Thomas C. Dolly, November 12, 1990, Dolly papers, Freeman/Lozier Library, Special Collections, Bellevue University, Bellevue, NE.

"hoss and buggy system": Dick McDonald, interviewed in *David Halberstam's the Fifties, Vol. 6: The Rage Within and the Road to the Sixties,* directed by Alex Gibney, New York: History Channel, A&E Home Video, distributed by New Video Group, 1997.

"Levittown on a bun.": Jane Stern, interviewed in *David Halberstam's the Fifties.*

Dick deviously posed: Letter from Richard J. McDonald to Thomas C. Dolly, June 17, 1993, Dolly papers, Bellevue University.

Offering choice, the brothers said: Ray Kroc with Robert Anderson, *Grinding It Out: The Making of McDonald's* (Chicago: Henry Regnery, 1977), 66; and Love, *McDonald's,* 9–29.

they choreographed an assembly line:

Dolly, "Pure Americana" (print version), 23.

costly issue of personnel: "Twelve x Sixteen Foot Restaurant Space Sells One Million Hamburgers and 160 Tons of French Fries a Year," *American Restaurant Magazine,* July 1952, 44; and "French Fries, 10-Cents," *Food Service News,* June 1951, reprinted in "For You with an Ambition to Own Your Own Business," McDonald's Offering Plan.

painting of a rising thermometer: Dolly, "Pure Americana" (print version), 14.

a wizard of the spud: Kroc, *Grinding It Out,* 9.

Would-be imitators arrived: Philip Langdon, "Burgers! Shakes! How the Evolving Architecture of Fast-Food Chains Has Shaped the Character of America's Roadside Landscape," *The Atlantic,* December 1, 1985, 74–77.

"The Most Important Sixty Seconds . . .": Advertisement, *American Restaurant Magazine,* September 1952, 27.

he thought their name "lucky": David Halberstam, *The Fifties* (New York: Villard Books, 1993), 160.

Finding an architect: Alan Hess, "The Origins of McDonald's Golden Arches,"

465

Journal of the Society of Architectural Historians 45, no. 1 (March 1986): 60–67.

Bold, even wild, designs: Langdon, *Orange Roofs, Golden Arches,* 47.

cooked them up during a nightmare: Ibid., 84.

in Stanley Meston: Dirk Sutro, "Architect's Arches Got the Job Done," *Los Angeles Times,* January 5, 1989, SD-D1.

In 1953, store number three: Alan Hess (architectural historian), e-mail to author, October 15, 2013.

The dairy supplier Carnation: Dolly, "Pure Americana," 33.

a franchise agent, William Tansey: Ibid., 38.

Prince Castles, they were called: Elizabeth Braham Spencer, *One-in-a-Million: The Cock Robin and Prince Castles Story,* Naperville Community Television: 2004, accessed online November 20, 2015, http://www.naperville-lib.org/content/one -million.

three gallons a person: Associated Press, "Prohibition Booms Ice Cream Sales," *Daily Illini* (Champaign, IL), October 17, 1922.

The year 1936 inspired two: Chris Stach, "The Land of the Last One-in-a-Million," *Riverside-Brookfield* (IL) *Landmark,* September 13, 2005, accessed online January 23, 2016, http://www.rblandmark.com/News/Articles/9-13-2005/ The-land-of-the-last-One_In_A_Million.

state-of-the-art contraption: Ray Kroc, interviewed by Tom Snyder, *Tomorrow,* NBC, season 4, episode 154, June 16, 1977.

chain of Liggett's soda fountains: Advertisement, Liggett's, *Wilkes-Barre* (PA) *Record,* January 11, 1929, 5.

forty Prince Castles across Illinois: Spencer, *One-in-a-Million.*

The sales pitch: "Twoallbeefpattiesgoldarchesand$400million," *Palatine Herald* (Palatine, IL), April 12, 1975, 1.

"cocky and probably annoying . . .": Kroc, *Grinding It Out,* 19.

"Shave and a haircut, two bits": Ibid., 16.

after a semester, he dropped out: Ibid., 18.

nearby town of Paw-Paw Lake: Ibid., 21; and Elaine Cotsirilos Thomopolous, *Resorts of Berrien County* (Charleston, SC: Arcadia, 2005), 61.

his non-musical talent: talking: Ray Kroc, interviewed by Tom Snyder, *Tomorrow.*

Sam and Henry "lousy,": Kroc, *Grinding*

It Out, 25.

Ray couldn't relax: Ibid., 26.

3,500 drugstore soda fountains: Langdon, *Orange Roofs, Golden Arches,* 9.

free tour of this emerging paradise: Susan Gillis, *Fort Lauderdale: The Venice of America* (Charleston, SC: Arcadia, 2004), 30.

"I'd call them and fill them in": Kroc, *Grinding It Out,* 29.

his good luck disappeared: Ibid., 32.

quit in an insolent huff: Ibid., 42.

shown Ray their Multimixer: Harold Keen, "Kroc Talks," *San Diego Magazine,* March 1977.

Heeding Ray's enthusiasm: Elizabeth Braham Spencer (documentary filmmaker), telephone conversation with author, June 23, 2015; and Ted Fredenhagen (son of Multimixer cofounder), e-mail to author, June 25, 2015.

"veritable opera of Wagnerian strife.": Kroc, *Grinding It Out,* 73.

self-styled brand of hypnosis: Ibid., 57.

Soda Fountain Service *reincarnated itself: Langdon, *Orange Roofs, Golden Arches,* 93.

Prince and Fredenhagen had had it: Elizabeth Braham Spencer, June 23, 2015; and Ted Fredenhagen (son of Multimixer cofounder) e-mail to author, September 27, 2013.

"devil of a lot of milk shakes": Keen, "Kroc Talks."

in Los Angeles, the Apple Pan: Sunny Sherman (owner of Apple Pan), telephone conversation with author, August 12, 2015; and Stacy Perman, *In-N-Out Burger: A Behind-the-Counter Look at the Fast-Food Chain That Breaks All the Rules* (New York: Harper Business, 2010), 68.

". . . these guys have got something": Robert Tallon, "The Burger That Conquered the Country," *Time,* September 17, 1973.

"eh-pit-o-mee of the eh-pit-o-mee": Keen, "Kroc Talks."

Requests to franchise continued: Thomas C. Dolly, "McDonald's and Ray Kroc: The Early Years," *The Bottom Line* newsletter, Entrepreneurial Leadership Center, Bellevue University, vol. 10, no. 4 (Winter 1993–1994): 1.

a farmer called McDonald?: Max Boas and Steve Chain, *Big Mac: The Unauthorized Story of McDonald's* (New York: E. P. Dutton, 1976), 44.

It was "all-inclusive . . .": Ray Kroc interview, posted online November 26, 2011, accessed online April 27, 2016,

https://www.youtube.com/watch?v=vK
-Jb0zmlGQ.

he knew raw talent when he saw it: "Empire Is Built on 15-Cent Hamburgers," *Chicago Tribune,* October 22, 1972, section 10, 3.

To deal with inclement weather: Ray Kroc, interviewed by Phil Donahue, *Donahue,* May 1977 (Princeton, NJ: Films for the Humanities and Sciences, 1989), VHS.

he tried to cajole Earl Prince: Ted Fredenhagen, September 27, 2013.

Ray set about corralling: "Twoallbeefpattiesgoldarchesand400 million . . . ," *Palatine Herald* (IL), April 12, 1975, 1.

She had done without for years: Charles Nerger (great-nephew of Ethel Kroc), e-mail to author, March 21, 2015.

a life-or-death situation: Love, *McDonald's,* 47.

To soak up the routine: Alan Hess, e-mail to author, October 15, 2013.

Finally, on April 15, 1955: "Twoallbeefpatties . . . ," *Palatine Herald,* 1.

Chapter 3: Blond Beauty

The Criterion was considered: Brian Horrigan, "Minnesota State Capitol Architectural History," Minnesota Historical

Society, accessed online December 14, 2015, http://sites.mnhs.org/historic-sites/minnesota-state-capitol/architectural-history.

the Criterion's popovers: Linda A. Wendfeldt, e-mail to author, April 30, 2015.

A perfectly positioned mirror: Ibid.

Her blond hair elegantly styled: Choney, "Joan Kroc: A Year of Wins, and Losses."

"Baby Girl" Mansfield: August 26, 1928, Ramsey County, Minnesota, Birth Certificate 47178.

a star ice-skater: Perry, "Philanthropy That Was Deeply Personal."

perhaps, a veterinarian: Granberry, "Action: Helping People . . ."

Her GPA at Humboldt High: Daniel Liljedahl (librarian, archivist, Humboldt High School, St. Paul, MN), e-mail to author, January 14, 2015.

Joan excelled in the music lessons: Granberry, "Action: Helping People . . ."

instead of listening to a symphony: Wayne Wagstad, "Widow of McDonald's Founder Named as Anonymous Donor to Flood Victims," *Star-Tribune,* May 20, 1997.

"Hitler's death reported": Humboldt High School "Life," 1945, St. Paul, MN, 30–31.

"Joan will set men's hearts afire": Ibid., 25.

summer job as a pianist: Linda A. Wendfeldt, letter to author, April 2, 2015.

had just returned to his hometown: Linda A. Wendfeldt, e-mail to author, April 1, 2015.

pharmacist's mate in the navy: Rawland F. Smith, Notice of Separation from U.S. Naval Service, May 1946, Bureau of Naval Personnel, #3258.

age on the marriage certificate as twenty-one: Rawland F. Smith and Joan Mansfield marriage license, Certificate 9399, State of Montana, county of Flathead, July 19, 1956.

local broadcasting pioneer Stanley Hubbard: "Stanley E. Hubbard," *National Radio Hall of Fame,* http://www.radiohof .org/stanley_e_hubbard.htm, 2011.

he invested in one of the nation's: "KSTP Continues Pioneering Tradition in Public Service and Equipment Innovations," *Broadcast News,* vol. 113, May 1962, 34–58, accessed online December 14, 2015, http://www.americanradio history.com/Archive-RCA-Broadcast -News/RCA-113.pdf.

One of the news readers: Stanley S. Hubbard (son of Stanley E. Hubbard and chairman, Hubbard Broadcasting), telephone conversation with author, January 12, 2013.

One snippy patron: Tom Blair, *San Diego Union,* October 17, 1986, B1.

The Criterion music songbook: "Northwest's Finest: The Criterion Restaurant Songbook," undated.

her favorite song: Burl Stiff, "An Unscheduled Duet Is the Evening's Hit," *San Diego Union-Tribune,* March 23, 2003, E4.

To tout the latest shows: Love, *McDonald's,* 215.

"Mr. Multimixer" had tried: Peter Zien (son of James Zien, Criterion restaurant owner), conversation with author, January 11, 2013.

one of the drinks the Delecato: Kroc, *Grinding It Out,* 59.

"McDonald's Speedee Service Drive-Ins": McDonald's Offering Plan, 1.

"Here is a restaurant that . . .": *Drive-In Restaurant and Highway Café Magazine,* July 1952, 4.

"A merchandising trend through the country . . .": *American Restaurant Magazine,* July 1952, 44.

"It's the McDonald's System . . .": "For You with an Ambition to Own Your Own

Business," McDonald's Offering Plan, 2.

Ray's enthusiasm belied his years: Donald R. Conley, *Flying over the Golden Arches* (Edina, MN: Beaver's Pond Press, 2010), 99.

There were thirty-four stores: Dolly, "McDonald's and Ray Kroc: The Early Years," 1.

He'd quiz Dick and Mac: Ray Kroc to Dick and Mac McDonald, Ray Kroc/ McDonald Brothers Dictaphone tapes, 1957, Disc B, D.

Dick and Mac would parry: Dick McDonald to Ray Kroc, Ray Kroc/McDonald Brothers Dictaphone tapes, 1957, Disc B, D.

all day on the weekends there: Ray Kroc Deposition, September 24, 1969, 37, June Sonneborn v. Harry J. Sonneborn, 69C 279 (Il. Northern District, Eastern Division, Chicago).

"funny bone feeling": Ray Kroc quoted in Schupack v. McDonald's System, Inc. 264 N.W. 2d 827 (1978) 200 Neb. 485, 7 (Supreme Court of Nebraska).

plastered the name "Sandy's" on it: Ray to Dick McDonald, Ray Kroc/McDonald Brothers Dictaphone tapes, September 1958, Disc K.

One of the worst infractions: Love, *Mc-*

Donald's, 76.

"cooking with gas": Kroc, *Grinding It Out,* 90.

Right off the bat: Love, *McDonald's,* 81.

when Sandy Agate deigned to contract with Pepsi: Ibid., 82.

"The individual seeking to go into . . .": Ray Kroc to Dick McDonald, Ray Kroc/ McDonald Brothers Dictaphone tapes, March 1958, Disc F.

That he was Jewish: Ibid., October 1959, Disc R.

college dropout named Fred Turner: Kroc, *Grinding It Out,* 87.

married a musician: Sylvester Nelson and Marilyn Kroc, Marriage License 2679467, State of Illinois, County of Cook, April 27, 1959.

an exact replica of the vanity kit: Fred Turner, interviewed in *David Halberstam's the Fifties, Vol. 6: The Rage Within and the Road to the Sixties,* directed by Alex Gibney, New York: History Channel, A&E Home Video, distributed by New Video Group, 1997.

tales of his earlier days: Don Freeman, "Point of View," *San Diego Union,* January 17, 1984, D4; and Kroc, *Grinding It Out,* 19.

" 'Come to Jesus' in the key of C":

Freeman, "Point of View," *San Diego Union,* D4.

stunned by her blond beauty: Kroc, *Grinding It Out,* 111.

Chapter 4: First Fruits

unseasonable cold spell: "Cold Due to End Today: Warmer Air from Plains Brings Relief," *Chicago Daily Tribune,* November 18, 1959, 1.

"This deal smells to high heavens,": "Chamber President Presses Attack on City Council in Fight over Drive-in Permit," *St. Louis Park Dispatch* (St. Louis Park, MN), December 5, 1957.

Peavey himself was a catalyzing force: William J. Brown, *American Colossus: The Grain Elevator 1843–1943* (Brooklyn: Colossal Books, 2009), 222.

"Peavey's Folly," they mockingly called: Joseph Hart, "Peavey's Folly," *City Pages,* November 22, 1995, accessed online December 14, 2015, http://www.citypages.com/books/peaveys-folly-6720580.

"To be successful we must . . .": Stephen George, *Enterprising Minnesotans: 150 Years of Business Pioneers* (Minneapolis: University of Minnesota Press, 2003), 32.

"the magnificent first fruits . . .": Mardges Bacon, *Le Corbusier in America: Travels in the Land of the Timid* (Cambridge, MA: MIT Press, 2001), 114.

A citizen named Leo Schultz: "Fight Brews on Permit for Drive-in," *St. Louis Park Dispatch* (St. Louis Park, MN), November 21, 1957.

"monument of neon and tile": Letters, "Citizen calls mayor, council's stand on drive-in 'obstinate,' " *St. Louis Park Dispatch* (St. Louis Park, MN), January 23, 1958.

"towering, blinking monstrosity of a sign": "Huge Sign for Drive-in Approved," *St. Louis Park Dispatch* (St. Louis Park, MN), November 21, 1957.

Chamber president Meyers: "Drive-in Discussion Prompts Library 'Offer,' " *St. Louis Park Dispatch* (St. Louis Park, MN), December 12, 1957.

something else with the land: "The Case of the Disputed Drive-in," *St. Louis Park Dispatch* (St. Louis Park, MN), December 5, 1957.

franchise vision a bit "pie-in-the-sky,": Conley, *Flying over the Golden Arches,* 110.

a modest $150 a week: Ibid., 120.

"If he does that much business,": "Planners Get Drive-in Squabble," *St. Louis Park Dispatch* (St. Louis Park, MN), November 28, 1957.

the restaurant rang up $23,000 in sales: "McDonald's," St. Louis Park Historical Society website, accessed online July 17, 2012, revised website no longer has the page. http://www.slphistory.org/history/mcdonalds.asp.

"If you've never seen a sign . . .": "Sign, Burgers in Contrast at Zein's [*sic*] Drive-in," *St. Louis Park Dispatch* (St. Louis Park, MN), June 12, 1958.

Small talk gave way to duets: Kroc, *Grinding It Out,* 112.

off to see the St. Paul Saints: Joan Explains the Date in Nick Canepa, "Joan Kroc's Only Regret Is That Ray Isn't Here to Enjoy the Fun," *San Diego Tribune,* September 21, 1984, E1.

sanctity of marriage: Kroc, *Grinding It Out,* 112.

"Go home, your mother's calling,": Canepa, "Joan Kroc's Only Regret."

Rollie worked backbreaking twelve-hour days: Linda A. Wendfeldt, letter to author, April 2, 2015.

mere sound of her voice: Kroc, *Grinding It Out,* 112.

An invention called videotape: Max Cooper, telephone conversation with author, February 15, 2015.

After stints writing comedy: Greg Bass, "Remembering Max Cooper: Broadway Producer and Fast Food Tycoon," WBHM blog, posted online September 3, 2015, accessed online December 1, 2015, https://news.wbhm.org/feature/2015/remembering-max-cooper-broadway-producer-and-fast-food-tycoon; "Our (Baseball) Man in Havana: Adman Recalls Efforts to Bring U.S. Audiences TV Games from Cuba in 1959," *Advertising Age,* April 19, 1999, accessed online December 14, 2015, http://adage.com/article/opinion/baseball-man-havana-adman-recalls-effort-bring-u-s-audiences-tv-games-cuba-1959/62708.

a pinup magazine: Ben Burns, *Nitty Gritty: A White Editor in Black Journalism* (Jackson: University Press of Mississippi, 1996), 205.

Cooper negotiated a deal: "Baseball Becomes New Winter TV Sport," *Chicago Tribune,* November 11, 1959, Part 3, Section 2, 4.

very first, very pricey video recorders: Sylvie Castonguay, "50 Years of the Video Cassette Recorder," *WIPO Magazine* (Geneva), issue 6, December 2006, 8, accessed online December 15, 2015, http://www.wipo.int/export/sites/www/wipo_magazine/en/pdf/2006/wipo_pub_121_2006_06.pdf.

Winter Baseball, Cooper called: Max Cooper, February 15, 2015.

When Castro, who'd played the game: Kathy Hagood, "Success on a Sesame Seed Bun," *Business Alabama,* January 2011, accessed online December 14, 2015, http://www.businessalabama.com/Business-Alabama/January-2011/Success-on-a-Sesame-Seed-Bun.

two of Cooper's associates: Max Cooper, conversation with author, February 5, 2015.

Burns had spotted an ad: Burns, *Nitty Gritty,* 208; and Sonia Holesnikov-Jessop, "The Elder Statesman of PR," *International Herald Tribune,* August 29, 2008, accessed online December 14, 2015, http://www.nytimes.com/2008/08/30/business/worldbusiness/30iht-WBSPOT30.1.15685352.html?_r=0. Max Cooper's cohorts Al Golin and Ben Burns each take credit for having had the idea of calling on Ray and McDonald's. Once Burns had gone back to journalism, Golin took over the agency after Cooper joined the executive staff at McDonald's. McDonald's has been Golin's client ever since and the involvement of the other two men in the early encounters with Kroc has faded from the background.

The noisy din: Kroc, *Grinding It Out,* 127.

a note posted on the corporate bulletin board: Love, *McDonald's,* 178.

A builder had just defaulted: Kroc, *Grinding It Out,* 105–106.

"A University of Omaha student,": "Daly Diary," *Chicago American,* reprinted in *McDonald's: The Drive-in with the Arches* newsletter, April 1961, A. Bernie Woods papers, 1942–2001 (bulk 1960s), Archives Center, National Museum of American History, Smithsonian Institution, Series 3, McDonald's Corporation 1960–1985, Subseries 3, Newsletters 1960–1964, 1983, Box 20, File 12. (Hereafter A. Bernie Woods papers.)

America had gone mad: Hal Boyle, "Hal Boyle Writes: Hamburgers Made Him a Millionaire," *Nevada Daily Mail* (Nevada, MO), September 17, 1959, 2.

cleaning the holes of a mop wringer: Love, *McDonald's,* 143.

"I put the hamburger on . . .": Hal Boyle, "Roving Reporter," Associated

Press, September 15, 1959.

"He's Getting Rich . . .": Hal Boyle, "Hal Boyle Says: He's Getting Rich on Hamburgers," *Denton Record-Chronicle* (Denton, TX), September 15, 1959, 6.

"$25 Million in Lowly . . .": Hal Boyle, "$25 Million in Lowly Hamburger," *Winona Daily News* (Winona, MN), October 3, 1959, 4.

"Burger King Keeps Making . . .": Hal Boyle, "Burger King Keeps Making Huge Fortune," *Courier News* (Blytheville, AR), September 15, 1959, 3.

Chapter 5: Wretched City

On my trips to Rapid City, I met with people who knew Mrs. Kroc back when she was Mrs. Smith, thanks to the invaluable assistance of Jean Kesseloff and Kim Morey of Historic Rapid City. I also spoke at the local library about her, where a number of others shared stories. An indispensable resource that brought the Rapid City of old to life for me is the Oral History Project, Rapid City Public Library, Rapid City Public Library Foundation, https://vimeo.com/channels/oralhistoryproject.

YOU MUST BE A PERFECTIONIST: McDonald's Owner/Operator Manual, October 1958, 4, collection of Joe Maguire, Wolverine Development, son of early McDonald's operator in Lansing, MI.

it was a religion: Dave Smothers, "Big Mac Man of McDonald's Believes in Wholesomeness, Religion, Baseball," United Press International, May 19, 1974; and June Martino Deposition, February 5, 1970, Sonneborn v. Sonneborn, No. 69C 279 (N.D. Ill.).

"Your parking lot . . .": McDonald's Owner/Operator Manual, October 1958, 10.

skittish National Park Service: Todd David Epp, "Alfred Hitchcock's 'Expedient Exaggerations' and the Filming of 'North by Northwest' at Mount Rushmore," *South Dakota History* 23, no. 3 (Fall 1993): 181–196.

on a Hollywood back lot: "North by Northwest," The Alfred Hitchcock Wiki, accessed online January 23, 2016, http:// the.hitchcock.zone/wiki/Mount_Rushmore,_South_Dakota.

As for the cleanliness: McDonald's Owner/Operator Manual, October 1958, French Fried Potatoes, 57–60, stainless steel, 62–67.

he looked forward to dipping: Linda A.

Wendfeldt, e-mail to author, June 21, 2015.

Rollie had earned a cash bonus: Love, *McDonald's*, 233; and Railroad Retirement Board file, Rawland F. Smith; for 1957, Rollie earned $4,175.74 for his work as yard fireman/helper on the Chicago, Milwaukee, St. Paul, and Pacific Railroad.

one dollar and fifty-six cents: Vyonne Glaze (resident of Rapid City and friend of Joan Smith), conversation with author, November 10, 2015.

Allentown, Pennsylvania, had been the other: Linda A. Wendfeldt, June 21, 2015.

happy as a couple of kittens: Ray Kroc to Dick McDonald, Ray Kroc/McDonald Brothers Dictaphone tapes, 1957, Tape E.

the power to make people laugh or cry: Barbara Fredricks (wife of Bob Fredricks, executive director of Joan Kroc's Operation Cork), conversation with author, March 13, 2014.

ghosts in the fancy Alex Johnson Hotel: "A Haunted Hotel?," accessed online January 23, 2016, http://www.alexjohnson.com/about-us/hauntings.

earn seventy-five cents an hour: Ed Borgman (early employee of Main Street Rapid City McDonald's), e-mail to author, April 12, 2014.

"Anyone can make and sell . . .": McDonald's Owner/Operator Manual, 27.

"No hearts, lungs, dyes . . .": Ibid., 13.

Joan placed her order: Love, *McDonald's*, 132.

"Two hamburgers, two sodas, and two shoes,": *McDonald's: The Drive-in with the Arches*, November 1960.

sneak into his swimming pool: Prominent businessman in Rapid City, telephone conversation with author, August 2015.

lean in across the table: Ibid.

mind her daughter for a few days: Vyonne Glaze, conversation with author, November 10, 2015.

"Wretched City": Linda A. Wendfeldt, e-mail to author, April 9, 2015.

her knight in shining armor: Judy Klemesrud, ". . . And a Program for the Families," *New York Times*, July 10, 1978, D9.

an average of more than $17,000: *McDonald's: The Drive-in with the Arches* newsletter, September 1960.

Banks were wary: Harry Sonneborn deposition, Sonneborn v. Sonneborn 69C279 (1969).

precipitous march toward bankruptcy: Kroc, *Grinding It Out*, 100.

the McDonald's floor, "Hamburger

Heaven,": *McDonald's: The Drive-in with the Arches,* May 1961.

"an Eskimo in a hothouse": Virginia Lee, "Queen of Coast to Coast Drive-in," *Chicago American,* September 4, 1961.

"I am broke": June Martino deposition, Sonneborn v. Sonneborn, 69C279 (N.D. Ill. 1974).

"Let's go for it,": McDonald's Partners newsletter, Summer/Fall 1991, 41, reprinted on the June Martino Memorial Website, accessed online January 23, 2016, http://www.junemartino.org/site/epage/21899_504.htm.

as a four-year-old from a phrenologist: Kroc, *Grinding It Out,* 40.

more than merely supportive: McDonald's Partners newsletter, Summer/Fall 1991.

the suburb of Glen Ellyn: "Gal Adds Relish to Hamburger Empire: Helps Guide McDonald's," *Daily Herald* (Chicago), December 12, 1963, 48.

company meeting on a Friday: Love, *McDonald's,* 95.

Ray rewarded June 10 percent: Kroc, *Grinding It Out,* 84.

resembled Abe Lincoln: Ibid., 82.

had left his job: Harry Sonneborn deposition, January 9, 1969, Sonneborn v. Sonneborn, 69C279 (N.D. Ill. 1974), 24.

Harry had initially bristled: Conley, *Flying over the Golden Arches,* 103; and Love, *McDonald's,* 99.

Its modern roots sprouted: Scott A. Shane, *From Ice Cream to the Internet: Using Franchising to Drive the Growth and Profits of Your Company* (Upper Saddle River, NJ: FT Press, 2005).

Howard Johnson had been selling: Ibid., 47.

Root-beer stands called A&W: Ibid., 60.

Ray and Harry could have opted to charge: Love, *McDonald's,* 153.

He sniffed at the frozen hamburgers: Ray Kroc to Dick and Mac McDonald, Ray Kroc/McDonald Brothers Dictaphone tapes, October 1958, Disc M.

own its real estate: Harry Sonneborn deposition, Sonneborn v. Sonneborn, 69C279 (N.D. Ill. 1974), 72; Kroc, *Grinding It Out,* 82–83; Love, *McDonald's,* 153.

upgraded from a single-engine plane: Conley, *Flying over the Golden Arches,* 138–148; and Love, *McDonald's,* 163.

a hundred hours a month: Harry Sonneborn deposition, Sonneborn v. Sonneborn, 69C279 (N.D. Ill. 1974), 100–101.

Harry remained as emotionally in-

vested: Love, *McDonald's,* 178.

"Development accounting," he called it: Kroc, *Grinding It Out,* 140.

As part of the lifesaving agreement: Ibid., 237.

Rollie's vivacious wife and: Ibid., 130; and Love, *McDonald's,* 234. (Corporate historian John Love mentions the first attempt at marriage between Ray and Joan, based on his interviews with each of them, while in his memoir Ray omits the fact that he and Joan came close to marrying in 1961.)

Joan's now fourteen-year-old daughter: Linda A. Wendfeldt, e-mail to author, April 9, 2015.

wait out the requisite six weeks: Mella Rothwell Harmon, "Illuminating Reno's Divorce History," University of Nevada, Reno, Library, http://www.renodivorce history.org.

"forget that you have a daughter": Love, *McDonald's,* 234.

"Will you state your name . . .": Kroc v. Kroc, Superior Court of Cook County, Case 62S-7583, April 18, 1962.

news that Ray planned to leave: Charles Nerger, e-mail to author, September 15, 2015.

Mae and her husband had seized:

Charles Nerger, e-mail to author, October 25, 2015; and *McDonald's: The Drive-in with the Arches* newsletters, January 1961, February 1961, May 1961, File 12, Folder 13, and February 1962, March 1962, April 1962, File 12, Folder 14, A. Bernie Woods papers.

"Dry rot" had long been: Kroc, *Grinding It Out,* 57.

Ray cosigned a loan: Ray Kroc, interviewed by Tom Snyder, *Tomorrow;* and ibid., *Grinding It Out,* 112.

"Loses Kroc, Wins Pot": United Press International, "Loses Kroc, Wins Pot," *The Pantagraph* (Bloomington, IL), April 19, 1962, 26.

splurge purchase of twin lamps: Charles Nerger, e-mail to author, September 12, 2015.

In 1960 alone, their slice of the royalty: Love, *McDonald's,* 189.

The increasing drumbeat of press: Charles Ebeling, "Breakfast with Mr. McDonald," *The Chicago Literary Club,* October 26, 2009, accessed online December 10, 2015, http://www.chilit.org.

They'd refused Ray's demand: Letter from Richard J. McDonald to Thomas C. Dolly, March 18, 1993, Dolly papers, Bellevue University.

The brothers had a new idea: Dolly, "Pure Americana," 59.

one-time cash payment of $2.7 million: Kroc, *Grinding It Out,* 114; and Richard McDonald, *Pure Americana.*

"Where am I going to get . . .": Ibid., 60.

"The only reason we sell . . .": Love, *McDonald's,* 200.

"the Twelve Apostles": Kroc, *Grinding It Out,* 114.

he exploded in a rage: Love, *McDonald's,* 195.

when Mac became ill: Letter from Richard J. McDonald to Thomas C. Dolly, November 20, 1989, Dolly papers, Bellevue University.

like a lovesick schoolboy: Kroc, *Grinding It Out,* 132.

his best friend, Art Trygg: Ibid., 139; and George Wright, "Trigger Finger Arthur Trygg — A Parole Error; Puts Pistol to Victim's Head and Fires," *Chicago Tribune,* December 10, 1938, 2.

The night Ray lopped off: Ibid.

wrote up the incident: *McDonald's: The Drive-in with the Golden Arches* newsletter, January 1962, Box 20, File 14, A. Bernie Woods papers.

he hated being a bachelor: Kroc, *Grinding It Out,* 133.

defy her mother's disapproval: Love, *McDonald's,* 233.

Chapter 6: The J and R Double Arch Ranch

magic-carpet ride into a fairy-tale life: Skipi L. Smoot, telephone conversation with author, August 20, 2015.

Swiss mountain the Matterhorn: John Frost, "Matterhorn Celebrates 55th Anniversary," The Disney Blog, June 18, 2014, http://thedisneyblog.com/2014/06/18/matterhorn-celebrates-55th-anniversary.

Jane's "sweet disposition": Kroc, *Grinding It Out,* 133.

on February 23, 1963, they were married: Ray Kroc and Jane Green marriage, California Marriage Index, State file number 10258, accessed online December 15, 2015, Ancestry.com.

confessed to his new love: Skipi L. Smoot, August 20, 2015.

the new bride asked for wisdom: Love, *McDonald's,* 251.

ramp up . . . over the next decade: "McDonald's Move into Real Estate Was a

Financial Necessity," *Restaurant Finance Monitor* 20, no. 2 (2009): 3.

Those "codfish aristocrats": "Empire Is Built on 15-Cent Hamburgers," *Chicago Tribune,* October 22, 1972; and Karen Blecha, "Burger Baron: Blood, Sweat Tears, Look What they Got — A Guy Like Ray Kroc," *Palatine Herald* (Palatine, IL), September 2, 1975.

required cash deposit: Love, *McDonald's,* 255.

phone to talk to his protégé: Donn Wilson (early McDonald's executive), telephone conversation with author, August 19, 2015.

a popular daily half-hour radio show: *The Joy Boys,* commemorative website, accessed online January 23, 2016, http://thejoyboys.com; and Willard Scott, *Willard Scott's The Joy of Living* (New York: Putnam, 1982), 133.

". . . Drive-in keeps growing, my friend": McDonald's radio commercial, *The Joy Boys* commemorative website, accessed online January 23, 2016, http://www.thejoyboys.com/sound/d206t7.mp3.

his own dramatic flourish: James Barron, "After 50 Years, Revisiting a TV Encounter with a Famous Clown," *New*

York Times City Room (blog), published February 19, 2012, accessed online January 23, 2016, http://cityroom.blogs .nytimes.com/2012/02/19/after-50-years -revisiting-a-tv-encounter-with-a-famous -clown.

irresistible to kids: Scott, *The Joy of Living,* 133.

". . . advertise, advertise, advertise": Boas and Chain, *Big Mac,* 107.

"Forty-five cents for a three course meal": Love, *McDonald's,* 216.

double their ad buy: Ibid.

reached forty-six million Americans: *McDonald's: The Drive-in with the Arches,* January 1961, Box 20, File 13, A. Bernie Woods papers.

skilled use of mass media: "McDonald's, Wertheim and Company Research Report," Robert Schweich, December 1, 1965.

"newest and most hamburger-eatingist clown": McDonald's Ronald McDonald commercial with Willard Scott, 1963, posted February 27, 2008, accessed online January 23, 2016, https://www.youtube .com/ watch?v=SO8-A396Lt4.

new character "Archie McDonald": Andrew F. Smith and Bruce Kraig, *The Oxford Encyclopedia of Food and Drink in*

America, Volume 1 (New York: Oxford University Press, 2004), 152.

local franchisee offered up the character: Love, *McDonald's,* 223.

chef or an animated hamburger: Ray Kroc to Dick and Mac McDonald, Ray Kroc/McDonald Brothers Dictaphone tapes, 1958, Disc O.

people confused it with *another* Speedy: "Cool Things-McDonald's Sign," Kansas Historical Society, accessed online January 23, 2016, https://www.kshs.org/kansapedia/cool-things-mcdonald-s-sign/10232.

roller-coastering stock market in 1965: Ed More, "New Stock Market High in 1965," *Nevada Herald,* December 21, 1965, 4.

stock market debut of McDonald's: *Securities and Exchange Commission News Digest,* issue no. 65-3-9, March 11, 1965, accessed online January 4, 2016, https://www.sec.gov/news/digest/1965/dig031165.pdf.

net worth on paper: Love, *McDonald's,* 241.

suggested posting the daily closing stock price: Ibid., 252.

Harry celebrated by redecorating: Ibid.

burgers sent onto the trading floor: "On the Big Board," *Racine Journal-Times* (Racine, WI), July 8, 1966.

"greatest growth . . . restaurant business": "Growth Has Been Called Greatest in History of the Restaurant Business," *Colorado Springs Gazette-Telegraph* (Colorado Springs, CO), July 6, 1966.

with Jane on a six-week cruise: Kroc deposition, Sonneborn v. Sonneborn, 69C279, US District Court Northern District Eastern Division, Kroc Deposition, September 24, 1969, 137; and Love, *McDonald's,* 243.

Happy Canyon Road: If you can't get to Happy Canyon Road in the Santa Ynez Valley yourself, here's a video made by some motorcyclists: https://www.youtube.com/watch?v=qfL7vEJUxgw.

facsimile of a Danish village: Ann Dittmer, "The History of Solvang's Danish Look," Elverhoj Museum of History and Art, http://www.elverhoj.org/history2.html.

Pea Soup Andersen's: History, Pea Soup Andersen's, accessed online December 9, 2015, http://www.peasoupandersens.net/historySantaNella.html.

he joined the on-duty pianist: Mary Ann Norton, "Bill Powell: The Valley's Piano

Man Knows the Score," *Santa Ynez Valley News,* June 21, 2015.

her husband had hit the jackpot: Skipi L. Smoot, August 20, 2015.

established another research facility: "Restaurant Chain Has Research Lab," *Arlington Heights Herald* (Arlington Heights, IL), March 19, 1964, 46.

franchisee in Wisconsin, Edward Traisman: Dennis Hevesi, "Edward Traisman, 91, Dies; Helped Create Iconic Foods," *New York Times,* June 7, 2007.

patented his frozen fry formula: Method for preparing frozen French fried potatoes, US Patent US3050404 A, August 21, 1962, accessed online December 1, 2015, https://www.google.com/patents/US3050 404 .

in favor of milk shake mix: Ray Kroc, interviewed by Tom Snyder, *Tomorrow,* June 16, 1977.

raised the eyebrows of nutritionists: Boas and Chain, *Big Mac,* 73.

What impact did this food . . . have on kids: A pioneering group called Action for Children's Television worked to remove commercial messages embedded in and around kid-focused programs. Carol Lawson, "Guarding the Children's Hour on TV," *New York Times,* January 24,

1991, accessed online December 20, 2015, http://www.nytimes.com/1991/01/24/garden/guarding-the-children-s-hour-on-tv.html?scp=5&sq=Action%20 for%20Children's%20Television&st=cse.

"What do all those nurtitionists . . .": Novak, "The McDonald's Man."

Ray turned to his only brother: Letter from Robert L. Kroc to Samuel Rosenthal, October 10, 1972, Series 6, Subseries 2, Box 111, Mss 61, Kroc Foundation Archives, Department of Special Collections, Davidson Library, University of California, Santa Barbara (Hereafter Kroc Foundation Archives).

drugs involving the hormone relaxin: "In Memoriam: Robert L. Kroc: A Relaxin Pioneer, and So Much More," *Society for the Study of Reproduction,* accessed online December 20, 2015, http://www.ssr.org/sites/ssr.org/files/uploads/attachments/node/74/kroc_memorial.pdf.

Bob had dispatched a polite: Letter from Robert Kroc to Allen-Edmonds, March 28, 1978, Subseries 2, Box 113, Kroc Foundation Archives.

"The" when referring to the foundation: Letter from Robert L. Kroc to Eve Marsh, January 7, 1977, Subseries 2, Box 112, Kroc Foundation Archives.

Since diabetes and arthritis: Elayne Smith, "Ray Kroc's Wealth Is Foundation of War against Disease," *San Diego Union,* May 5, 1978, D1.

The scholarly, scientific nature: Letter from Robert L. Kroc to Alvin Golin, March 16, 1972, Series 6, Subseries 1, Box 106, Kroc Foundation Archives.

a gigantic hamburger: Even today, pedestrians strolling on the road say they've heard that a giant hamburger once topped the hillside.

upscale design magazine *Architectural Digest:* "Experience in Living Ranch-Style," *Architectural Digest,* Fall 1968, vol. XXV, no. 2, 18–32; and Joanne Rife, "Kroc Foundation Seeks Answers through Medical Research," *Santa Ynez Valley News,* January 30, 1975, 7A.

the automated bar: "Experience in Living Ranch-Style," 27.

Those glasses came from Tiffany: Letter to Bob Kroc from Waddy Pratt, March 3, 1975, Series 6, Subseries 1, Box 109, Kroc Foundation Archives.

His bids to buy Baskin-Robbins . . . failed: Love, *McDonald's,* 414.

renowned pastry chef Boston Strause: Patricia McCune, "Apple, Pumpkin Pies Are Favorite Treat All Year," *Pasadena*

Independent, December 12, 1968, 18.

offered the actor Fess Parker $50 million: Love, *McDonald's,* 414–416; William R. Chemerka, *Fess Parker: TV's Frontier Hero* (Albany, GA: BearManor Media, 2011), 210; and Ashley Parker (daughter of Fess Parker), e-mail to author, July 22, 2013.

bought her a convertible: Confidante of Joan Kroc, conversation with author, December 4, 2012.

didn't love Jane the way he loved Joan: Love, *McDonald's,* 235; and Kroc, *Grinding It Out,* 140.

"Yes," he blurted out: Kroc, *Grinding It Out,* 133.

vice president of equilibrium: Ibid., 126.

beer garden . . . called Hottinger's: Love, *McDonald's,* 413; and Jane Loring, "Front Views and Profiles," *Chicago Tribune,* July 16, 1965, 14.

Harry began stepping onto: Love, *McDonald's,* 244.

company's national debut: Smith and Kraig, *The Oxford Encyclopedia of Food and Drink in America, Volume 1,* 152.

tabled his disdain of Ronald McDonald: Max Cooper, telephone conversation with author, February 5, 2015.

ad to run in the debut Super Bowl: Terry Lefton, "How McDonald's Has Used Sports to Package the Perfect Pitch during Most of Its 50 Year History," *Sports Business Daily,* May 20, 2005.

Willard Scott was deemed unfit: Love, *McDonald's,* 246; and "Michael Polakovs," *The Telegraph,* December 15, 2009, http://www.telegraph.co.uk/news/obituaries/culture-obituaries/6819508/Michael-Polakovs.html. Some speculate that Willard Scott was denied the role because of his weight. A quick look at the commercials shows he was actually quite svelte at the time.

fifty Ronalds would be cast: Robert Tallon, "The Burger That Conquered the Country," *Time,* September 17, 1973, 84.

the outgoing president sold: Scott P. Janik (friend of Harry and Aloyis Sonneborn), telephone conversation with author, August 17, 2015; Love, *McDonald's,* 270; and Kroc, *Grinding It Out,* 147.

indulged his passion for collecting: *Highly Important Federal and State Constitutions, from the Collection of Harry J. Sonneborn,* Sotheby Parke Bernet, New York, Sale Number 4389, June 5, 1980; and *The Distinguished Autograph Collection of Harry J. Sonneborn,* Sotheby Parke Bernet, New York, Sale Number 3655, Tuesday, June 11, 1974.

Lincoln College in Illinois: Larry Shreyer, "Lincoln Speaker in London for Accused Killer of King," *Pantagraph* (Bloomington, IL), June 11, 1968, 6.

an errant McDonald's cup: Garry Mitchell, "For Sale: Alabama Estate; a Steal at $4.2 million," *Star-News* (Wilmington, NC), September 29, 1985, 8D.

June also received the promise of: Novak, "The McDonald's Man."

daughter, Linda, finished high school: Linda A. Wendfeldt, e-mail to author, April 10, 2015.

parties that quickly became local legend: David T. Olsen (builder and resident of Rapid City who worked on condo building where Smiths moved), conversation with author, November 11, 2015.

pick up a pastry at the grocery store: Mary Lou Lowery (former shopkeeper, Rapid City), conversation with author, November 10, 2015.

Vanity Fair sleepwear and lingerie: Sylvia Conrad (former shop clerk, Haggerty's department store, Rapid City), conversation with author, November 9, 2015.

outfitted in splendor: Press photo, Cooper and Golin, McDonald's 1,000th Restaurant Opening, 1101 Oakton Avenue, Des Plaines, IL, 1968.

call three hundred owners: Confidante of Ray Kroc, telephone conversation with author, April 29, 2014.

"like throwing gasoline on the fire": Love, *McDonald's,* 272.

at the sight of his blond beauty: Kroc, *Grinding It Out,* 155.

". . . except one thing": Ibid.

how hard Ray was working: Fred Turner, interviewed in "Ray Kroc: Fast Food Mc-Millionaire," *Biography,* A&E Television Network, 1998.

". . . top out of control": Kroc, *Grinding It Out,* 150.

last his way out of the harbor: Ibid., 157.

laying out the terms of the deal: Skipi L. Smoot, August 20, 2015; Love, *McDonald's,* 273; Kroc, *Grinding It Out,* 157. Love says Ray announced the divorce at the party; Ray omits from his memoir the fact that he asked his lawyer to break the news to Jane.

Joan and Rollie's marriage officially over: Smith v. Smith divorce decree, Clark County Case 163727, February 28, 1969.

Ray and Jane's bonds of matrimony: Kroc v. Kroc divorce decree, Clark County

Case A63469, March 5, 1967.

the story circulated that Ray: Former McDonald's executive, telephone conversation with author, March 5, 2016.

register for a marriage license: "Hamburger King Plans to Marry," *Lompoc Record* (CA), March 7, 1969, 3A.

The newlyweds embraced: This picture of Ray and Joan from their wedding appears briefly in "Ray Kroc: Fast Food Mc-Millionaire."

Chapter 7: The JoniRay

Potter Palmer had: "Chicago: City of the Century," *American Experience,* PBS, http://www.pbs.org/wgbh/amex/chicago/peopleevents/p_ppalmer.html.

finally won her hand: "Death of Potter Palmer: Chicago Millionaire Passes Away Unexpectedly at Home," *New York Times,* May 5, 1902, 9.

building the Mrs. a majestic, turreted palace: Barbara Mahaney, "Chicago's Palmer Castle," *Chicago Tribune,* undated, accessed online January 23, 2016, http://www.chicagotribune.com/news/nationworld/politics/chi-chicagodays-palmercastle-story-story.html.

"the embodiment of the new woman":

Amelia Dellos, *Love Under Fire: The Story of Bertha and Potter Palmer,* Chicago, 2013, accessed online December 1, 2015, http://www.eanderso.wix.com/#!bertha/c158d.

5,300-square-foot condo cost: Rudoph Unger, "Ray Kroc Sued over $163,464 by Decorator," *Chicago Tribune,* May 30, 1970, 22.

interior designer Raymond Jacques Dayan: Designer Dayan ultimately sued Kroc for nonpayment of bills for the design job. An even bigger dispute erupted years later after Dayan was granted the right to open McDonald's in France. See Jo Ellen Goodman, "Dayan vs. Kroc's McDonald's: Where Affection Turned Bitter," *Crain's Chicago Business,* March 27, 1980, 21.

Joan cloaked herself: Eleanor Page, "Praise for Recent Party Hosts and Guests," Social Life, *Chicago Tribune,* April 23, 1969, Sec. 2, 4.

"organ that hides in the wall . . .": Ibid.

A fleet of "Big Mac" buses: Letter from Whitey Anderson, McDonald's pilot, to Joan Kroc, Kroc Foundation Archives, Series 6, Subseries 2, Box 114, January 21, 1980.

a private rail car: Thomas W. Bush,

"Hamburger King Puzzled by New Toy: $63,000 Private Rail Car," *Los Angeles Times,* September 16, 1968, E11.

she'd indulge in a massage: Canepa, "Joan Kroc's Only Regret."

boosters of the underclass: Dubin, "She's More than the Padres' Madre."

spontaneous merriment would erupt: Eleanor Page, "This Fall Event Could Get Chilly," Paging People, *Chicago Tribune,* November 2, 1972, 2.

at the banquet in his honor: "Here's to the Ladies Who Do More than Lunch," *Sheridan Road* 6, no. 8, http://www .sheridanroadmagazine.com/ article.php/ vol/6/issue/8/title/article-1366749655484; and Renee Crown (prominent Chicago philanthropist), telephone conversation with author, September 1, 2015.

Horatio Alger Award: Michael Miner, "3 Rags-to-Riches Chicagoans Win Horatio Alger Awards," *Chicago Sun-Times,* October 15, 1972, 26.

he quit in a huff: Bob Olmstead, "Henrotin: Medical Caretaker of the Poor," *Chicago Sun-Times,* October 19, 1986, 20.

She bragged to total strangers: Sheldon Jacobs, *Investing without Wall Street: The Five Essentials of Financial Freedom*

(Hoboken: John Wiley and Sons, 2012). Author relates story of meeting Joan in the Rapid City airport when she was still Mrs. Smith and her boasts about McDonald's.

The unmanly Manhattan was Korczak's favorite: Sharon Cohen, "Crazy Horse and a Dream Stand Tall," *Los Angeles Times,* May 31, 1998, 1; and Rob Hiassen, "On Its Face, a South Dakota Monument Is a Tribute to the Great Sioux Leader Crazy Horse, but It's Also a Testament to the Outsized Dream of Its Creator," *Baltimore Sun,* June 4, 1998.

as if she were going crazy: Gerald T. Rogers (filmmaker commissioned by Joan Kroc to produce films for Operation Cork), telephone conversation with author, November 20, 2012.

she'd married her father: Dr. Vincent Pisani (licensed clinical psychologist/behavioral therapist who consulted with Operation Cork), conversation with author, May 23, 2014.

ferry him to suburban Arlington: "Two-allbeefpattiesgoldarchesand$400million," *Palatine Herald.*

The press loved this celebrity businessman: "Millionaires Say Must Enjoy Job," *Abilene Reporter-News* (TX), June 13,

1971, 3-E.

grand two-week tour: John Getze, "20 × 6 billions = McDonald's Success," *Los Angeles Times,* January 31, 1971.

Her strong will: Kroc, *Grinding It Out,* 133.

"hot tempered, emotional and . . .": Blecha, "Burger Baron: Blood, Sweat, Tears."

a place on the Intracoastal Waterway: Charles Maher, "Kroc: Big Money Kills the Do or Die Spirit," *Los Angeles Times,* February 13, 1971, D1.

A custom boat: *Burger Yard News,* Burger Boat Company, Manitowoc, WI, Fall 1971.

branded with an insignia: Maher, "Kroc: Big Money Kills the Do or Die Spirit."

gala Halloween brunch: Eleanor Page, "The Two Beauties," Paging People, *Chicago Tribune,* November 2, 1971, Sec. 2, 3.

The locks had been changed: Confidante of Ray and Joan Kroc, conversation with author, September 18, 2013.

"The defendant has a violent . . .": Joan B. Kroc v. Raymond A. Kroc, 71 D 21992, Cook County Circuit Court, November 11, 1971.

"Ray A. Kroc, 69 . . .": "Food Chain Chief's Wife Sued for Divorce," *Des*

Moines Register, November 12, 1971, 2.

signature chicken-crab gumbo: Susan Stewart, "Zee Man Who Made McNuggets," *Philadelphia Daily News,* August 18, 1984, F1.

Good Scout award: "Good Scout," *Chicago Community Publications,* December 8, 1971, 2.

offered Joan's attorney a franchise: Confidante of Joan Kroc, conversation with author, December 5, 2012.

His own attorney hinted: Ibid.

they shouldn't be apart: Scott Harris, "Joan Kroc Steps Up Ad Campaign to Bring a Halt to Nuclear Arms Race," *Los Angeles Times,* July 18, 1985, SD_A1.

her engaging head shots: Charles Nerger (great-nephew of Ethel Kroc), e-mail to author, September 14, 2015.

"You killed my sister": Confidante of Joan Kroc, conversation with author, December 4, 2013.

In her mid-forties now: It's not clear when Marilyn divorced her first husband, but she married James W. Barg on May 28, 1960, in Cook County, license D9302A8D-7C08-4725-8EB6-96E784C 35742.

an advance on the inheritance: Amendments to the Kroc v. Kroc divorce of

1961, 62 S 7583 Cook County, IL, detail the agreement between Ray and his daughter.

unlikely she'd outlive her father: Mark Ordower (son of attorney representing Marilyn Kroc), telephone conversation with author, December 3, 2012; and James T. Friedman (appointed guardian ad litem for Marilyn Kroc), telephone conversation with author, December 2, 2012.

cirrhosis of the liver: State of Illinois Certificate of Death 5553, September 11, 1973. Linda A. Wendfeldt, e-mail to author, April 14, 2015. Few people in Ray's orbit had ever met Lynn, and many were not even aware he had a daughter.

cover of *Time* magazine: Robert Tallon, "The Burger That Conquered the Country," *Time,* September 17, 1973, 84.

something to keep Joan busy: Confidante of Ray and Joan Kroc, conversation with author, March 31, 2014.

appointed her vice chairman: The Kroc Foundation 1965–1975 Annual Report, 12.

an investment proposal: Robert X. Leeds, *All the Comforts of Home: The Story of the First Pet Motel* (New York: Dodd, Mead, 1987), updated as *Love Is a Four-Legged*

Word (Las Vegas: Epic Publishing, 2001), 49–66; and Monty Hoyt, "American Pet Motel Is Hilton for the Animal in Your Family," *Christian Science Monitor News Service,* November 11, 1973.

make Leeds rich, too: Leeds, *All the Comforts of Home,* 62–63.

Ray made a fuss: Ibid., 65.

Even her butler observed: Eric Myers, *Uncle Mame: The Life of Patrick Dennis* (New York: St. Martin's Press, 2002), 274–276.

Fifteen inches, fallen in the span: "Disaster: Rapid City Flood 1972," Montana-Dakota Utilities Company, Rapid City Public Library's 1972 Black Hill Flood Oral History Project, accessed online December 21, 2015, https://vimeo.com/28328166; and "The Black Hills-Rapid City Flood of June 9–10, 1972: A Description of the Storm and Flood," USGS, http:// pubs.usgs.gov/pp/0877/report.pdf.

second-worst flood in the nation's history: "Disaster: Rapid City Flood 1972," Montana-Dakota Utilities Company.

meeting with the recently elected mayor: "Don V. Barnett," Black Hills Knowledge Network, accessed online December 21, 2015, http://www.rapidcity library.org/BHKN/KnowledgeNetwork/

includes/bios/barnett-bio.asp.

"Holy cow" was the mayor's: Don Barnett (mayor of Rapid City during historic 1972 flood), telephone conversation with author, October 22, 2013.

under strict orders not to utter: Longtime McDonald's employee, conversation with author, November 9, 2015.

proposed new name: "The Washington Padres?" *Ebbett's Blog: Musings of a Baseball History Junkie,* https://ebbetsblog .wordpress.com/2014/11/11/the-washington-padres/; and Maxwell Kates: "A Brief History of the Washington Stars," in Bob Brown, ed., *Monumental Baseball: The National Pastime in the National Capital Region, The National Pastime,* SABR, no. 39 (2009): 117–120.

cheer at Wrigley Field: Jack Murphy, "Padres Become Kroc's Hereafter," *San Diego Union,* January 24, 1974, D1.

one day own the Chicago Cubs: "Twoallbeefpattiesgoldarchesand$400million," *Palatine Herald.*

". . . the Chicago Cubs is one of them": Golin, *Trust or Consequences: Build Trust Today or Lose Customers Tomorrow* (New York: American Management Association, 2004); and Mary Ellen Podmolik, "A

Strong Brand of PR Man," *Chicago Tribune*, November 24, 2006.

Ray made one last inquiry: Ron Fimrite, "San Diego Finds a Sugar Padre," *Sports Illustrated*, February 11, 1974.

his old friend Jim Zien: Peter Zien (son of Jim Zien, owner of Criterion restaurant), conversation with author, February 11, 2013.

For Ray, $12 million: Buzzie Bavasi with John Strege, *Off the Record* (Chicago: Contemporary Books, 1987), 153.

shipping magnate George Steinbrenner: "New York Moment: This Day in NY Sports History," *Newsday* (Long Island, NY), January 3, 2010, A59.

husband was buying a monastery: Kroc, *Grinding It Out,* 171.

"I just wanted a hobby": Fimrite, "San Diego Finds a Sugar Padre."

his "one and only child, McDonald's": Dave Smothers, "Old McDonald's Has a Team . . . and Now Everybody Knows . . . ," *Playground Daily News* (Fort Walton Beach, FL), May 27, 1974, 48.

money had never been his motive: Steve Bisheff, "Baseball Too Protective of Weaker Sisters, Says Big Brother Kroc," *Sporting News,* May 12, 1979, 9.

work the same magic: Terry Mikelson,

" 'I Just Love to Watch Baseball,' Explains New Padre Owner Ray Kroc," *Yuma Daily Sun,* March 6, 1974, 13.

Topaz had first been hired: Jack Williams, "Danny Topaz, Entertainer Wowed Padres, Fans as Team Organist, *San Diego Union-Tribune,* August 22, 2005.

159 games to go: Bob Wolf, "Remember When," *Los Angeles Times,* June 20, 1990.

erupted in a hero's welcome: Bavasi, *Off the Record,* 154.

distinctive style of introducing the players: Wayne McBrayer and Rebecca Herman, "The Night Ray Kroc Took Over the Mic," Padres360.com blog, published August 14, 2014, accessed online January 24, 2016, http://padres360.com/2014/08/14/the-night-ray-kroc-took-over-the-mic.

"it's his crowd": John DeMott (announcer for San Diego Padres on night Ray took the mic), telephone conversation with author, January 7, 2015. I've relied on DeMott's explanation of the evening for my description of it, though Ray in his memoir claims to have seized the microphone.

Chapter 8: The Secret Everyone Knows

done what she could to avoid journalists: Beth Mohr, "Joan Kroc Offers Stoppers to Ease Drinking Problems," *San Diego Union,* date unknown, D1.

her own personal attorney: Paul D. Paganucci memo to John Kemeny and James Strickler, May 7, 1979, Dartmouth College, Box 7901, Folder Kroc Correspondence up to 1979, Manuscript DA-2, Subject Files of Paul D. Paganucci, 1900–1985, Rauner Special Collections Library, Dartmouth (hereafter cited as Subject Files of Paul D. Paganucci).

trade a $300,000 emerald: Judy Klemesrud, ". . . And a Program for the Families," *New York Times,* July 10, 1978, D9.

the right side of the menu: Joan Kroc toasts Ray, "The Ray Kroc 75th Birthday Tribute."

the idea that money equaled happiness: Alison Da Rosa, "Joan Kroc: Soft Life Is No Life," *Altoona Mirror* (Altoona, PA), October 17, 1978, 6.

Ray wanted to live on a yacht: Former employee of Ray Kroc, telephone conversation with author, April 28, 2014.

bought another house: Bavasi, *Off the Record,* 158.

best pitcher in baseball, Catfish Hunter: Hal Block, "Baseball's Emancipation: It Was Twenty Years Ago When Catfish Hunter, Sport's Best Pitcher, Was Declared a Free Agent," *Los Angeles Times,* December 11, 1994; and confidante/ former employee of Ray Kroc, e-mail to author, April 29, 2014.

stop reacting and start acting: Mohr, "Joan Kroc Offers Stoppers to Ease Drinking Problem."

believer in the "great hereafter": Jack Murphy, "Padres Become Kroc's Hereafter Right Now," *San Diego Union,* January 24, 1974, D1.

Those Latin Americans: Former employee of Ray Kroc, conversation with author, April 28, 2014. McDonald's actually opened its first outpost in Panama in 1971, according to http://www.mcspotlight .org/company/company_history.html.

edict prohibiting female employees: Love, *McDonald's,* 294.

Had he been drunk?: Kroc, *Grinding It Out,* 173.

"set baseball back fifty years": Jack Murphy, "Kroc's Cheerful about Hamburgers and Padres," *San Diego Union,* January 24, 1975.

"Kroc was washing down his hamburgers . . .": Dick Young, "It Ain't Hamburger," New York *Daily News,* April 12, 1974.

AA had been widely believed: William L.

White and Voices from the Profession, *The History of Addiction Counseling in the United States: Promoting Personal Family and Community Recovery* (Alexandria, VA: NAADAC, 2014).

Today, he said . . . a turning point: Testimony of Bill W., Hearings Before the Special Subcommittee on Alcoholism and Narcotics, July 24, 1969, accessed online December 8, 2015, http://silkworth.net/aahistory/print/congress1969_2.html.

a sudden spiritual awakening: Congressional testimony, *The Impact of Alcoholism,* July 23, 24, 25, 1969, http://silkworth.net/aahistory/print/congress1969_2.html.

". . . no more moral stigma than diabetes": United Press International, "Congress Urged to Attack Alcoholism," *Reading Eagle* (Reading, PA), July 24, 1969, 24.

Congress passed the Hughes Act: William L. White, *Slaying the Dragon: The History of Addiction Treatment and Recovery in America* (Bloomington, IL: Chestnut Health Systems, 1998), 266.

possible for a drinker: Memo from Paul Paganucci to President John Kemeny, Professor J. Brian Quinn, Dean Richard R. West, Dean James C. Strickler, Mr. Paul F. Doscher, and Ms. Patricia King, September 19, 1978, Box 7901, Folder Kroc Correspondence up to 1979, Manuscript DA-2, Subject Files of Paul D. Paganucci.

former first lady Betty Ford: United Press International, "Family Made Mrs. Ford Face the Truth," *Los Angeles Times,* October 17, 1978, 2.

". . . no embarrassment to me": United Press International, "Betty Ford Tells Story of Struggle over Drink," *Sarasota Herald-Tribune* (Sarasota, FL), October 18, 1978, 4A.

persuade him he had a problem: A number of people have talked about Ray's resistance to therapists and treatment, including Barbara Fredricks (wife of Bob Fredricks, former executive director of Joan Kroc's Operation Cork), conversation with author, March 13, 2014; Dr. Vincent Pisani, conversation with author, May 23, 2014; Dr. Peter Whybrow (former dean of Dartmouth Medical School and head of Project Cork), conversation with author, September 22, 2012; and Rev. John Keller (addiction counselor and former president of Operation Cork), conversation with author, May 29, 2014.

never suffer a hangover: Rev. John Keller, May 29, 2014.

attendance at meetings changed her

life: Richard Roth, "Joan Kroc: The Dynamo Who Is Operation Cork Talks about Turning Walls into Bridges," *Alcoholism: The National Magazine* 1 (May/June 1981), 5; Gerald T. Rogers, November 20, 2012; and Sandy McCullough (former trustee of Dartmouth College who courted the Krocs for donations), telephone conversation with author, December 5, 2014.

someone who drank to excess: Joan Kroc, interviewed by Glenn Jorgenson, *It's Great to Be Alive,* episode: "The Other Victims," KELO-TV and River Park Foundation, Pierre, South Dakota, first airdate, January 27, 1978.

launch a "social revolution": Da Rosa, "Joan Kroc: Soft Life Is No Life."

eight-page list of media: Roth, "Joan Kroc: The Dynamo . . . ," 13–16.

"Cork is Kroc spelled backward": Sandra Pesman, "She's Plugging the Cork on Alcohol Abuse: To Joan Kroc, Wife of the Hamburger King, It's No Rich Girl's Hobby," *Chicago Daily News,* June 10, 1977.

"putting the cork back in the bottle": *Operation Cork Update,* Operation Cork, La Jolla, CA, Summer 1981, 3.

Ray casually delivered the news: Bob

Kroc, undated notes, Box 116, Folder Operation Cork, Kroc Foundation Archives.

When Joan informed him: Ibid.

minimizing the importance of his work: Letter from Bob Kroc to Joan Kroc, November 29, 1976, Box 116, Folder Operation Cork, Kroc Foundation Archives.

Operation Cork gave Joan: Mohr, "Joan Kroc Offers Stoppers to Ease Drinking Problems."

diminished the importance of her message: Bob Crouch (graphic designer employed by Operation Cork), telephone conversation with author, June 16, 2014; and Cathleen Brooks (author commissioned by Joan Kroc to write *The Secret Everyone Knows* for Operation Cork), conversation with author, October 28, 2013.

Corky figurines made of solid gold: Gila Saks (former Operation Cork employee), conversation with author, January 31, 2014; and Cathleen Brooks, conversation with author, October 28, 2013; both mentioned this bauble. Around this time, Joan had commissioned jeweler Sidney Mobel to craft a 14K gold mousetrap, replete with diamond-encrusted cheese, as a present for Ray, which she presented with a note: "Thanks for catching me." It's likely but not proven that Mobel also created the gold Corky. Leslie Bennett, "Midas Touches the Mundane," *St. Petersburg Times* (St. Petersburg, FL), May 30, 2006, 1E.

"Hi! My name's Corky": Advertisement for Operation Cork, "Happy New You!" *San Diego Union,* January 11, 1977.

Joan wrote in the foreword: John E. Keller, *Alcohol. A Family Affair: Help for Families in Which There Is Alcohol Misuse* (La Jolla, CA: Operation Cork, 1977), iv.

prepared for a deluge of inquiries: Wendy Gross, conversation with author, April 14, 2014.

Abby ran the column: Abigail Van Buren, "Help Wanted for Drinking Problem," *Paris News* (Paris, TX), July 5, 1978, 2.

"I only have fifty cents": Da Rosa, "Joan Kroc: Soft Life Is No Life."

"Mom, you put salt in . . .": Bill Melendez, *Operation Cork Public Service Announcement,* 1978, posted online July 16, 2013, accessed online December 15, 2015, https://www.youtube.com/watch?v=i3WJM3ODotI.

The film *If You Loved Me:* Sherri Gilman-

Tompkins, "For Alcoholics, a New Video to Show the Way Out," *Chicago Tribune,* January 3, 1986, 43.

aired on PBS stations: A remake of *Soft Is the Heart of a Child,* produced by Hazelden Treatment Center, is still widely used today.

live conversation with experts: Memo from John Keller to Robert Kroc, October 3, 1979, Box 116, Folder Operation Cork, Kroc Foundation Archives.

sporting a pink diamond: Dubin, "She's More than the Padres' Madre."

a dilettante hobby: Ibid.

She'd started Cork because: Pat Kailer, "Alcohol: A Family Affair," *Albuquerque Journal,* December 29, 1977, B1.

the struggle of a cherished uncle: George Flynn, "San Ysidro Tragedy Struck at the Heart of Joan Kroc," *San Diego Union,* July 29, 1984, 1.

borrowing a cue from the AA pledge: Pesman, "She's Plugging the Cork on Alcohol Abuse."

". . . alcoholic's answer to Ronald McDonald": Fran Arman, "Speaking of People," *National Observer* (Washington, DC), undated.

". . . after all, well — a merchandiser": Kailer, "Alcohol: A Family Affair."

When Ray wanted to accept: Glenn Jorgenson (founder, River Park Treatment Center, and host/producer, *It's Great to Be Alive*), conversation with author, April 2, 2014.

The fact that she drank: Mohr, "Joan Kroc Offers Stoppers to Ease Drinking Problems."

copious amounts of alcohol: One of Bob Kroc's tasks at the ranch was ensuring the alcohol consumed at the bar was recorded and charged to the correct entity, and that the bar was restocked. The Kroc Foundation Archives contain many inventory sheets for the restocking and memos concerning alcohol.

Bob meticulously inventoried: Memo from Robert L. Kroc to Miss Margarete Wemlinger, Subject: Use of Liquor and Wine at Conference or Seminars, January 20, 1972, Series 6, Box 104, Kroc Foundation Archives.

Château Lafite Rothschild: Dr. Vincent Pisani, telephone conversation with author, May 10, 2014.

"God is among us": Jim Crouch (graphic designer for Operation Cork and guest at ranch), telephone conversation with author, June 16, 2014.

It's Great to Be Alive: Joan Kroc, interviewed by Glenn Jorgenson, *It's Great to Be Alive,* KELO-TV, Sioux Falls, SD, first aired January 27, 1978.

cover of *Alcoholism* magazine: Roth, "Joan Kroc: The Dynamo."

book designed to help children: Claudia Black (alcoholism counselor and author), telephone conversation with author, November 4, 2015. Her book *My Dad Loves Me My Dad Has a Disease* is still in print today.

"I want to tell you a secret": Cathleen Brooks, *The Secret Everyone Knows,* 8.

"The Secret Everyone Knows": Cathleen Brooks, conversation with author, October 28, 2013.

same disdain for professors: Dr. Peter Whybrow (Dartmouth Medical School and Project Cork), conversation with author, November 15, 2012.

"too many baccalaureates . . .": Kroc, *Grinding It Out,* 187.

alumnus of the school, Fred Fedeli: Love, *McDonald's,* 185.

one of the fleet of Big Mac buses: Paul Doscher (Dartmouth Tuck School employee), telephone conversation with author, September 8, 2015.

given away an incredible $30 million: Memo from Paul Paganucci to Professor

Roy J. Lewicki, December 8, 1976, Box 7901, Folder Kroc Correspondence up to 1979, Subject Files of Paul D. Paganucci.

no alma mater to sentimentally tug: Memo from Paul Paganucci, Associate Dean, to President John G. Kemeny, March 1, 1976, Box 7901, Folder Kroc Correspondence up to 1979, Manuscript DA-2, Subject Files of Paul D. Paganucci.

Ray's affinity for Early Times: Memo from Paul Paganucci to Paul Doscher, May 4, 1976, Box 7901, Folder Kroc Correspondence up to 1979, Subject Files of Paul D. Paganucci.

yield "big casino": Memo from Paul Paganucci to President David T. McLaughlin, August 20, 1981, Box 7901, Folder Ray Kroc Medical School, Subject Files of Paul D. Paganucci.

At a celebratory pre-graduation dinner: Dr. James Strickler (former dean, Dartmouth Medical School), telephone conversation with author, September 30, 2014.

Just as the nation was: Sandy McCullough, December 5, 2014.

bells in the campus clock tower: Paul Doscher, September 8, 2015.

in his, a picture of a naked woman: Dr. Peter Whybrow, conversation with author,

September 22, 2012.

five-page memo from Paul Paganucci: Letter from Paul Paganucci to Donald C. Lubin, September 15, 1977, Box 7901, Folder Ray Kroc Medical School, Subject Files of Paul D. Paganucci.

gift of twenty thousand shares: Kroc Medical School Fund Letter from Don Lubin to Paul Paganucci, November 22, 1977, Box 7901, Folder Ray Kroc Medical School, Subject Files of Paul D. Paganucci.

book release party: Eleanor Page, "There's a Lot of Ham in Burger King Ray Kroc," *Chicago Tribune,* May 18, 1977, and *Chicago Sun-Times,* May 18, 1977.

books bored him: Kroc, *Grinding It Out,* 15.

"We can trust a machine better . . .": Ray Kroc, interviewed by Tom Snyder, *Tomorrow.*

family-minded host grilled Ray: Ray Kroc, interviewed by Phil Donahue, *Donahue,* May 1977.

"Vegas would envy": Al Golin on "The Ray Kroc 75th Birthday Tribute."

Oscar-winning lyricist Sammy Cahn: Correspondence between Al Golin and Sammy Cahn, 1977, Series 7 Biography,

Ray Kroc file f1044, Sammy Cahn papers, Margaret Herrick Library, Academy of Motion Picture Arts and Sciences.

inventive lyrics that lampooned: "Songwriter Discovers Fun, Profit," *Wilmington Morning Star* (Wilmington, NC), January 23, 1979.

charity that McDonald's had adopted: Charles Ebeling, "The Chase: Afloat in the PR Whirl of the 1970s (the Golin Years)," Apple Pressings Blog, published June 13, 2014, accessed online January 20, 2016, https://applewoody.wordpress.com/2014/06/13/the-chase-afloat-in-the-pr-whirl-of-1970s-chicago-the-golin-years.

This was a riff: Kroc, *Grinding It Out,* 186; *Field Museum of Natural History Bulletin 55,* no. 1 (January 1984), accessed online April 24, 2016, https://archive.org/stream/fieldmuseumofnat55chic/fieldmuseumofnat55chic_djvu.txt.

In recent years, wage issues: "Clowning Around with Charity: How McDonald's Exploits Philanthropy and Targets Children," Michele Simon, published October 2013, accessed online January 17, 2016, http://www.eatdrinkpolitics.com/wp-content/uploads/Clowning_Around_Charity_Report_Full.pdf.

Who had seven hundred intimate friends?: Joan Kroc toasts Ray, "The Ray Kroc 75th Birthday Tribute."

Ray had informed Joan that: Memo from Paul Paganucci to President John G. Kemeny and Dean James C. Strickler, May 7, 1979, Box 7901, Folder Ray Kroc Medical School, Subject Files of Paul D. Paganucci.

not believe in funding buildings: Letter from Dr. Peter Whybrow to Joan Kroc, May 23, 1980, and from Joan Kroc to Dr. Peter Whybrow, May 23, 1980, Subject Files of Paul D. Paganucci.

"To you, Ray . . .": Joan Kroc toasts Ray, "The Ray Kroc 75th Birthday Tribute."

"Life's prize is not . . .": Ray's recitation of poem, "The Ray Kroc 75th Birthday Tribute." Poem by Carl A. Dragstedt, cited in William S. Middleton, "Intellectual Crossroads — an Appreciation of Ralph H. Major," *Perspectives in Biology and Medicine* 14, no. 4 (1971): 651–658, accessed online January 17, 2016, http://muse.jhu.edu/article405721.

Joan commissioned two more films: Both films are reviewed by George E. Vaillant, "Book Reviews," *New England Journal of Medicine* 306, no. 2 (1982): 115.

how sick and tired he was: Phil Collier,

"Man Upstairs Gives Word to Padres: 'Ycch,' " *Sporting News,* July 1, 1978.

cheerfully squired reporter Norm Clarke: Norm Clarke (former Associated Press baseball reporter), telephone conversation with author, April 14, 2014.

"baseball can go to hell": Associated Press, "Kroc Prefers Burgers to Baseball," *Daytona Beach Morning Journal* (Daytona, FL), August 25, 1979.

he suffered a stroke: Associated Press, "Kroc under Care following Stroke: Bout with Alcoholism Also Cited by Family," *Los Angeles Times,* January 4, 1980, SD_B1. Ray suffered a series of strokes beginning in late 1979.

Continuing to drink now: Choney, "Joan Kroc: A Year of Wins, and Losses."

If he didn't consent: Barbara Fredricks, conversation with author, March 13, 2014.

Chapter 9: 1984: Two Widows

blood had barely been mopped: Arthur Golden, "$1 Million Donated to Survivors," *San Diego Union,* July 21, 1985, A1.

"My father could never . . .": Vicki Torres, "San Ysidro Massacre: Gunman Storms Border Restaurant," *San Diego Tribune,* July 19, 1984, A1.

"Society has had their chance . . .": Arthur Golden, "Wife: Slayer Heard 'Voices,' " *San Diego Union,* July 20, 1984, A1.

"You should have let me kill myself": Ibid.

In nineteen years of marriage: Mike Granberry, "A Bitter Harvest," *Los Angeles Times,* October 19, 1984, A3.

He tossed French fries: United Press International, "McDonald's Killer Threw Food at Victims," *Gazette* (Montreal), August 3, 1984, 8.

in a little over an hour: Golden, "Wife: Slayer Heard 'Voices.' "

written an open letter: Murray Dubin, "Clues to a Massacre Motive," *Philadelphia Inquirer,* July 20, 1984, A1.

"I am truly sorry . . .": United Press International, "Etna Huberty's Letter: I'm Truly Sorry," *Los Angeles Times,* July 21, 1984, 26.

magnitude of Huberty's actions: Barry M. Horstman, "Killer Called 'Angry at World,' " *Los Angeles Times,* July 21, 1985, A1.

Rolls-Royce that arrived to deposit Joan: Linda A. Wendfeldt, e-mail to author, August 18, 2015.

Its assets of more than $30 million:

Marc Cooper, "A Crusader's Rebellion," *MacLean's,* September 30, 1985, 10. IRS Tax Form 990 for Joan B. Kroc Foundation, 1984, shows assets of $33,017,733.

memorial ad and service: Charles Ebeling, "Breakfast with Mr. McDonald," *Chicago Literary Club,* published October 26, 2009, accessed online December 10, 2015, http://www.chilit.org.

their marriage's happiest: Leeds, *Love Is a Four-Legged Word,* 264.

off the McDonald's payroll: Love, *McDonald's,* 412.

Chef René Arend: "Top Chef Helps McDonald's Develop Products," *Gazette* (Montreal), December 10, 1986, E5.

Turner still refused: Fred Turner, "In Memory of Ray Kroc," *Crews Views,* McDonald's Corporation, February 1984, 12.

commissioned a portrait: Love, *McDonald's,* 270.

signed off on an $11 million deal: One-time Padres general manager Jack McKeon quoted in "Triumph and Tragedy: 1984 San Diego Padres," Major League Baseball Network, accessed online December 17, 2015, https://www.youtube.com/watch?v=aylyiwAAJC4.

salaries had continued to zoom: Paul D.

Staudohar, "Baseball's Changing Salary Structure," *Compensation and Working Conditions,* Fall 1997, 2–9, accessed online December 29, 2015, http://www.bls.gov/opub/mlr/cwc/baseballs-changing-salary-structure.pdf.

flown at half-staff: Lynn Emmerman, "His 'Family' Pays Kroc Last Honors," *Chicago Tribune,* January 21, 1984.

The music was fitting: *Memorial Service for Ray A. Kroc,* Christ Church of Oak Brook, Oak Brook, IL, January 20, 1984.

son-in-law Ballard: Emmerman, "His 'Family' Pays Kroc Last Honors."

a second father, said Turner: Turner, "In Memory of Ray Kroc."

A jury had concluded: Warren, Kelly and Tybor, "How Jurors Had It Their Way at McDonald's Expense," *Chicago Tribune,* February 7, 1984, Sec. 3, 1.

crystal flutes of pink Dom Pérignon: Susan Rosser with Charlie Smith and Trevor Schaefer, *The Boy on the Lake: He Faced Down the Biggest Bully of His Life and Inspired Trevor's Law* (New York: Morgan James Publishing, 2013), 150.

variety of voices commenting: Confidante of Joan Kroc, telephone conversation with author, February 13, 2013.

buying a radio station: Ted Leitner (Padres broadcaster and friend/neighbor of Joan Kroc), telephone conversation with author, January 30, 2014.

she'd underwritten its production: Bob Thomas, "Husband, Father, Golfer, Director . . . and Actor," *Indiana Gazette,* June 27, 1980, 12.

actor named John Travolta: Larry Turman (producer of *Mass Appeal*), e-mail to author, November 16, 2013.

a dedication to Ray: Bill C. Davis (writer of *Mass Appeal*), telephone conversation with author, November 16, 2013.

Diagnosed with a mysterious illness: Norman Cousins, interviewed by James Day, *Day at Night,* CUNY TV, March 12, 1974, accessed online December 13, 2015, https://www.youtube.com/watch ?v=O344DBKkm0s.

about the aging process, she'd convened: Letter from John Keller to Robert Kroc, October 11, 1979, Subseries 1, Box 107, Kroc Foundation Archives.

after which she had a face-lift: Phyllis Jorgenson (wife of River Park addiction treatment founder Glenn Jorgenson), conversation with author, April 2, 2014; and Wendy Gross, conversation with author, April 25, 2014.

care of the elderly: Memo from James

Strickler to Paul Paganucci, December 1983, Box 7901, Subject Files of Paul Paganucci.

Cousins trekked the few hours: Norman Cousins, *Head First: The Biology of Hope* (New York: E. P. Dutton, 1989), 196.

flew up on her helicopter: George Freeman Solomon, *From Psyche to Soma and Back: Tales of Biopsychosocial Medicine* (Los Angeles: Xlibris, 2000), 251.

How did hope: Cousins, *Head First,* 199.

called her a "patsy": George Flynn, "San Ysidro Tragedy Struck at the Heart of Joan Kroc," *San Diego Union,* July 29, 1984, B1.

"I didn't hear no gunshots . . .": Robert Locke, "They Waited Out Attacker's Rampage," *San Diego Tribune,* July 20, 1984, A1.

this grave scene: Christopher Reynolds, "McDonald's Will Establish Fund," *San Diego Union,* July 20, 1984, A14.

formation of a victims' fund: "Chains Pull Ads; Kroc's Widow Sets Up Fund," *Philadelphia Daily News,* July 20, 1984, 12.

he'd have done the same: Jeanette Valentine, "McDonald's to Donate $1 Million to Fund for Survivors of Massacre," *Los Angeles Times,* July 21, 1984, SD_A1.

top executives in Oak Brook: Robert

Blair Kaiser, conversation with author, October 22, 2012; and confidante of Joan Kroc, telephone conversation with author, December 4, 2013.

modest donations poured in: John Farine and Maria Puente, "Donations Pour In for Survivors," *San Diego Union,* July 24, 1984, A1.

Sports star Jimmy Connors: Gina Lubrano, "Mayor Opens Talks on Memorial Park," *San Diego Union,* July 26, 1984, B3.

dispatched the Rolls back down: "Town Says Mass for Massacre Dead," *Los Angeles Times,* July 22, 1984.

ferry Etna and her daughters: "Ohio Man Had 'Gun in Every Corner,' " *Los Angeles Times,* July 19, 1984, A1.

bishop of the San Diego diocese: David Hassemyer and Vicki Torres, "Hundreds of Mourners Say Farewell to Victims of San Ysidro Massacre," *San Diego Tribune,* July 21, 1984, A1.

a thousand-dollar payout: David Freed, "Funds Given to Huberty's Widow Set Off a Protest," *Los Angeles Times,* July 27, 1984, 19.

he thought such a film: Larry Spivey (Hollywood producer who wanted to make a TV movie about Huberty), telephone interview with author, May 12,

2014; and Diane Lindquist, "Opposition to Film on Massacre Increases," *San Diego Union,* March 7, 1985, B1.

"Now some of the victims are feeling more pain . . .": Joe Gandelman, "Cousins Says He Gave Funds to Hubertys," *San Diego Union,* July 28, 1984, B1.

Joan had been enrolling: Mike Sund (former PR director for Joan B. Kroc Foundation), telephone conversation with author, September 10, 2012.

hiring the fallen pitcher Bo Belinsky: Milton Richman, "Bo Belinsky, Evangelist: The Left-Hander Was Wild and He Was High," *Los Angeles Times,* December 12, 1980, G1.

made her erase the logo: Gerald T. Rogers, November 20, 2012.

nice man named Willie Stargell: Barry Lorge, "Sports," *San Diego Union,* March 23, 1986, H1.

Legendary baseball executive Buzzie Bavasi: Hal D. Steward, "Excitement in San Diego," *Daily Chronicle* (Centralia, WA), September 26, 1977, 2.

agent for shortstop Ozzie Smith: Ozzie Smith, *Wizard* (Chicago: Contemporary Books, 1988), 35.

rename Desert Sun Stadium: Phil Collier, "Yuma Names Stadium in Memory of Kroc," *San Diego Union,* March 10, 1984, C7.

Einstein Middle School: Christopher Reynolds, "School Board Makes It Official: Ray Kroc Displaces Einstein," *San Diego Union,* May 8, 1985, B3.

testosterone-infused brawls: Demetrius Bell, "That Time When the Padres and Braves Had a Mini-riot in 1984," SB Nation/Talking Chop blog, posted online October 2, 2014, accessed online December 5, 2015, http://www.talkingchop.com/2014/10/2/6880557/throwback-thursday-braves-padres-brawl-1984-classic-fight.

John Birch Society: Ray Ratto, "The Weird Saga of the Padres," *San Francisco Chronicle,* September 10, 1986, 57.

Tim McCarver asked her: Details of Game 5 in the playoffs from Major League Baseball Classics, NLCS Game 5, Chicago Cubs v. San Diego Padres, posted online October 1, 2010, https://www.youtube.com/ watch?v=QuOauPWip_8.

Gossage swore later: Don Freeman, "Point of View," *San Diego Union,* March 19, 1985, D9.

"She's one of us . . .": Dave Distel, "Carrying On the Dream: Owner Joan Kroc Has Earned Padres Respect and Affection," *Los Angeles Times,* October 3,

1984, SD_B1.

full-page newspaper ad: Newspaper ad by Joan Kroc, "I Am Proud to Be a San Diegan," *San Diego Union,* August 13, 1984.

San Diego Press Club voted her: "It's Unanimous: Headliners a Hit," *Foghorn,* San Diego Press Club, March 1985, 1. Ray was a unanimous winner, too, in 1974.

St. Joan of the Arches: Choney, "Joan Kroc: A Year of Wins, and Losses."

done with the now vacant lot: Andrea Skorepa (president and chief executive, Casa Familiar, a social service provider in San Ysidro, CA, that assisted the community and Joan Kroc after the massacre), e-mail to author, March 12, 2014.

surprised a crowd of five thousand: Paula Parker, "5,000 Cheer Walter Mondale in San Diego: Supporters Upbeat," *Los Angeles Times,* October 28, 1984, SD_A1.

La Jolla Christmas Parade: Tom Blair, *San Diego Union,* November 19, 1984, B1.

"DREAMS! CAN COME TRUE": Neil Morgan, *San Diego Tribune,* December 21, 1984, B1.

hosted the first party she'd thrown: David Freed, "Billy Humble: Unusual Success in Cops' Macho World," *Los Angeles Times,* March 10, 1985.

$16 million Gulfstream III: Tom Blair, *San Diego Union,* December 12, 1984, B1.

reproduction of the Declaration of Independence: Zenia Cleigh, "Auction Ends an Episode in Dominelli Soap Opera," *San Diego Tribune,* November 19, 1984, C1. Joan also bought autographs that evening of Einstein, Andrew Carnegie, and Alexander Hamilton.

Chapter 10: "Dear World, I Really Love You"

National Women's Conference: Lloyd Grove, "The Sexes and the War Machines," *Washington Post,* September 13, 1984, accessed online January 24, 2016, http://www.washingtonpost.com/archive/lifestyle/1984/09/13/the-sexes-and-the-war-machines/22f7203b-5e9a-4218-b8d8-07d521b8973b.

Oscar-winning actress Joanne Woodward: Kathy Larkin, "She's Working for World Peace," *Lawrence Journal World* (Lawrence, KS), September 12, 1984, 23.

"We're not anti-men": Judy Klemesrud, "Rallying Women on Nuclear War Issues," *New York Times,* September 9, 1984.

backdrop for this austere occasion: Cannon Caucus Room, accessed online December 8, 2015, http://history.house.gov/Exhibitions-and-Publications/Cannon-Building/Caucus-Room.

"It's Up to the Women": Conference program, "National Women's Conference to Prevent Nuclear War," Washington, DC, September 11–12, 1984, accessed online October 25, 2015, http://bcrw.barnard.edu/archive/militarism/national_womens_conference.pdf.

convince world leaders to enact disarmament: Charles Mohr, "200 Women Turn Out for Parley to Seek Ways to Halt Arms Race," *New York Times,* September 13, 1984, A18.

the "psychosexual element": Grove, "The Sexes and the War Machines."

A reviewer for the *Christian Science Monitor:* Burke Wilkinson, "Dr. Caldicott's Remedy for a Fevered Missile Race," *Christian Science Monitor,* October 1, 1984.

The doctor had just arrived: Helen Caldicott, *A Desperate Passion: An Autobiography* (New York: W. W. Norton, 1997), 304.

budget for nuclear weapons: Ibid.

the "corporate prostitutes": Grove, "The Sexes and the War Machine."

The well-dressed blonde: Caldicott, *A Desperate Passion,* 324.

the editor Norman Cousins: Akira Tashiro and Masami Nishimoto, "The Moral Adoption of Hiroshima's A-Bomb Orphans, Part 1," Hiroshima Peace Media Center, February 1, 2009, accessed online December 29, 2015, http://www .hiroshimapeacemedia.jp/?p=23336.

"the conscience of America": Daisaku Ikeda, "Norman Cousins: The Conscience of America," *SGI Quarterly,* April 2004, accessed online December 29, 2015, http://www.sgiquarterly.org/global2004 Apr-1.html.

"I can't talk to the Russians": Dartmouth Conference, Kettering Foundation website, accessed online December 16, 2015, https://www.kettering.org/ dartmouth-conference.

if his competition was drowning: Fred Turner relays the oft-repeated Ray Kroc maxim in the documentary "Ray Kroc: Fast Food McMillionaire."

he was in love with her: David Nelson, "Society," *Los Angeles Times,* June 27, 1985, 3; and Nancy Scott Anderson, "Salute to Joan Kroc," *San Diego Tribune,* June 20, 1985.

"unrequited love of keyboards": Norman Cousins, interviewed by James Day, *Day at Night:* "Norman Cousins, Author, Journalist, Peace Advocate," CUNY TV, March 12, 1974, posted online December 19, 2011, accessed online January 24, 2016, https://www.youtube.com/watch?v=O344DBKkm0s.

an expensive electrical organ: Candis Cousins (daughter of Norman Cousins), e-mail to author, March 13, 2014.

stole off with him: Neil Morgan, *San Diego Tribune,* June 28, 1990, B1.

Preventing a nuclear holocaust: Barbara O'Neil, "Kroc's Ad Campaign Condemns Arms Race," *San Diego Union,* May 31, 1985, B1.

apologized for shifting gears: Glenn Jorgenson (founder of River Park addiction treatment facility and friend of Joan Kroc), telephone conversation with author, December 5, 2015.

too much time focused on material things: Joan Kroc, interviewed by George Lewis, *NBC Nightly News with Tom Brokaw,* July 16, 1985.

on a "nuclear bender": "Joan Kroc Is Honored by B'nai B'rith," *San Diego Union,* June 20, 1985, B3.

Dr. Caldicott was breathless: Caldicott, *A Desperate Passion,* 304.

backed off on her promise: Dr. Helen Caldicott (author and activist), telephone conversation with author, August 22, 2012.

struck a deal with the publisher: Harris, "Joan Kroc Steps Up Ad Campaign . . ."

insisted on excising a passage: Dr. Helen Caldicott, *Missile Envy: The Arms Race and Nuclear War,* first edition (New York: William Morrow and Co., 1984), 324.

"weaving spiders come not here": Mark Dice, *The Bohemian Grove: Facts and Fiction* (San Diego: The Resistance Manifesto, 2015).

"The productive drunk is the bane . . .": Philip Weiss, "Masters of the Universe Go to Camp: Inside the Bohemian Grove," *Spy,* November 1989, 69.

"It is obvious that the Bohemian Grove . . .": Caldicott, *Missile Envy,* 324.

Turner had even referenced: Turner, "In Memory of Ray Kroc."

hospitalized for days to recover: Dr. Helen Caldicott, August 22, 2012; and confidante of Ray and Joan Kroc, conversation with author, September 10, 2015.

touch a chord with women: Marylouise Oates, "On the Circuit," *Los Angeles Times,* May 2, 1985.

check of appreciation for $100,000:

Lionel Van Deerlin, "Joan Kroc's Concern Runs Deep," *San Diego Tribune,* August 3, 1985.

executive director Chuck Bieler: Chuck Bieler (emeritus director of San Diego Zoo), conversation with author, March 7, 2013.

"What can we do for the humans?": Ibid.

how could she *not* write the check: Lew Scarr, " 'It Just Seemed Like the Buck Stopped with Me,' Says Kroc," *San Diego Union,* April 26, 1985, A18.

give her a rock-star welcome: Robert Blair Kaiser, "A Magical Night for Joan Kroc," *San Diego Tribune,* April 16, 1984, C1.

calling her "hamburger queen": Glenn Jorgenson, telephone conversation with author, December 3, 2015.

Joan shooed Linda: Kaiser, "A Magical Night for Joan Kroc."

local musician Steve Vaus: The second was "Thunderin' Lumber," from *Sounds of Success: Music of a Winning Season,* posted online October 10, 2012, accessed online November 15, 2015, https://www.youtube.com/watch?v=8_X60gKJnFU.

would never have bought a baseball

team: Kaiser, "A Magical Night for Joan Kroc."

Before it had been moved: Memorial Day History, Office of Public Affairs, US Department of Veterans Affairs, accessed online November 15, 2015, http://www.va.gov/opa/speceven/memday/history.asp.

"military-industrial complex": James Ledbetter, *Unwarranted Influence: Dwight D. Eisenhower and the Military-Industrial Complex* (New Haven: Yale University Press, 2011), 78.

"Every gun that is made . . .": Quotation in peace ad placed in national newspapers by Joan B. Kroc Foundation citing Eisenhower speech, May 30, 1985.

half a million dollars: "Ad Campaign Urges Citizens to Speak Against Nuclear War," *Marketing News* 19, no. 18 (August 30, 1985): 1.

more than four thousand letters had arrived: Tom Greeley, "Kroc Pleads for Peace in Nation's Newspapers," *Los Angeles Times,* May 31, 1985.

shove her Chicken McNuggets: "Kroc Ads Deplored, Lauded," *San Diego Tribune,* June 5, 1985, B10.

"To take President Eisenhower's words . . ." Scott Harris, "Kroc Turns Up the Heat to Aid Peace Effort," *Los*

Angeles Times, October 13, 1985, B1.

Such criticism was: Helmut Sorge, "So haben alle etwas davon," *Der Spiegel,* June 24, 1985, 144.

God, she believed: Harris, "Joan Kroc Steps Up Ad Campaign . . ."

"all shared in the same search . . .": Robert Blair Kaiser, "Kroc, Pope Share Hope for World Peace," *San Diego Tribune,* June 5, 1985, D-1.

J and R Double Arch Ranch: In 1986, Joan donated the ranch to the Ronald McDonald Children's Charities for use as a camp for kids. Neighbors complained, and the ranch was listed for sale, with the proceeds going to the charity. See "A Ranch That Billions of Burgers Built: Kroc Estate Selling for $14 Million," *San Bernardino Sun,* August 13, 1989, 58; and Ruth Ryon, "Hot Property: Beverly Hills New Principal Resident," *Los Angeles Times,* August 13, 1989.

"Dear world, I really love you": Steve Vaus, "Dear World, I Really Love You," Joan B. Kroc Foundation, 45 rpm, 1985.

"I am praying . . .": Kaiser, "Kroc, Pope Share Hope for World Peace."

"Please stop all nuclear weapons . . .": Harris, "Joan Kroc Steps Up Ad Campaign . . ." (The zip code for the White

House was printed incorrectly in the ad, according to Tom Blair, *San Diego Union,* July 21, 1985.)

Joan fielded questions: Associated Press, "Joan Kroc Places Ads to Make Plea for World Peace," July 18, 1985.

issue that transcended politics: Barbara O'Neil, "Kroc Pays $750,000 on a Second Set of Ads," *San Diego Union,* July 9, 1985, B-1.

enabled her to spread the word: Harris, "Joan Kroc Steps Up Ad Campaign . . ."

sung and recorded in Japanese: Steve Vaus (songwriter commissioned by Joan Kroc), conversation with author, January 25, 2013.

Tom Brokaw informed his audience: George Lewis segment on Joan Kroc, *NBC Nightly News with Tom Brokaw,* July 16, 1985.

He was so revered in Japan: Michael Sund, e-mail to author, August 5, 2015.

"a kind of bridge . . .": Don Wycliff, "A Tribute to Notre Dame's Father Hesburgh," *Chicago Tribune,* February 27, 2015.

he had come to San Diego: The Reverend Theodore M. Hesburgh, "The Nuclear Threat to Humanity," Eugene M. Burke C.S.P. Lectureship, University of

California, San Diego, April 3, 1985, posted online September 22, 2011, accessed online November 15, 2015, https://www.youtube.com/watch?v=fhE4Tubh fTI.

Hesburgh believed every college student: Laura Gritz, "Peace on Campus," *Scholastic: Notre Dame's Student Magazine,* vol. 130, no. 7, October 13, 1988, 5.

"McNut," one conservative columnist: Cal Thomas, "Joan Kroc Should Stay in the Kitchen," *Los Angeles Times,* October 31, 1985, C7.

"the whole world is chauvinistic": Distel, "Joan Kroc: Madre Who Owns the Padres."

"great deal more than just . . .": Norman Cousins, "A Controversial Spokeswoman for the Peace Movement," *Christian Science Monitor,* January 17, 1986, accessed online November 15, 2015, http://www.csmonitor.com/1986/0117/hkroc.html.

Linda had become involved: Linda A. Wendfeldt, letter to author, April 2, 2015.

They'd been floated: Rick Shaughnessy, "Kroc-Smith Turn Down Idea of Mother-Daughter Ticket," *San Diego Tribune,* April 6, 1987, B3.

attentive blond woman: Emily Paladino, "Spirit of Philanthropy," *Scholastic: Notre*

Dame's Student Magazine, vol. 145, no. 6, November 13, 2003, 14.

The name Joan Kroc: "Malloy's Reflection on Hesburgh," *Observer* (South Bend, IN), March 4, 2015, accessed online November 15, 2015, http://ndsmcobserver.com/2015/03/malloy-on-hesburgh.

a check for a million dollars: Confidante of Joan Kroc, conversation with author, December 4, 2013.

letters in response to this cartoon: Paul Conrad, Speech to San Diego Press Club, September 26, 1985, Paul Conrad Papers 1950–2005, the Huntington Library, San Marino, CA.

Conrad was ruining their breakfast: James Rainey, "Paul Conrad Dies at 86; Pulitzer Prize–Winning Political Cartoonist Helped Bring the Times to National Prominence," *Los Angeles Times,* September 5, 2010, A1.

caricatures of each of them: Beverly Beyette, "Putting Works in Their Mouths," *Los Angeles Times,* July 12, 1998, 2.

Robert Blair Kaiser had become: Robert Blair Kaiser (journalist and friend of Joan Kroc), e-mail to author, October 15, 2012.

an ordained Jesuit priest: Thomas C.

Fox, "Robert Blair Kaiser Dies at 84 on Holy Thursday," *National Catholic Reporter,* April 3, 2015, accessed online December 29, 2015, http://ncronline.org/blogs/ncr-today/robert-blair-kaiser-passes-84-holy-thursday.

not only had arranged the trip: Kaiser, "Kroc, Pope Share Hope for World Peace."

permitted him to write about the trip: Paul Krueger, "The Inside Story," *San Diego Reader,* June 20, 1985, 8.

animal rights activist Cleveland Amory: Robert Blair Kaiser, "Cleveland Amory: Wildlife Crusader," *San Diego Tribune,* July 4, 1985, E1.

tantalizing rumor and speculation: Virtually anyone in the orbit of the Krocs whispers about Joan's varied romantic connections, most of which I have not been able to substantiate.

"Do you know what a romance . . .": Choney, "Joan Kroc: A Year of Wins, and Losses."

Love affairs and marriage: Ibid.

far too independent: Chuck Bieler, conversation with author, March 7, 2013.

using the word "dating": Paul Krueger, "The Inside Story," *San Diego Reader.* However, Kaiser did use the word years later in an e-mail to the *Chain Reaction* organizers, July 3, 2012, as well as in a conversation with author on October 22, 2012.

President Reagan had extended: Kaiser, "A New Force: Joan Kroc's Out of Shadow . . ."

Kaiser rushed up to him: Kay Conrad (wife of Paul Conrad), conversation with author, June 20, 2013; and Robert Blair Kaiser, October 22, 2012.

passionate self-taught musician: Tom Longden, "Paul Conrad," *Des Moines Register* Data Central blog, http://data.desmoinesregister.com/famous-iowans/paul-conrad.

sketched out a stubby snarl: Kay Conrad, June 20, 2013.

wrote a check to the Democratic Party: Associated Press, "Kroc Gives Democrats $1 Million: Widow of McDonald's Founder Breaks Record," *Los Angeles Times,* August 13, 1987, 2.

Joan sat happily perched: Roger Genser (Santa Monica arts commission member at time of Joan's gift), conversation with author, July 23, 2013; and Katharine King (guest on Joan's yacht), e-mail to author, December 3, 2015.

first ran for public office: Frank Macomber, "Newly-Elected Woman Praises Gung-ho Youth," *Rome* (NY) *News Tribune,* Copley News Service, December 5, 1971, 2F; and "Transcription of Interview with Councilwoman Maureen O'Conner [*sic*], conducted by Richard H. Glass," April 27, 1973, Women in Politics archive, San Diego State University, accessed online April 24, 2016, http://library.sdsu.edu/sites/default/files/O%27Connor MaureenTranscript.pdf.

The Wonderful World of Sports: "Swimming Sisters," *Montreal Gazette,* September 17, 1964, 40.

ventured to City Hall: Patricia Murphy, "She Fought City Hall, Now Sits in It," *Los Angeles Times,* November 10, 1971, F7.

"be a slipper": Jennings Parrott, "Can't Be a Slipper, 'Cinderella' Says," *Los Angeles Times,* November 4, 1971, A2.

he dubbed Topsy's: Tony Perry, "Robert O. Peterson, Founder of Jack in the Box Restaurants, Dies," *Los Angeles Times,* April 20, 1994, 3; Jack Williams and Patricia Dibsie, "R. O. Peterson, Jack in the Box Founder, Dies," *San Diego*

Union-Tribune, April 20, 1994, A-1; and *Nation's Restaurant News,* May 2, 1996, 24.

a Renaissance man: Gary Shaw, "Bob Peterson's Influence beyond the Public Inkling," *San Diego Daily Transcript,* April 21, 1994, 1.

a sense of responsibility: Barry M. Horstman, "O'Connor Overcomes Aloof Image in Winning San Diego Mayor's Chair," *Los Angeles Times,* June 5, 1986.

campaign finance scandal: Ralph Frammolino, "Hedgecock Always Wanted to Be in Charge," *Los Angeles Times,* February 14, 1985, 1.

Maureen jumped into the race: Barry M. Horstman, "O'Connor: Wants to Be 'Nobody's Mayor but Yours,' " *Los Angeles Times,* May 18, 1986, SD_4.

"You should know": Alison Da Rosa, "Mayor Samples Lifestyle of the Homeless," *San Diego Tribune,* September 5, 1988, A1.

to buy cigarettes at a discount: Todd G. Buchholz, *New Ideas from Dead CEOs: Lasting Lessons from the Corner Office* (New York: HarperBusiness, 2007), 139.

at the home of Dr. Salk: Jordan Bonfante, "Lady Power in the Sunbelt," *Time,* March 10, 1990, 21.

fortune now approached a billion: Ed Jahn, "Philanthropists Say Giving Is the Reward," *San Diego Union,* May 12, 1985, B1.

Dr. Doris Howell: John Wilkens, "Hospice Pioneer Reflects on Closure," *San Diego Union-Tribune,* February 15, 2013, accessed online January 12, 2016, http://www.sandiegouniontribune.com/news/2013/feb/15/hospice-pioneer-reflects-on-closure.

secretive "Howard Hughes" nature: Michael Smolens, "Hospice Talks Break Down over Access," *San Diego Union,* October 22, 1985, B1.

reveal her identity: Ralph Frammolino, "Council to Reconsider Issue; Mystery over Plan to Buy Vauclain Point Cleared," *Los Angeles Times,* January 4, 1986, SD_1.

"What we are talking about . . .": Ralph Frammolino, "Council OKs Plan to Buy Vauclain Point as Hospice Site," *Los Angeles Times,* January 7, 1986, SD_A1.

"best shelter in the free world": St. Vincent de Paul Village, San Diego, World Habitat Awards, Building and Social Housing Foundation, September 27, 1988, http://www.worldhabitatawards.org/winners-and-finalists/project-details.cfm

?lang=00&theProjectID=107; and Tom Blair, *San Diego Union,* September 27, 1988.

AIDS clinic in Palm Springs: Robert Hopwood and Darby Wright, "Desert AIDS Project: 30 Years of Hope," *Desert Sun* (Palm Springs, CA), March 30, 2014, http://www.desertsun.com/story/life/2014/03/30/desert-aids-project-years/7077615.

"He's a human . . .": Associated Press, "Students Weep over Boy Leaving School," *Kokomo Tribune* (IN), September 11, 1987, 15.

throwing out the first pitch: Carmen Valencia, "Visiting 12-Year-Old Stars at Padres Game," *San Diego Union,* May 16, 1988, B2.

her "beautiful attitude": "Star Teacher Inspires Kroc Gift," *Chicago Tribune,* February 11, 1988, 20.

Playing guardian angel was: Mark Kreidler, "No Second Thoughts: Kroc Tired of Ownership Responsibilities," *San Diego Union,* October 19, 1989, F1.

tired of the rising cost: Tom Cushman, "Baseball Not Kroc's Game, but She Kept Padres Here," *San Diego Union-Tribune,* November 9, 2003, C4.

maitre d' in the owner's box: Scott Miller, "Joan Kroc's Farewell: Her Last Big

Game's Tonight," *Los Angeles Times,* July 27, 1990, SD_1.

Ballard had unceremoniously dumped: Dick Williams, *No More Mr. Nice Guy: A Life of Hardball* (New York: Harcourt, 1990), 228.

she fired Williams anyway: Ibid., 280; and Barry Bloom, "Kroc Gives Her Views of What Happened and Why in Dick Williams Saga," *San Diego Tribune,* February 6, 1986, D1.

Gossage blew a gasket: Richard Gossage, *The Goose Is Loose* (New York: Ballantine Books, 2000), 238.

a $25,000 donation: Barry Bloom, "Kroc Owned Her Share of Highs and Lows," *San Diego Tribune,* July 28, 1990, C1.

A deal to sell the Padres: Miller, "Joan Kroc's Farewell."

Major League Baseball brass wouldn't have it: Barry Lorge, "Kroc Wanted to Give Padres to City," *San Diego Union,* July 29, 1990, H1.

Joan put *him* in charge: "Kapstein Gives Up Control of Padres Daily Operation," *Los Angeles Times,* April 19, 1990, SD_C10.

finally found a buyer: Kirk Kenney, "Roseanne Barr's Anthem Still Anathema," *San Diego Union-Tribune,* July 24,

2015; and Tom Cushman, "For Joan the Decision to Sell Was a Natural," *San Diego Tribune,* November 21, 1986, E-1.

Shame had been part: S. D. Liddick, "Destiny, Dynasty, and the Copleys," *San Diego Magazine,* October 30, 2006; Gail Sheehy, "Cinderella West: California's Unknown New Queen of the Press," *New West,* May 24, 1976, 50–59; and Alexander Auerbach, "Helen Copley: Novice Takes Control," *Los Angeles Times,* July 19, 1975.

The esteemed publisher plucked: Sheehy, "Cinderella West"; and Matt Potter, "Mysterious End of an Era," *San Diego Reader,* April 9, 2004, accessed online October 30, 2015, http://www.sandiegoreader.com/news/2004/apr/08/mysterious-end-era.

Copley's marriage had collapsed: Gregory Alan Gross, "Helen K. Copley's Legacy," *San Diego Union-Tribune,* August 27, 2004, A1.

described herself as "pathetically shy": Sheehy, "Cinderella West."

Courts ruled she owed: Sheehy and Ted Vollmer, "Copley Children Win $10 Million in Court Ruling," *Los Angeles Times,* September 2, 1978, D3.

"I don't know about any . . .": Steve Schmidt, "Copleys Helped Shape City," *San Diego Union-Tribune,* May 10, 2009, A1.

the multimillionaire lady publisher: Janny Scott, "Resignation of USD Trustee Brings Out a Touchy Issue," *Los Angeles Times,* March 30, 1986, SD_1.

"Hire good editors": James O. Goldsborough, "On Owning Newspapers," *Voice of San Diego,* August 10, 2006, http://www.voiceofsandiego.org/topics/opinion/on-owning-newspapers.

fuse her flagship holdings: Greg Johnson, "Circulation Drop Behind Merger Plan," *Los Angeles Times,* September 12, 1991, SD_1; and Dennis McLellan, "Obituaries: Helen Copley, 81; Headed Newspaper Chain," *Los Angeles Times,* August 27, 2004, B10.

donation to the San Diego Zoo: Neil Morgan, *San Diego Tribune,* October 4, 1991, B1.

The Krocs picked "JoRayK": At thirty-eight, the gorilla JoRayK is alive and well at Utah's Hogle Zoo. She's had seven children, and lives with her eleven-year-old daughter Jabali and twenty-three-year-old son Husani, reports Erin Jones (Great Ape Senior Keeper), e-mail to author,

September 9, 2015.

Time **magazine declared:** Jordan Bonfante, "Lady Power in the Sunbelt," *Time,* March 19, 1990, 21–24.

the spurned creator of Ronald McDonald: Willard worked in a passing on-air reference to the fact that he knew Joan, even though he didn't explain how.

"When they come down": Matt Potter, "The Egg Women," *San Diego Reader,* June 10, 1989, 4.

your Academy Award–winning friend: Dennis McLellan, "Mercedes McCambridge, 87; Radio Actress Played Strong Characters in Films," *Los Angeles Times,* March 18, 2004, B13.

sailed through the Panama Canal: Douglas Keating, "No Looking Back, The Past and Its Tragedies Are a Closed Chapter for Mercedes McCambridge," *Philadelphia Inquirer,* November 3, 1991, H1.

"the greatest living radio actress": "Mercedes McCambridge," *Telegraph* (London), March 19, 2004, http://www.telegraph.co.uk/news/obituaries/1457195/Mercedes-McCambridge.html.

"There was no point in trying . . .": Mercedes McCambridge, *The Quality of Mercy* (New York: Times Books, 1981), 14.

"nasty sister, the nasty mother . . .": Margaret Harford, "Mercedes Back with a New Outlook," *Los Angeles Times,* September 5, 1967, E1.

the actress chain-smoked: McCambridge, *The Quality of Mercy,* 94.

Marlene Dietrich flew: Ibid., 183.

delivered a healthy baby: Mercedes McCambridge, interviewed by Chuck Schaden, recorded October 29, 1976, accessed online January 24, 2016, http://www.speakingofradio.com/interviews/mccambridge-mercedes.

Before she became sober: McCambridge, *The Quality of Mercy,* 149–173.

president of a rehab center: Ellen L. Slott, "Oscar Winner Heads Rehabilitation Center," *Pittsburgh Press,* March 13, 1977, A5.

"I was essentially raised . . .": Mark Carnopsis, "Suicide Letter Lashes Out," *Arkansas Democrat,* April 18, 1989, 1.

dispatching *Impromptu:* Lamar James, "Father Kills Family, Himself, Police Say," *Arkansas Gazette,* November 17, 1987, 1; and Donnali Fifield (daughter of Mercedes McCambridge's first husband), e-mail to author, September 22, 2015.

sent a terse acknowledgment: Ron Lackmann, *Mercedes McCambridge: A Biogra-*

phy and Filmography (Jefferson, NC: Mc-Farland and Co., 2005), 131.

"Life is a bitch,": Pearl Sheffy Gefen, " 'Life Is a Bitch, but You Have to Survive,' " *Globe and Mail* (Toronto), March 23, 2004, C8.

After thirty years as the assistant: Liz Fedor, "Mayor Inspires Grand Forks as Dad, 92, Evacuates Farm," *Grand Forks Herald,* April 21, 1997, A1.

"Look in Webster's": Chuck Haga, "Owens Earns Her Stripes, Trust as Mayor," *Minneapolis Star Tribune,* April 18, 1997, 22A.

largest evacuation of an American city: Byron Dorgan (US senator, North Dakota, during floods), telephone conversation with author, August 4, 2012.

"this little fox": Pat Owens (mayor of Grand Forks, ND, during 1997 floods and recipient of Kroc gift), telephone conversation with author, February 6, 2014.

such an enormous donation: Carol J. Castaneda, "A Ray of Hope — and Money in the Bank," *USA Today,* May 1, 1997, A, 4:1.

thirty-eight pieces of western art: Fred Tully (board member, Crazy Horse Foundation), telephone conversation with author, November 15, 2015.

new museum in Rapid: Joan B. Kroc letter to Joe Rovere, chairman, Museum Alliance of Rapid City, April 4, 1994, Minnilusa Historical Society. Joan had intended to donate the $1 million worth of art, including pieces by Frederic Remington and Charles Marion Russell, to a new museum being built in Rapid, but the city did not comply with the terms of the gift and the offer was rescinded. A full list of the work is available at www.rayandjoan .com.

an intrepid reporter searched: Sorge, "So haben alle etwas davon."

paid expenses for family members: Don Bell, "How It All Came Together: The History of a Relationship That Led to 27 Kroc Centers," *Carin* 19, no. 2 (Summer 2012): 18–21.

invited them to lunch: David Montgomery, "Billions Served: McDonald's Heiress Joan Kroc Took Her Philanthropy and Supersized It," *Washington Post,* March 14, 2004, D1.

"If I said, 'Oh, she was great . . .' ": David Nelson, "Dick Freeman," *San Diego Magazine,* vol. 56, no. 6, April 2004, 38.

stingy with benefits: Confidante of Joan Kroc, telephone conversation with author, September 8, 2015.

forty-ninth richest in the world: Greg Johnson, "San Diegans on the 400 Richest List," *Los Angeles Times,* October 13, 1987, SD_G2A.

via hired limo to Atlantic City: Confidante of Joan Kroc, conversation with author, December 4, 2012.

skip the show and go to dinner: Amanda Latimer, conversation with author, March 31, 2015.

romance with Phil Bifulk: Tom Blair, *San Diego Union,* March 10, 1991, B1.

tooled around the country: Maria Puente, "Did Wings Cost 'Angel' Anonymity," *USA Today,* May 20, 1997; and Phil Bifulk (companion of Joan Kroc), telephone conversation with author, July 15, 2012.

she found a lost dog: Tom Gorman, "She Believes Dog Is Telling (That's Right) the Truth," *Los Angeles Times,* February 5, 1989, 55; and Jim Okerblom, "A Lost Dog, a Therapist, and Joan Kroc," *San Diego Union,* February 3, 1989, B1.

When Norman Cousins died: Candis Cousins, e-mail to author, March 12, 2014.

offer to write an essay: Stuart Elliott, "Essays for McDonald's Concentrate on Quality," *San Bernardino Sun,* April 12,

1989, B10; and Ebeling, "The Chase: Afloat in the PR Whirl of the 1970s (the Golin Years)," Apple Pressings blog.

won a $100,000 award: "Awards of Excellence Gala," Ronald McDonald House Children's Charities website, accessed online November 15, 2015, http://www.rmhc.org/awards-of-excellence-gala.

handsome checks of support: Letter from Joan Kroc to Mr. and Mrs. Fred Rogers, December 6, 1993, and letter from Nancy Trestick (Joan Kroc's secretary and coexecutor) to Mr. and Mrs. Fred Rogers, November 16, 1994 ($400,000), Fred Rogers Center for Early Learning and Children's Media, St. Vincent College, Latrobe, PA.

serve on the board: Family Communications, Inc., Tax Exempt Form 990, 2003, accessed online November 15, 2015, CitizenAudit.org.

When the recipient: Alison Da Rosa, *San Diego Tribune,* October 29, 1986, B1.

a check for $5 million: Confidante of Joan Kroc, conversation with author, December 4, 2012.

she wasn't doing enough: Ted Leitner (Padres broadcaster and friend/neighbor of Joan Kroc), telephone conversation with author, January 30, 2014.

heiresses halted the car frequently: Perry, "Philanthropy That Was Deeply Personal."

she contacted . . . the Salvation Army: Maria Nobles, "Slow Going for Kroc Centers," *Nonprofit Times,* November 1, 2006, accessed online December 30, 2015, http://www.thenonprofittimes.com/news-articles/ slow-going-for-kroc-centers.

Members adhered to: Key Principles, The Salvation Army International, accessed online November 15, 2015, http://www.salvationarmy.org/ihq/healthprinciples.

"Think big," she told them: Perry, "Philanthropy That Was Deeply Personal."

The most expensive one: Person involved with the building of the Kroc Center project, conversation with author, January 16, 2016.

zeroed in on a run-down lot: Rebecca Go, "Transformation of a Neighborhood," *San Diego Union-Tribune,* April 12, 2008, C21.

nearby Mexican border: Jim Newland, "A Brief History of Rolando, a Community of San Diego, California," accessed online November 15, 2015, http://www.rolandovillage.com/history.

"working of the Holy Spirit": Donald Bell, "Bell Recalls Kroc's 'Stealth

Philanthropy,' " *New Frontier Chronicle,* vol. 22, no. 1, January 20, 2004.

". . . put up a shack or something": "The History behind the Salvation Army Kroc Center San Diego," Salvation Army Ray and Joan Kroc Corps Community Center, posted online July 21, 2012, accessed online December 8, 2015, https://www.youtube.com/watch?v=fNpMowwn-1I.

ten more could be built: Person involved with building Kroc Centers, January 16, 2016.

". . . build bigger swimming pools": Fred Rogers keynote speech in "Ray and Joan Kroc Corps Community Center Grand Opening," Salvation Army Ray and Joan Kroc Corps Community Center, June 19, 2002, posted online November 12, 2013, https://www.youtube.com/watch?v=dupfehtm5Po.

there'd be a Starbucks: In May 2015, the Salvation Army issued a study on the "Halo Effect" the community centers have had on their respective neighborhoods. Researchers concluded that the centers had an over $258 million impact. A brief of the report is available online at https://s3.amazonaws.com/usn-cache.salvationarmy.org/8f3d0cfe-dca6-467f-8c59

-f97963adf793_Kroc+Halo+Effect+One +Pager.pdf.

a surprise guest emerged: David Moye, "Joan of Arches: San Diego Hero Serves (and Donates) Billions," *Pacific San Diego Magazine,* July 24, 2012, accessed online December 4, 2015, http://www.pacific sandiego.com/joan-of-arches; and Burl Stiff, "An Unscheduled Duet Is the Evening's Hit," *San Diego Union-Tribune,* March 23, 2003, E4.

Chapter 12: St. Joan

16,000-square-foot estate: "Kroc Home in Fairbanks Ranch," *San Diego Source,* January 25, 2007, accessed online December 17, 2015, http://www.sddt.com/news/ article.cfm?SourceCode=20070125tdf#. VnMgRDZh1p8.

serious medical condition: Letter from Joan Kroc to Helen Copley, August 4, 2003.

Like so many: Ken Stern, *With Charity for All: Why Charities Are Failing and a Better Way to Give* (New York: Doubleday, 2013), 129.

a tour of their new facility: Doug Myrland (former general manager, KPBS), conversation with author, February 13, 2013.

NPR's Klose, on the other hand: Stern, *With Charity for All,* 128; and ibid.

ensure good "McKarma": Steve Harvey, "Weather That Suits Shoppers," *Los Angeles Times,* April 1, 1998, 3; and Patt Morrison, "California and the West," *Los Angeles Times,* April 7, 1998, 3.

Joan invited Commissioner Linda Bond: Linda Bond, "She Forced Us to Dream Big," *New Frontier Chronicle,* vol. 22, no. 1, January 20, 2004, accessed online December 30, 2015, http://www .usw.salvationarmy.org/usw/www_newfron tierpub.nsf/15814db8a702449f88256e 3f007b7ddd/7fa89da1f512917288256e2 1005d6dda.

that she get a pet: Linda Bond, "My Friendship with Joan Kroc: A Gift to the Salvation Army," *Caring,* vol. 19, no. 2, Summer 2012, 26–29.

a stuffed bear — covered in mink: Linda Bond, "My Three Bears, a Reminder of Gracious Giving," *Pipeline: The Salvation Army Australia Eastern Territory,* vol. 15, issue 2, February 2011, 5.

rebuffed the San Diego Gay Men's Chorus: Travis D. Bone, "Gay Men's Chorus Pays Tribute to Lost Friend: December

Concerts to Be Dedicated to Philanthropist Joan B. Kroc," *Gay and Lesbian Times* (San Diego), issue 825, October 16, 2003, 26.

she gifted the chorus: Kevin Filer (treasurer, San Diego Gay Men's Chorus), e-mail to author, January 18, 2016.

"step into Grandma's boots": Choney, "Joan Kroc: A Year of Wins, and Losses."

the Four Flowers: Four Flowers Foundation, incorporated August 5, 1997, dissolved February 2, 1998, accessed online November 30, 2015, http://www.californiacorporates.com/corp/1090872.html.

McDonald's had come to dominate: Jaime DeLage, "Obituary: Jay Chadima, 85, Was Twin Cities-Area McDonald's Franchisee," *St. Paul Pioneer Press,* June 19, 2015.

call-in astrology numbers: Chuck Bieler, conversation with author, March 7, 2013.

feeding cash into a paper shredder: Timothy Clancy, telephone conversation with author, January 19, 2015.

might write a book about her: Amy Ragen (granddaughter of Joan Kroc), conversation with author, June 27, 2014; and Amanda Latimer, conversation with author March 31, 2015.

"... great things together": David Folkenflik, "Kroc's Dedication to News Inspired Her Gift to NPR," *Los Angeles Times,* December 9, 2003, E15.

if she left her house: Bond, "My Friendship with Joan Kroc," 27.

Figure in a Shelter: "San Diego Honors Generous Spirit of Joan Kroc," *New Frontier Chronicle,* vol. 22, no. 1, January 20, 2004, accessed online December 30, 2015, http://www.newfrontierchronicle.org/san-diego-honors-generous-spirit-of-joan-kroc.

"... Every one of us is a facet ...": Fred Rogers at opening of Salvation Army Ray and Joan Kroc Corps Community Center, June 19, 2002, accessed online December 15, 2015, https://www.youtube.com/watch?v=dupfehtm5Po.

Her office issued a statement: "Philanthropist Joan B. Kroc Passes Away," October 12, 2003, accessed online April 24, 2016, http://www.prnewswire.com/news-releases/philanthropist-joan-b-kroc-passes-away-72470707.html.

"The world has lost a true ...": "McDonald's Statement on Joan B. Kroc, Philanthropist and Wife of McDonald's Founder Ray Kroc," October 12, 2003, accessed online April 24, 2016, http://

www.prnewswire.com/news-releases/
mcdonalds-statement-on-joan-b-kroc
-philanthropist-and-wife-of-mcdonalds
-founder-ray-kroc-72470737.html.
"Lord, make me an instrument . . .":
Information about the genesis of the peace
prayer, written anonymously in 1915 and
frequently attributed erroneously to St.
Francis, is available at https://franciscan
-archive.org/patriarcha/peace.html.

Postscript

a copy of the trust: Linda Bond, "When I
First Heard the News," *New Frontier
Chronicle,* vol. 22, no. 1, January 20, 2004,
accessed online December 30, 2015,
http://www.newfrontierchronicle.org/
when-i-first-heard-the-news.

"gift from God": Jessi Hempel, "How to
Spend $1.5 Billion Windfall," *Bloomberg
Business News,* February 1, 2004, accessed online January 5, 2015, http://www
.bloomberg.com/bw/stories/2004-02-01/
how-to-spend-a-1-dot-5-billion-windfall.

start writing down zeroes: Noah Adams,
David Folkenflik, Renee Montagne, Cokie
Roberts, Ari Shapiro, Susan Stamberg,
John Ydstie, *This Is NPR: The First Forty
Years* (San Francisco: Chronicle Books,

2010), 225.

brought in Big Macs at lunch: Ibid.

Christmas and the lottery: Jacques Steinberg, "Money Changes Everything," *New York Times,* March 19, 2006, 2:1.

changing her name to "McStamberg": Jacques Steinberg, "Billions and Billions Served, Hundreds of Millions Donated," *New York Times,* November 7, 2003, E3.

$10 million a year: Mike Janssen, "Kroc's $200 Million Gift Frees Pubradio's Dreams," *Current: The Newspaper about Public TV and Radio in the US,* November 17, 2003, accessed online December 30, 2015, http://current.org/files/archive-site/npr/npr0309kroc.shtml.

NPR administrators had hatched a plan: Mike Janssen, "Kroc Gift Lets NPR Expand News, Lower Fees," *Current: The Newspaper about Public TV and Radio in the US,* May 24, 2004, accessed online January 5, 2016, http://current.org/files/archive-site/npr/npr0409krocgift.shtml.

about $2.7 billion: Joan's daughter, Linda, believes her mother had been called by God to give away her fortune. In an e-mail to author, October 25, 2015, she wrote, "She searched relentlessly over the years, in her own way, to find faith and trust in Jesus' unconditional love. She believed in

His teachings and example, and in the last few months of her life, I honestly believe she was guided by her love for Him to tend the poor and make life better for perhaps countless thousands of people."

Appendix: Where Did the Fast-Food Fortune Go?

"There are so many gifts you don't know about . . .": Father Carroll quoted in Reilly Capps and Paul Farhi, "Kroc's Generosity No Surprise to Her Friends," *St. Paul Pioneer Press,* November 9, 2003.

"I hope . . . it's sold to some crazy . . .": Tom Blair, *San Diego Union,* June 7, 1989, B1.

BIBLIOGRAPHY

McDonald's maintains an exhaustive corporate archive that is off-limits to researchers unaffiliated with the corporation, like this author. Information about the company's history is tightly controlled, and virtually every work cites the same sources. Chief among them are Ray Kroc's 1977 autobiography, *Grinding It Out,* and the 1986 company-commissioned *McDonald's: Behind the Arches* by John Love, a business journalist who was furnished unprecedented access to key figures in order to produce a comprehensive corporate history. As I worked to cut through the pervasive mythology of the McDonald's story, I sought fresh, unvarnished accounts. An interesting one proved to be the federal case from 1969 involving the first McDonald's president, Harry Sonneborn, and his ex-wife, June, who sued him for $21 million after their divorce for allegedly misrepresenting the value of his stock, which was worthless at the time they separated. (She lost.) The depositions offer insights to both Sonneborn's and Ray's right-hand woman and secretary, June Martino, integral figures in the birth of the company who are, today, lesser known. In addition, the research of a former A&W franchisee, the late Thomas Dolly, also proved invaluable. As an adult student studying at Bellevue University, Dolly wrote a book and several articles, and coproduced a documentary, based on extensive interviews with Dick McDonald. He offers the story from the brothers' perspective. Also helpful was the essay published online "Breakfast with Mr. McDonald," written from the vantage point of a McDonald's public relations man, Charles Ebeling, assigned to manage Dick McDonald's frustration with his waning place in corporate history. Don Conley's *Flying over the Golden Arches* offered personal insights into his role as the company's first pilot and franchise manager, although he omits details about his acrimonious falling-out with Kroc for, among other things, forming the dissident McDonald's Operators Association. He only hints at trips he made with Ray to St. Paul to see Joan. Early McDonald's newsletters, found in the A. Bernie Woods collection in the Smithsonian, also contained invaluable information from the early years. As I find additional sources, I'll post them on my website, www.rayandjoan.com.

Adams, Noah, David Folkenflik, Renee Montagne, Cokie Roberts, Ari Shapiro, Susan Stamberg, and John Ydstie. *This Is NPR: The First Forty Years.* San Francisco: Chronicle Books, 2010.

Bavasi, Buzzie, with John Strege. *Off the Record.* Chicago: Contemporary Books, 1987.

Black Hills Oral History Project, Historic Rapid City, Rapid City (SD) Public Library. https://vimeo.com/channels/oralhistoryproject.

Boas, Max, and Steve Chain. *Big Mac: The Unauthorized Story of McDonald's.* New York: E. P. Dutton, 1976.

Brooks, Cathleen. *The Secret Everyone Knows.* San Diego: Operation Cork, 1981.

Burk, Robert F. *Marvin Miller: Baseball Revolutionary.* Champaign: University of Illinois Press, 2015.

Burns, Ben. *Nitty Gritty: A White Editor in Black Journalism.* Jackson: University Press of Mississippi, 1996.

Ben Burns Papers, Vivian G. Harsh Research Collection of Afro-American History and Literature, Chicago Public Library.

Sammy Cahn papers, Margaret Herrick Library, Academy of Motion Picture Arts and Sciences, Beverly Hills, CA.

Caldicott, Helen. *A Desperate Passion: An Autobiography.* New York: W. W. Norton, 1997.

———. *Missile Envy: The Arms Race and Nuclear War.* First edition. New York: William Morrow, 1984.

———. *Missile Envy: The Arms Race and Nuclear War.* Revised edition. New York: Bantam Books, 1986.

Capps, Reilly, and Paul Farhi. "Magnaminity & McMuffins," *Washington Post,* November 7, 2003, C1.

Chase, Chris. *The Great American Waistline: Putting It On and Taking It Off.* New York: Coward, McCann & Geoghegan, 1981.

Chemerka, William R. *Fess Parker: TV's Frontier Hero.* Albany, GA: BearManor Media, 2011.

Choney, Suzanne. "Joan Kroc: A Year of Wins, and Losses," *San Diego Union,* October 19, 1984, A1.

Conley, Donald R. *Flying over the Golden*

Arches. Edina, MN: Beaver's Pond Press, 2010.

Conrad, Barnaby. *Time Is All We Have: Four Weeks at the Betty Ford Center.* New York: Arbor House, 1986.

Conrad, Paul. *Paul Conrad: Drawing the Line: The Collected Works of America's Premier Political Cartoonist.* Los Angeles: Los Angeles Times, 1999.

Paul Conrad Papers, 1950–2005, the Huntington Library, San Marino, CA.

Cousins, Norman. *Anatomy of an Illness as Perceived by the Patient.* New York: W. W. Norton, 1979.

———. *Head First: The Biology of Hope.* New York: E. P. Dutton, 1989.

———. *Modern Man Is Obsolete.* New York: Viking Press, 1945.

———. *The Pathology of Power.* New York: W. W. Norton, 1987.

Norman Cousins Papers, Department of Special Collections, Charles E. Young Research Library, University of California, Los Angeles.

Christie's. *Important American Paintings, Drawings and Sculpture.* Thursday, November 30, 2006. New York.

———. *19th Century European Art.* Wednesday, April 19, 2006. New York.

Davis, Bill C. *Mass Appeal.* Directed by Glenn Jordan. Universal Studios. December 6, 1984.

Charles T. Davis Papers. James Weldon Johnson Collection in the Yale Collection of American Literature, Beinecke Rare Book and Manuscript Library, Yale University, New Haven, CT.

Dice, Mark. *The Bohemian Grove: Facts and Fiction.* San Diego: The Resistance Manifesto, 2015.

Dolly, Tom. *Pure Americana: The Founding of McDonald's.* Unpublished thesis. Bellevue, NE: Bellevue University, 2009.

————. *Pure Americana: The Founding of McDonald's,* 1995, VHS.

Thomas C. Dolly Papers, Freeman/Lozier Library, Special Collections, Bellevue University, Bellevue, Nebraska.

Domhoff, G. William. *The Bohemian Grove and Other Retreats.* New York: Harper and Row, 1974.

Ebeling, Charles. *Breakfast with Mr. McDonald.* The Chicago Literary Club, October 26, 2009. http://www.chilit.org.

Ford, Betty, with Chris Chase. *Betty: A Glad Awakening.* Garden City, NY: Doubleday and Company, 1987.

————. *The Times of My Life.* New York:

Harper and Row, 1978.

George, Stephen. *Enterprising Minnesotans: 150 Years of Business Pioneers.* Minneapolis: University of Minnesota Press, 2003.

Gibney, Alex, Susan Motamed, and Tracy Dahlby. *David Halberstam's the Fifties.* New York: History Channel, A&E Home Video, distributed by New Video Group, 1997.

Golin, Al. *Trust and Consequences: Build Trust Today or Lose Your Market Tomorrow.* New York: American Management Association, 2004.

Gossage, Richard. *The Goose Is Loose.* New York: Ballantine Books, 2000.

Graham, Ellen. "McDonald's Pickle," *Wall Street Journal,* August 15, 1991, A1.

Halberstam, David. *The Fifties.* New York: Villard Books, 1993.

Harris, Neil. *Chicago Apartments: A Century of Waterfront Luxury.* New York: Acanthus Press, 2004.

Heimann, Jim. *Car Hops and Curb Service: A History of American Drive-In Restaurants 1920–1960.* San Francisco: Chronicle Books, 1996.

Hesburgh, Theodore. *God, Country and Notre Dame: The Autobiography of Theo-*

dore M. Hesburgh. Notre Dame, IN: University of Notre Dame Press, 2000.

Hess, Alan. *Googie: Fifties Coffee Shop Architecture.* San Francisco: Chronicle Books, 1986.

————. *Googie Redux: Ultramodern Roadside Architecture.* San Francisco: Chronicle Books, 2004.

Hollis, Tim. *Hi There, Boys and Girls!: America's Local Children's TV Programs.* Jackson: University Press of Mississippi, 2001.

Hughes, Harold, with Dick Schneider. *The Man from Ida Grove: A Senator's Personal Story.* Lincoln, VA: Chosen Books, 1979.

Jakle, John A., and Keith A. Sculle. *Fast Food Roadside Restaurants in the Automobile Age.* Baltimore: Johns Hopkins University Press, 1999.

Jorgenson, Glenn. *It's Great to Be Alive.* Video archives. http://www.riverparksd .com.

"June Martino, 1917–2005." http://www .junemartino.org.

Keller, John E. *Alcohol. A Family Affair.* San Diego: Operation Cork, 1977.

————. *Ministering to Alcoholics.* Minneapolis: Augsburg Fortress, 1991.

Kerst, Adrienne Merola, Jean Oleson-

Kessloff, and Patrick D. Roseland. *Rapid City: Historic Downtown Architecture.* Charleston, SC: Arcadia Publishing, 2007.

Kincheloe, Joe L. *The Sign of the Burger: McDonald's and the Culture of Power.* Philadelphia: Temple University Press, 2012.

Kinney, Jean. "Project Cork Database: Authoritative Information on Substance Abuse." http://www.projectcork.org.

Kroc Foundation, Annual Reports and 990s, 1965–1975, 1979, 1980, 1981, 1982, Joseph and Matthew Payton Philanthropic Studies Archive, Indiana University–Purdue University Indianapolis University Library.

Kroc Foundation Archives. Mss 61. Department of Special Collections, Davidson Library, University of California, Santa Barbara.

Ethel Kroc v. Ray Kroc, Superior Court of Cook County, Case 62S-7583, April 18, 1962.

Joan B. Kroc Foundation Annual Reports and 990s, 1984–1988, Joseph and Matthew Payton Philanthropic Studies Archive, Indiana University–Purdue University Indianapolis University Library.

Joan B. Kroc v. Raymond A. Kroc, (71-d) 21992, Cook County Circuit Court, November 11, 1971.

Ray Kroc/McDonald Brothers Dictaphone Tapes, 1957–1959.

"The Ray Kroc 75th Birthday Tribute." Private press, 33 1/3 rpm LP. Recorded at Continental Plaza, Chicago, October 8, 1977.

Kroc, Ray, with Robert Anderson. *Grinding It Out: The Making of McDonald's.* Chicago: Henry Regnery, 1977.

Kroc, R. L., and A. Kroc. *The Kroc Foundation: 1965–1985.* Santa Barbara: R. L. and A. Kroc, 1985.

Kuhn, Bowie. *Hardball: The Education of a Baseball Commissioner.* New York: Times Books, 1987.

Bowie K. Kuhn Collection, BA MSS 100, National Baseball Hall of Fame Library, A. Bartlett Giamatti Research Center, Cooperstown, New York.

Lackmann, Ron. *Mercedes McCambridge: A Biography and Filmography.* Jefferson, NC: McFarland & Company, 2005.

Langdon, Philip. *Orange Roofs, Golden Arches: The Architecture of American Chain Restaurants.* New York: Alfred A. Knopf, 1986.

Ledbetter, James. *Unwarranted Influence: Dwight D. Eisenhower and the Military-*

Industrial Complex. New Haven: Yale University Press, 2011.

Leeds, Robert X. *Love Is a Four Legged Word: One Man's Revolution in the Pet Care Industry.* Las Vegas: Epic Publishing, 2001.

———. *All The Comforts of Home: The Story of the First Pet Motel.* New York: Dodd, Mead, 1987.

Lewis, Sinclair. *Free Air.* New York: Harcourt, Brace and Howe, 1919.

Love, John F. *McDonald's: Behind the Arches.* New York: Bantam Books, 1986.

Luxemberg, Stan. *Roadside Empires: How the Chains Franchised America.* New York: Viking Press, 1985.

McCambridge, Mercedes. *The Quality of Mercy.* New York: Times Books, 1981.

Mercedes McCambridge Papers. Women & Leadership Archives. Loyola University Chicago.

McDonald's: The Drive-in with the Arches, Newsletters 1960–1964, A. Bernie Woods papers, Archives Center, National Museum of American History, Smithsonian Institution.

McDonald's Offering Plan, 1958.

McDonald's Owner/Operator Manual, October 1958.

McGee, William. *The Divorce Seekers:*

Memoir of a Nevada Dude Wrangler. St. Helena, CA: BMC Publications, 2004.

McLamore, James W. *The Burger King: Jim McLamore and the Building of an Empire*. New York: McGraw-Hill, 1997.

Madigan, Tim. *I'm Proud of You: My Friendship with Fred Rogers*. New York: Gotham Books, 2006.

Neil Morgan Papers, MSS 0038. Mandeville Special Collections Library, University of California, San Diego.

Myers, Eric. *Uncle Mame: The Life of Patrick Dennis*. New York: St. Martin's Press, 2000.

Multer-Wellin, Barbara, and Jeffrey Abelson. *Paul Conrad: Drawing Fire*. Alexandria, VA: PBS Home Video, 2006.

The Henri J. M. Nouwen Archives and Research Collection, John M. Kelly Library, University of St. Michael's College, Toronto.

Ozersky, Josh. *The Hamburger*. New Haven: Yale University Press, 2008.

Paul D. Paganucci, Subject Files of, Records of the VP and Treasurer of Dartmouth College, Series 1110, Dartmouth Rauner Special Collections Library, Hanover, NH.

Perman, Stacy. *In-N-Out Burger: A Behind-the-Counter Look at the Fast-Food Chain*

That Breaks All the Rules. New York: Collins Business, 2009.

Poseley, Judy. *The Park: A History of the City of St. Louis Park.* 1976.

Pursch, Joseph. *Dear Doc: The Noted Authority Answers Your Questions on Drinking and Drugs.* Minneapolis: CompCare Publications, 1985.

Rapid City Public Library. Oral History Project, Rapid City Public Library Foundation. https://vimeo.com/channels/oralhistoryproject.

Carl R. Rogers collection. HPA Mss 32. Department of Special Collections, University Libraries, University of California, Santa Barbara.

Rogers, Gerald T. *Alcohol and the Physician.* San Diego, CA: Operation Cork. Center City, MN: Distributed by Hazelden Educational Foundation, 1981.

———. *Dugout.* San Diego: Operation Cork, 1981.

———. *If You Loved Me.* San Diego: Operation Cork, 1977.

———. *Our Brother's Keeper.* San Diego: Operation Cork, 1980.

———. *Soft Is the Heart of a Child.* San Diego: Operation Cork, Center City, MN: Distributed by Hazelden Educational Foundation, 1978.

Ross, Ishbel. *Silhouette in Diamonds: The Life of Mrs. Potter Palmer.* New York: Harper and Brothers, 1960.

Rosser, Susan, with Charlie Smith and Trevor Schaefer. *The Boy on the Lake: He Faced Down the Biggest Bully in His Life and Inspired Trevor's Law.* New York: Morgan James Publishing, 2012.

Schlosser, Eric. *Fast Food Nation: The Dark Side of the All-American Meal.* Boston: Houghton Mifflin, 2001.

Schupack v. McDonald's System, Inc. 264 N.W. 2d 827 (1978) 200 Neb. 485, 7 (Supreme Court of Nebraska).

Scott, Willard. *Willard Scott's The Joy of Living.* New York: Coward, McCann & Geoghegan, 1982.

Shane, Scott A. *From Ice Cream to the Internet: Using Franchising to Drive the Growth and Profits of Your Company.* Upper Saddle River, NJ: FT Press, 2005.

Simon, Michele. "Clowning Around with Charity: How McDonald's Exploits Philanthropy and Targets Children." http://www.eatdrinkpolitics.com/wp-content/uploads/Clowning_Around_Charity_Report_Full.pdf.

Smith, Ozzie. *Wizard.* Chicago: Contemporary Books, 1988.

Solomon, George Freeman, with Ping Ho. *From Psyche to Soma and Back: Tales of Biopsychosocial Medicine.* Los Angeles: Xlibris, 2000.

June Sonneborn v. Harry J. Sonneborn, 69C 279 (Il. Northern District, Eastern Division, Chicago).

Sotheby Parke Bernet, Inc. *The Distinguished Autograph Collection of Harry J. Sonneborn.* Sale number 3655. Tuesday, June 11, 1974. New York.

————. *Highly Important Federal and State Constitutions from the Collection of Harry J. Sonneborn.* Sale number 4389. June 5, 1980. New York.

Stern, Ken. *With Charity for All: Why Charities Are Failing and a Better Way to Give.* New York: Anchor Doubleday, 2013.

Tennyson, Jeffrey. *Hamburger Heaven: The Illustrated History of the Hamburger.* New York: Hyperion, 1993.

Turman, Lawrence. *So You Want to Be a Producer.* New York: Three Rivers Press, 2005.

Vaus, Steve. "Dear World, I Really Love You." Joan B. Kroc Foundation, 45 rpm, 1985.

Waechter, T. Richard, Jr. *The Pot of Gold under the Arches: Ray Kroc and Entrepre-*

neurship. Unpublished thesis, Seeley G. Mudd Manuscript Library, Princeton University, Princeton, NJ, 1984.

Wagner, Benjamin. *Mister Rogers and Me: A Deep and Simple Documentary Film.* New York: Wagner Bros. Film, 2010.

Weinstein, Greg. "Ray Kroc: Fast Food McMillionaire." *Biography.* New York: A&E Television Networks. December 7, 1998.

White, William L. *The History of Addiction Treatment and Recovery in America.* Bloomington, IL: Chestnut Health Systems, 1998.

————. *The History of Addiction Counseling in the United States: Promoting Personal, Family and Community Recovery.* Alexandria, VA: NAADC, 2014.

Williams, Dick. *No More Mr. Nice Guy.* San Diego: Harcourt Brace Jovanovich, 1990.

Witzel, Michael Karl. *The American Drive-In: History and Folklore of the Drive-In Restaurant in American Car Culture.* Osceola, WI: Motorbooks, International, 1994.

A. Bernie Woods Papers, Archives Center, National Museum of American History, Smithsonian Institution, Washington DC.

Woster, Terry. *It's Great to Be Alive: Remembering River Park and Its Pioneering Addic-*

tion Treatment. Philadelphia: BookBaby, 2013.

In addition, I relied on the digital resources Ancestry.com, FamilySearch.com, News papers.com, NewspaperArchives.com, Pro-Quest, and NewsBank. Thanks, too, to the following libraries:

Joseph and Matthew Payton Philanthropic Studies Archives, IUPUI University Library; Special Collections, Bellevue University Freeman/ Lozier Library; Seeley G. Mudd Manuscript Library at Princeton University; Hesburgh Library, University of Notre Dame; National Archives at Chicago; San Diego Public Library; San Diego State University Special Collections and University Archives; Mandeville Special Collections Library, UCSD; Fred Rogers Center for Early Learning and Children's Media, Latrobe, PA; Boca Raton Public Library; The Little Rock (AK) Public Library; Minnesota Historical Society; Los Angeles Public Library; Pasadena Public Library; Rapid City Public Library; St. Paul Public Library; San Diego State University Library; South Dakota Historical Society; St. Louis Park Historical Society; Santa Monica Public Library; Beverly Hills Historical Society; Crazy Horse Foundation, Custer,

SD; Hazelden-Cork Library, Center City, MN; Minnilusa Historical Association, Rapid City, SD; Museum of Broadcast Communications, Chicago; Vanderbilt TV News Archive, Nashville, TN; Monticello College Archives; Paley Center, Beverly Hills, CA, and New York, NY.

The employees of Thorndike Press hope you have enjoyed this Large Print book. All our Thorndike, Wheeler, and Kennebec Large Print titles are designed for easy reading, and all our books are made to last. Other Thorndike Press Large Print books are available at your library, through selected bookstores, or directly from us.

For information about titles, please call:
  (800) 223-1244

or visit our Web site at:
  http://gale.cengage.com/thorndike

To share your comments, please write:
  Publisher
  Thorndike Press
  10 Water St., Suite 310
  Waterville, ME 04901